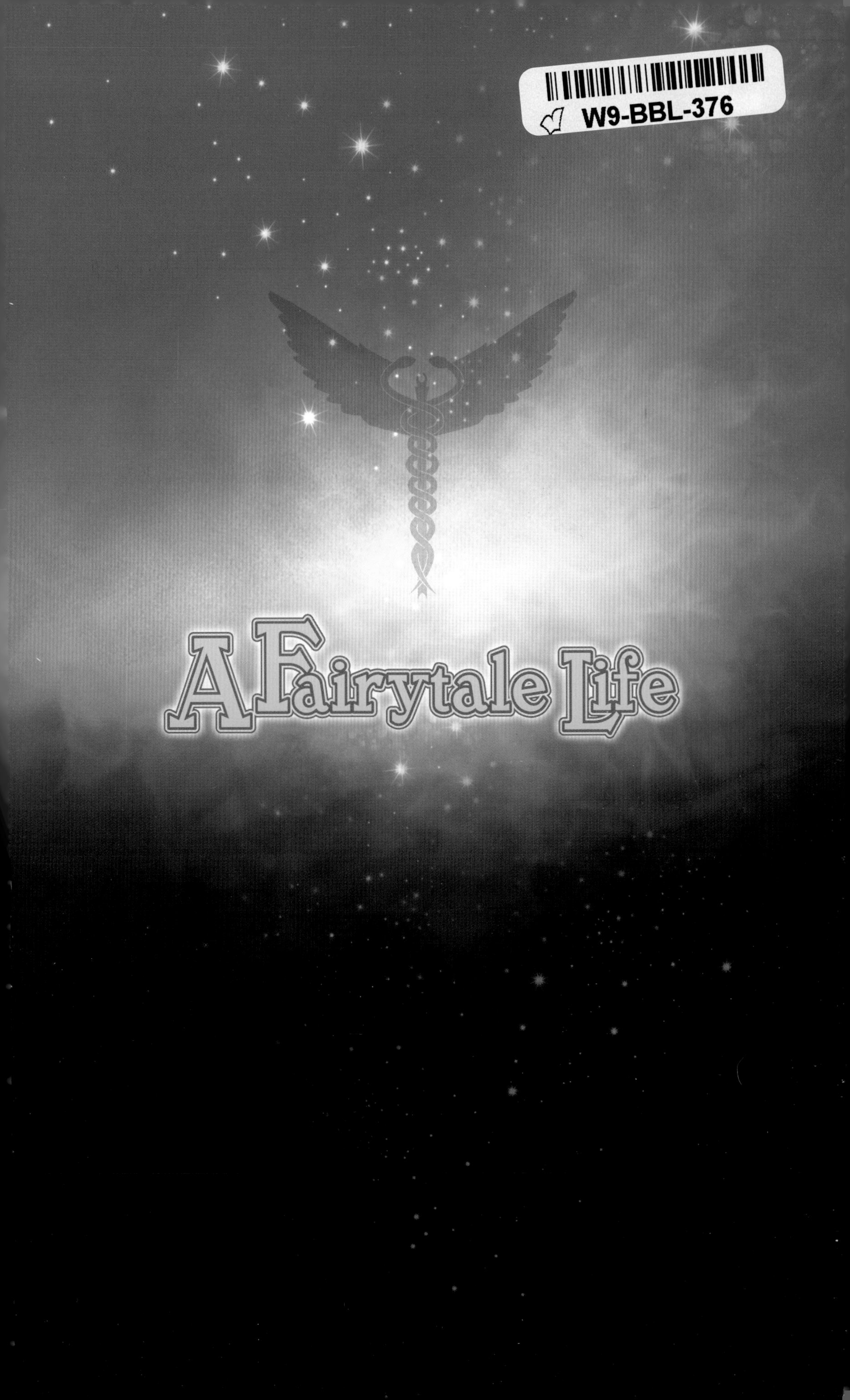
A Fairytale Life

DOCTOR DW WHO

A Fairytale Life

Written by
Matt Sturges

Pencils by
Kelly Yates & Brian Shearer

Inks by
Brian Shearer, Steve Bird, & Rick Ketcham

Colors by
Rachelle Rosenberg

Letters by
Shawn Lee & Neil Uyetake

Cover by
Mark Buckingham

Original Series Edits by
Denton J. Tipton

Collection Edits by
Justin Eisinger
& Alonzo Simon

Collection Design by
Ben D. Brown

Special thanks to Gary Russell, David Turbitt, and Ed Casey for their invaluable assistance.

ISBN: 978-1-61377-022-1   14 13 12 11   1 2 3 4

www.IDWPUBLISHING.com

Ted Adams, CEO & Publisher
Greg Goldstein, Chief Operating Officer
Robbie Robbins, EVP/Sr. Graphic Artist
Chris Ryall, Chief Creative Officer
Matthew Ruzicka, CPA, Chief Financial Officer
Alan Payne, VP of Sales

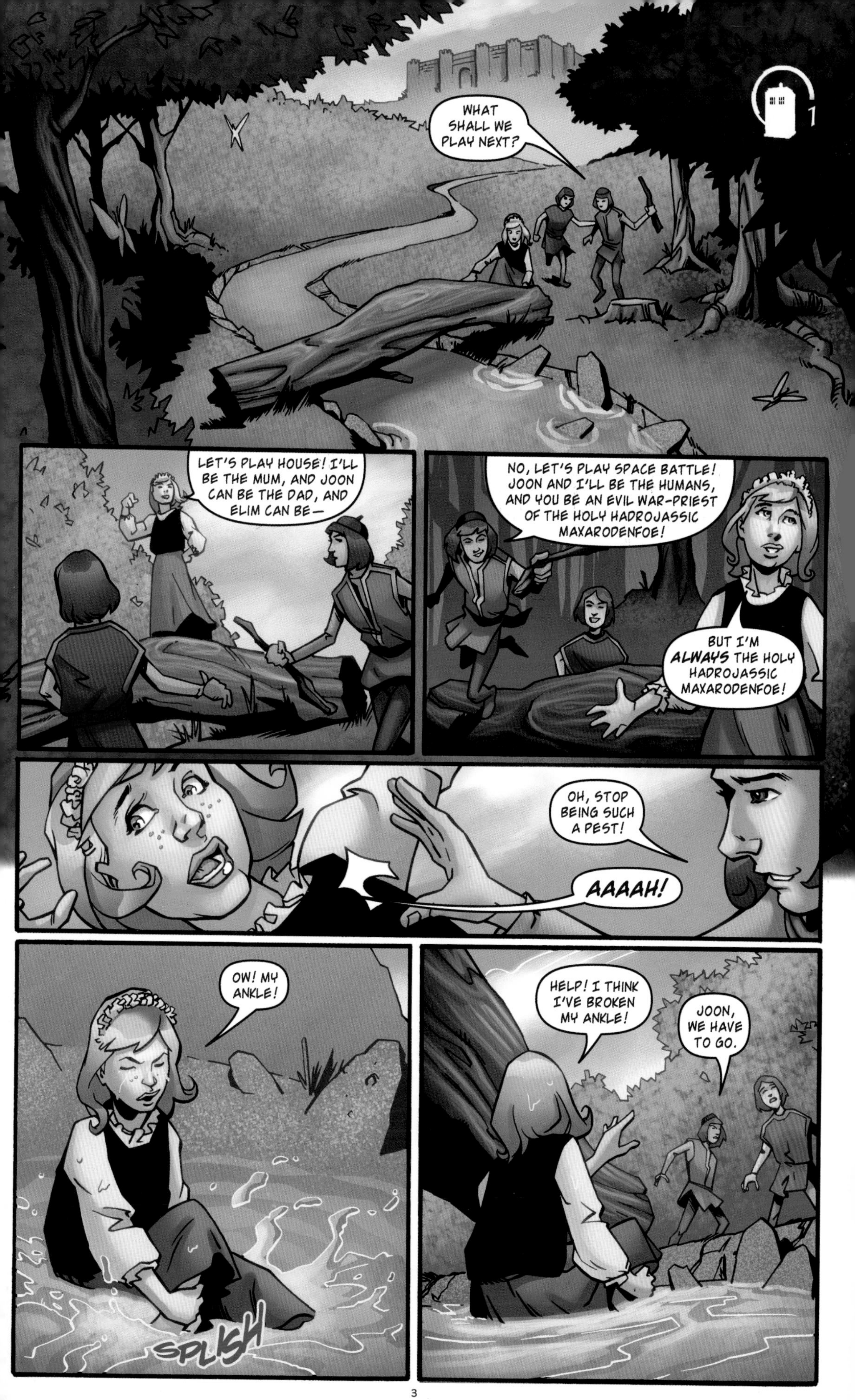

WHAT SHALL WE PLAY NEXT?
LET'S PLAY HOUSE! I'LL BE THE MUM, AND JOON CAN BE THE DAD, AND ELIM CAN BE—
NO, LET'S PLAY SPACE BATTLE! JOON AND I'LL BE THE HUMANS, AND YOU BE AN EVIL WAR-PRIEST OF THE HOLY HADROJASSIC MAXARODENFOE!
BUT I'M ALWAYS THE HOLY HADROJASSIC MAXARODENFOE!
OH, STOP BEING SUCH A PEST!
AAAAH!
OW! MY ANKLE!
SPLISH
HELP! I THINK I'VE BROKEN MY ANKLE!
JOON, WE HAVE TO GO.

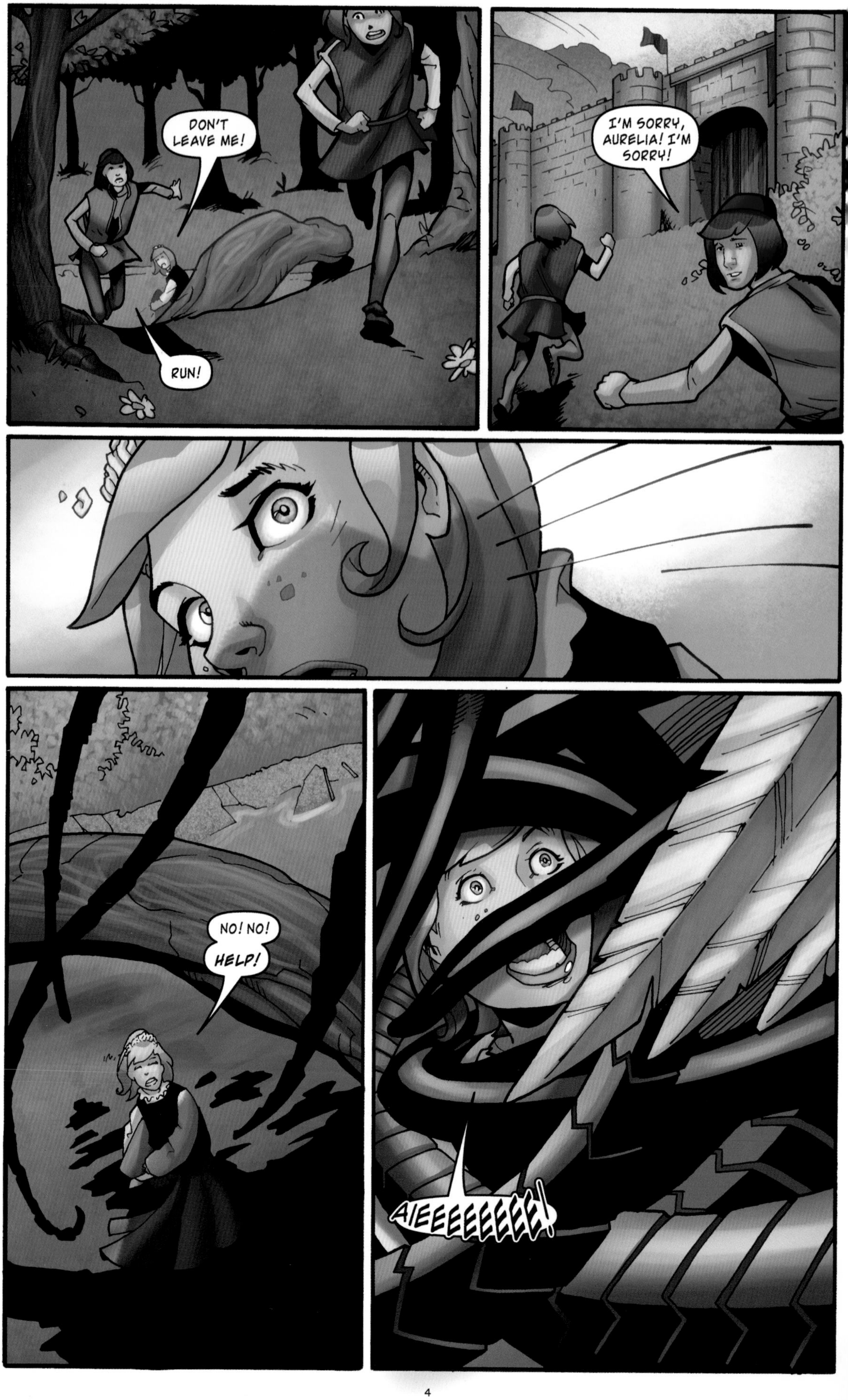
DON'T LEAVE ME!
RUN!
I'M SORRY, AURELIA! I'M SORRY!
NO! NO!
HELP!
AIEEEEEEEEE!

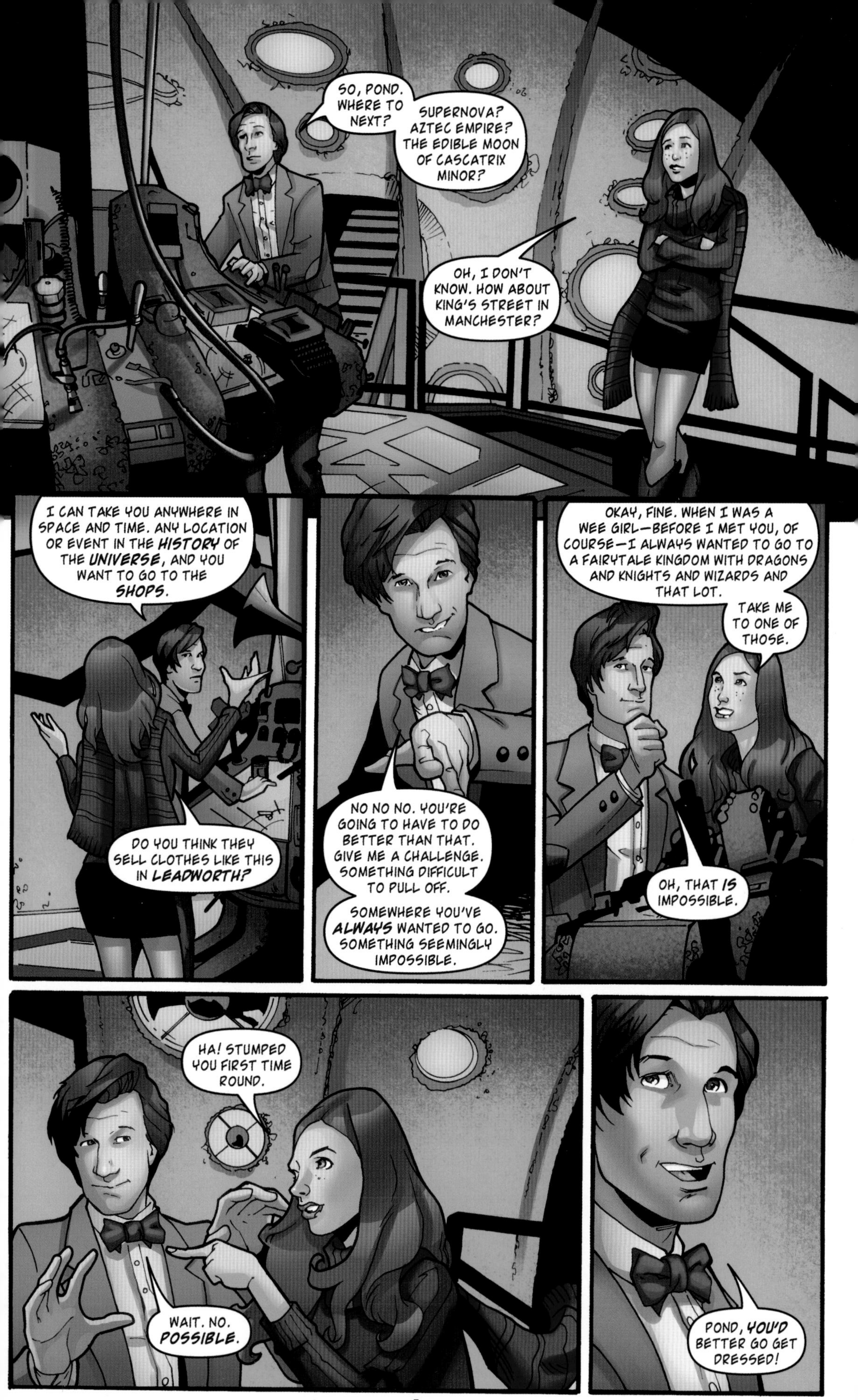

SO, POND. WHERE TO NEXT?
SUPERNOVA? AZTEC EMPIRE? THE EDIBLE MOON OF CASCATRIX MINOR?
OH, I DON'T KNOW. HOW ABOUT KING'S STREET IN MANCHESTER?
I CAN TAKE YOU ANYWHERE IN SPACE AND TIME. ANY LOCATION OR EVENT IN THE HISTORY OF THE UNIVERSE, AND YOU WANT TO GO TO THE SHOPS.
DO YOU THINK THEY SELL CLOTHES LIKE THIS IN LEADWORTH?
NO NO NO. YOU'RE GOING TO HAVE TO DO BETTER THAN THAT. GIVE ME A CHALLENGE. SOMETHING DIFFICULT TO PULL OFF.
SOMEWHERE YOU'VE ALWAYS WANTED TO GO. SOMETHING SEEMINGLY IMPOSSIBLE.
OKAY, FINE. WHEN I WAS A WEE GIRL—BEFORE I MET YOU, OF COURSE—I ALWAYS WANTED TO GO TO A FAIRYTALE KINGDOM WITH DRAGONS AND KNIGHTS AND WIZARDS AND THAT LOT.
TAKE ME TO ONE OF THOSE.
OH, THAT IS IMPOSSIBLE.
HA! STUMPED YOU FIRST TIME ROUND.
WAIT. NO. POSSIBLE.
POND, YOU'D BETTER GO GET DRESSED!

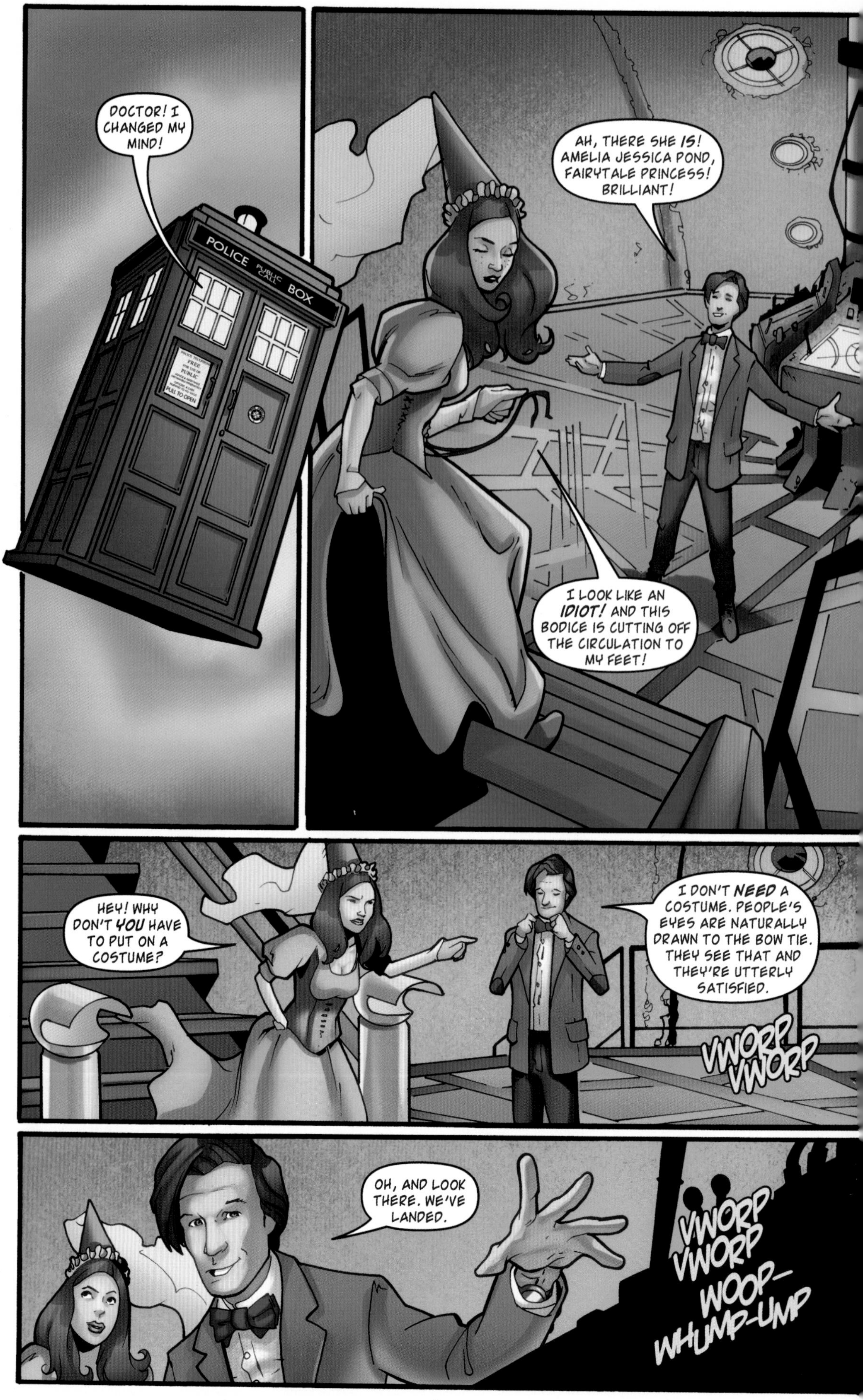
DOCTOR! I CHANGED MY MIND!
POLICE PUBLIC CALL BOX
AH, THERE SHE IS! AMELIA JESSICA POND, FAIRYTALE PRINCESS! BRILLIANT!
I LOOK LIKE AN IDIOT! AND THIS BODICE IS CUTTING OFF THE CIRCULATION TO MY FEET!
HEY! WHY DON'T YOU HAVE TO PUT ON A COSTUME?
I DON'T NEED A COSTUME. PEOPLE'S EYES ARE NATURALLY DRAWN TO THE BOW TIE. THEY SEE THAT AND THEY'RE UTTERLY SATISFIED.
VWORP VWORP
OH, AND LOOK THERE. WE'VE LANDED.
VWORP VWORP WOOP-WHUMP-UMP

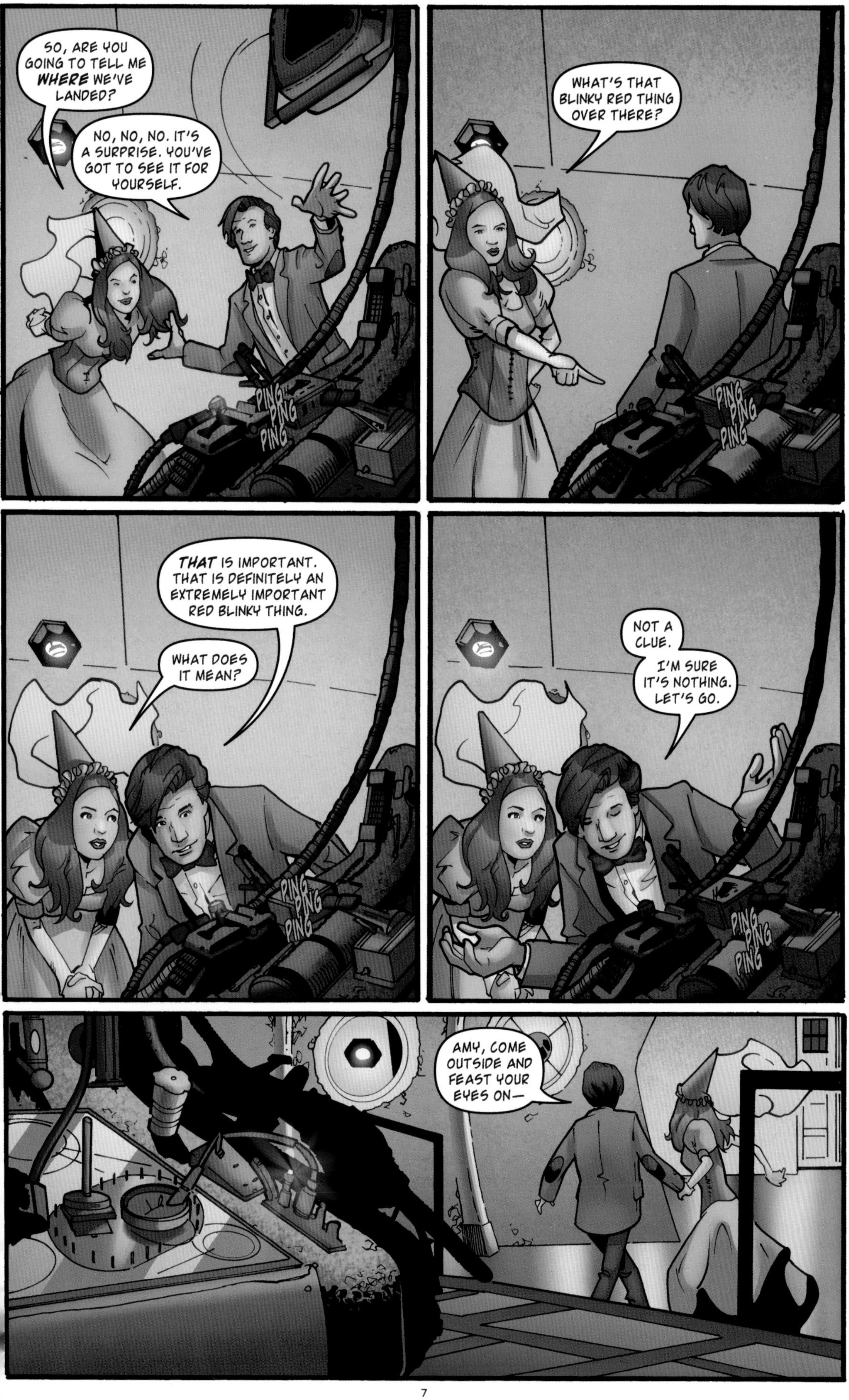
SO, ARE YOU GOING TO TELL ME WHERE WE'VE LANDED?
NO, NO, NO. IT'S A SURPRISE. YOU'VE GOT TO SEE IT FOR YOURSELF.
PING PING PING
WHAT'S THAT BLINKY RED THING OVER THERE?
PING PING PING
THAT IS IMPORTANT. THAT IS DEFINITELY AN EXTREMELY IMPORTANT RED BLINKY THING.
WHAT DOES IT MEAN?
PING PING PING
NOT A CLUE.
I'M SURE IT'S NOTHING. LET'S GO.
PING PING PING
AMY, COME OUTSIDE AND FEAST YOUR EYES ON—

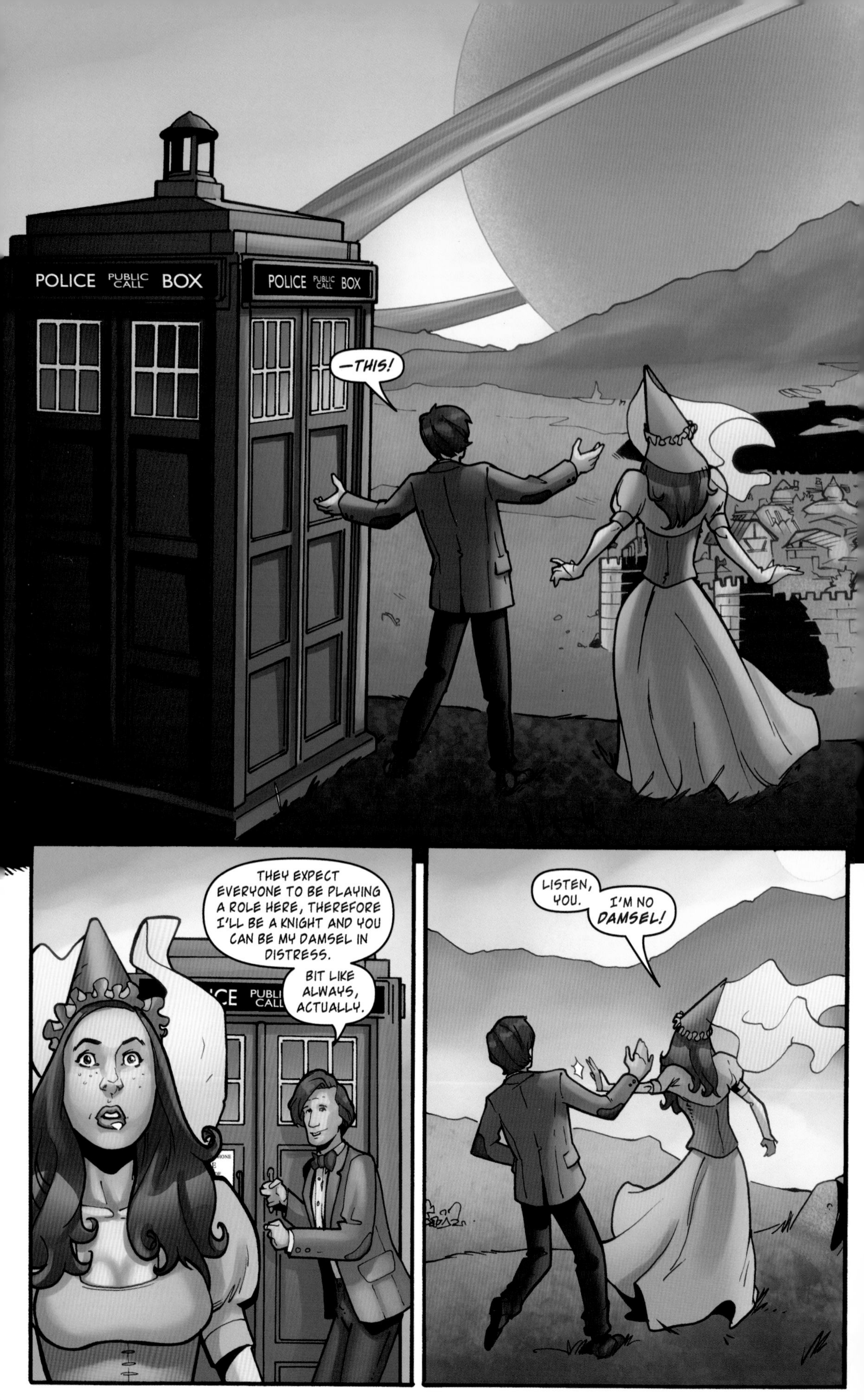
POLICE PUBLIC CALL BOX
POLICE PUBLIC CALL BOX
—THIS!
THEY EXPECT EVERYONE TO BE PLAYING A ROLE HERE, THEREFORE I'LL BE A KNIGHT AND YOU CAN BE MY DAMSEL IN DISTRESS.
BIT LIKE ALWAYS, ACTUALLY.
LISTEN, YOU.
I'M NO DAMSEL!

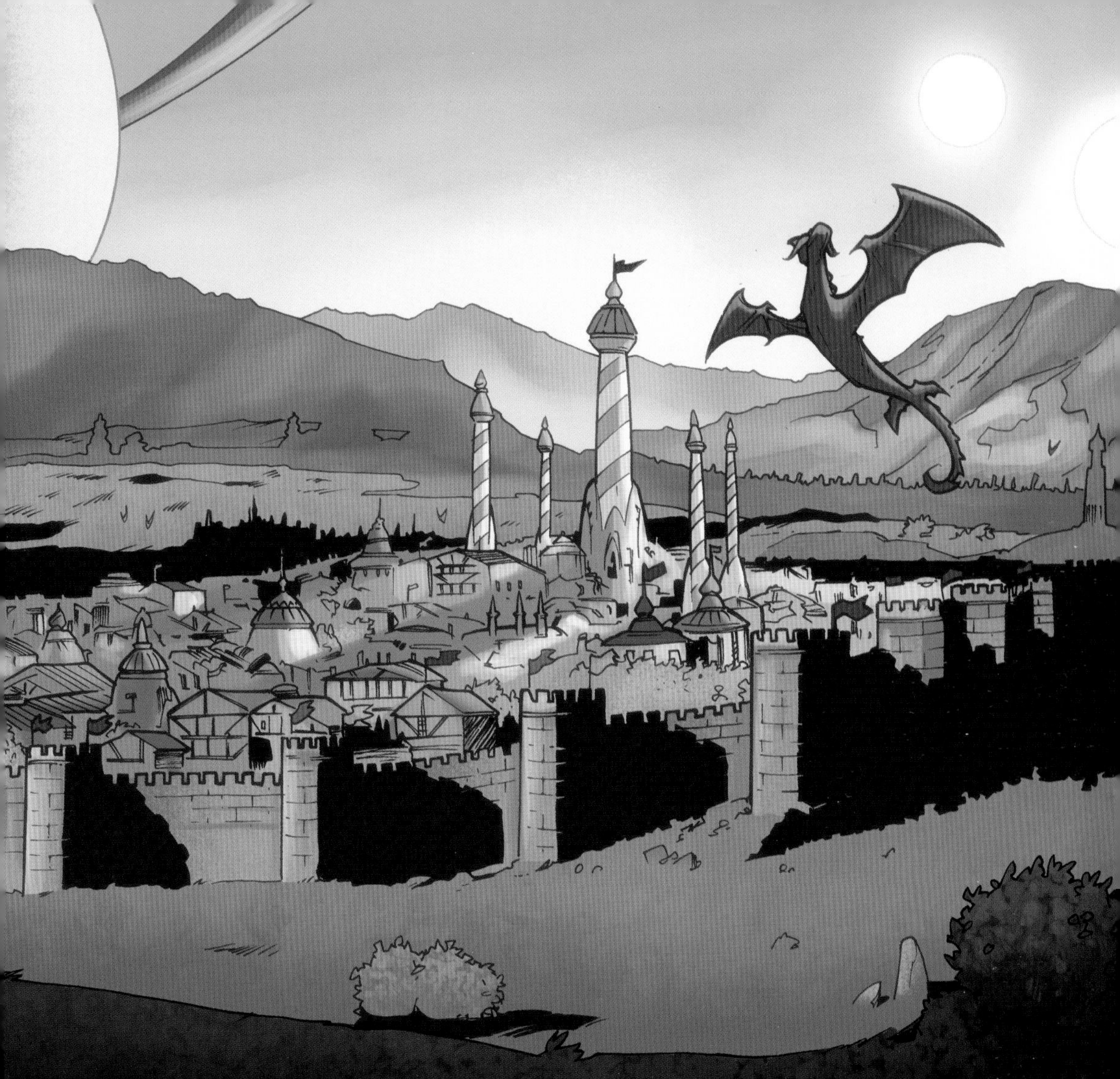

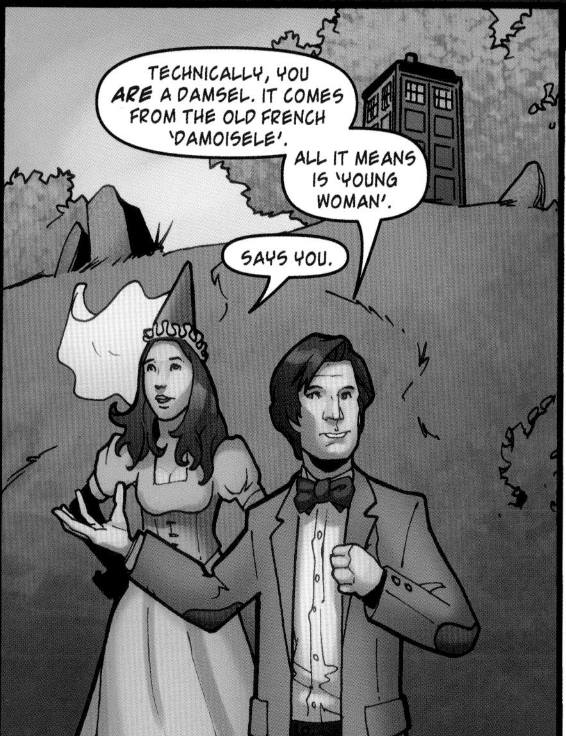
TECHNICALLY, YOU ARE A DAMSEL. IT COMES FROM THE OLD FRENCH 'DAMOISELE'.
ALL IT MEANS IS 'YOUNG WOMAN'.
SAYS YOU.

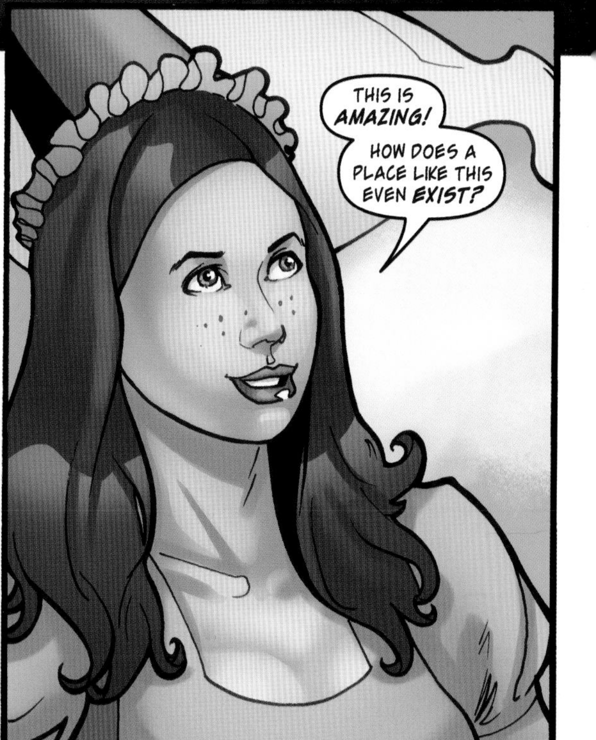
THIS IS AMAZING!
HOW DOES A PLACE LIKE THIS EVEN EXIST?

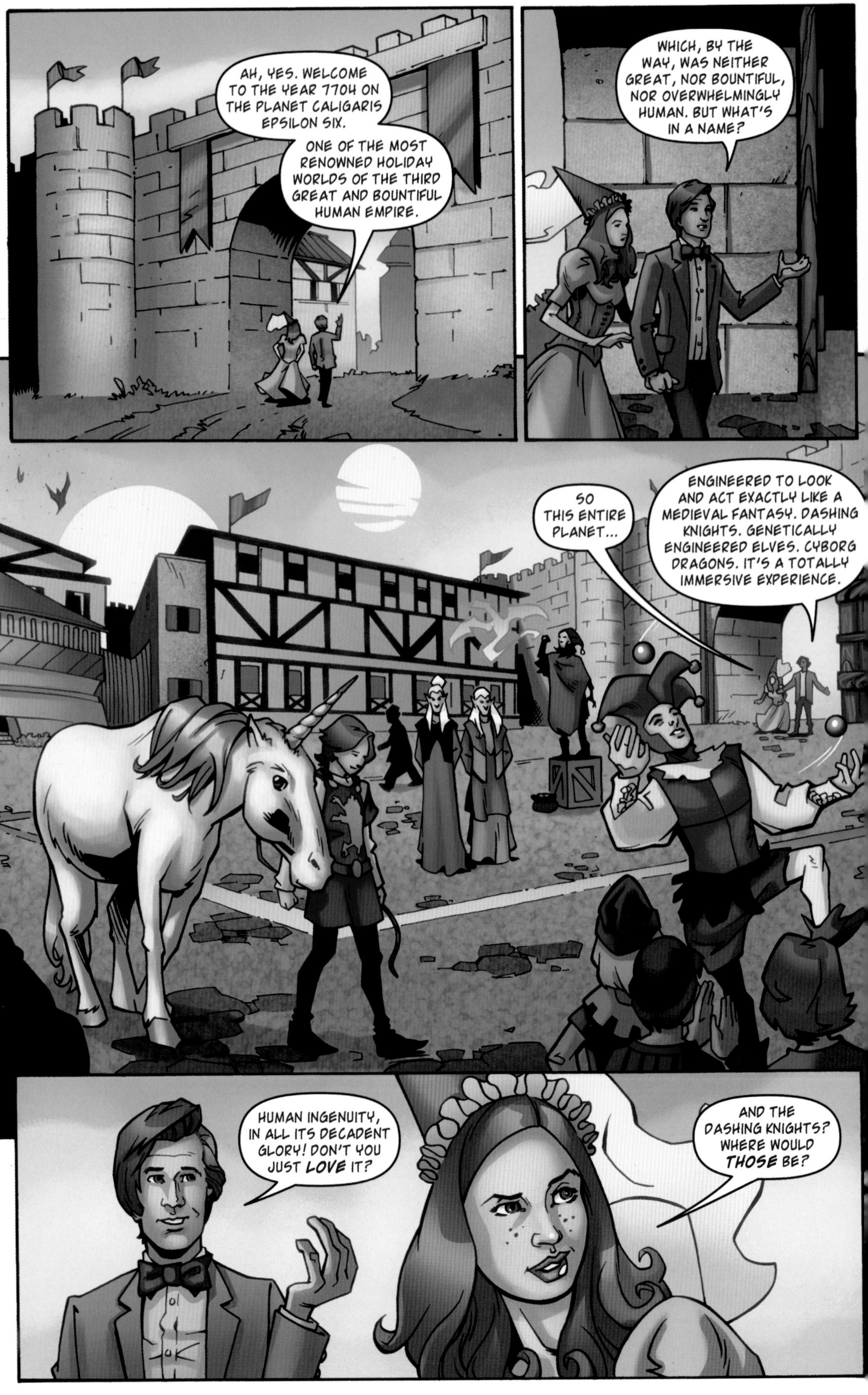
AH, YES. WELCOME TO THE YEAR 7704 ON THE PLANET CALIGARIS EPSILON SIX.
ONE OF THE MOST RENOWNED HOLIDAY WORLDS OF THE THIRD GREAT AND BOUNTIFUL HUMAN EMPIRE.
WHICH, BY THE WAY, WAS NEITHER GREAT, NOR BOUNTIFUL, NOR OVERWHELMINGLY HUMAN. BUT WHAT'S IN A NAME?
SO THIS ENTIRE PLANET...
ENGINEERED TO LOOK AND ACT EXACTLY LIKE A MEDIEVAL FANTASY. DASHING KNIGHTS. GENETICALLY ENGINEERED ELVES. CYBORG DRAGONS. IT'S A TOTALLY IMMERSIVE EXPERIENCE.
HUMAN INGENUITY, IN ALL ITS DECADENT GLORY! DON'T YOU JUST *LOVE* IT?
AND THE DASHING KNIGHTS? WHERE WOULD *THOSE* BE?

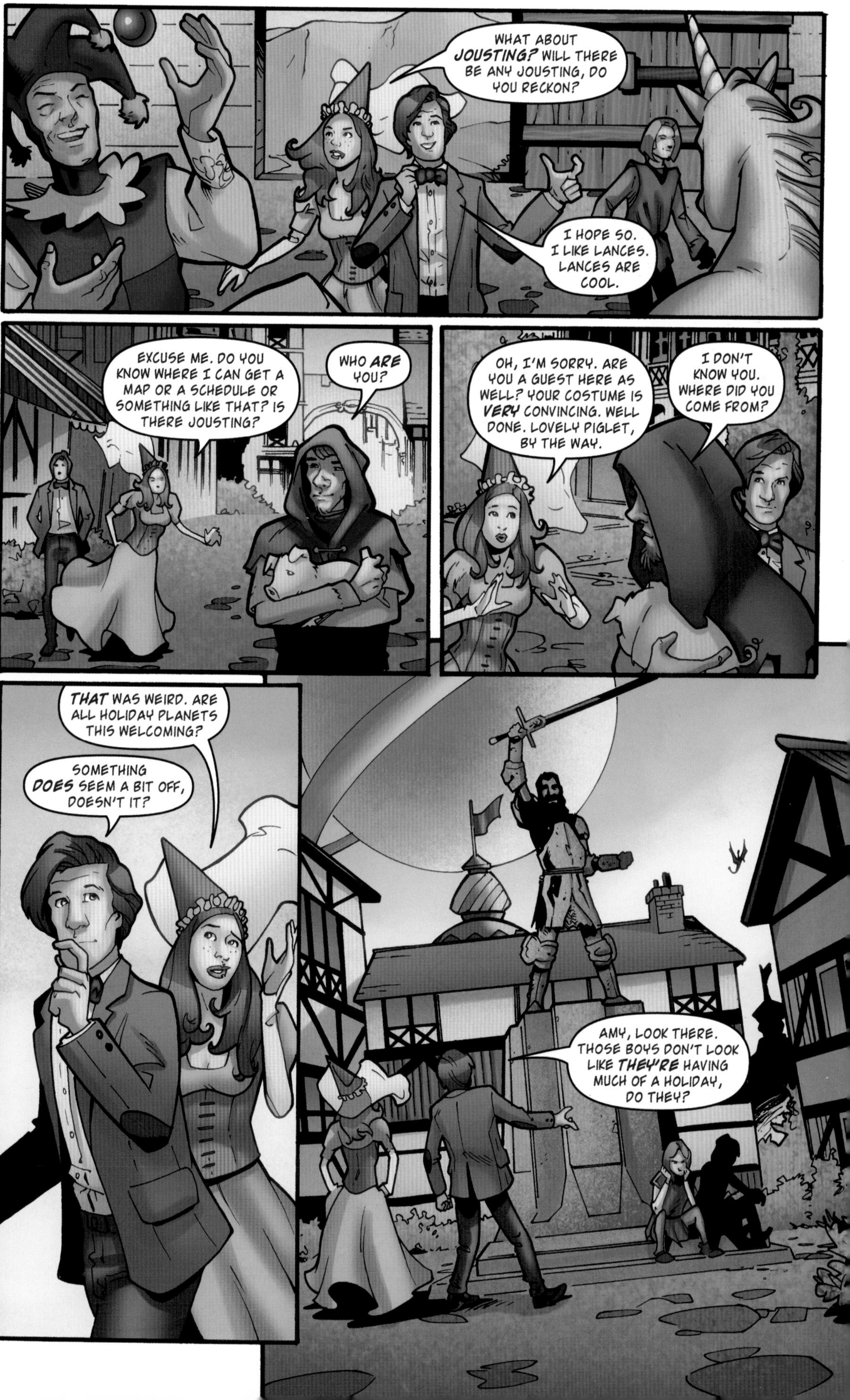
WHAT ABOUT JOUSTING? WILL THERE BE ANY JOUSTING, DO YOU RECKON?
I HOPE SO. I LIKE LANCES. LANCES ARE COOL.
EXCUSE ME. DO YOU KNOW WHERE I CAN GET A MAP OR A SCHEDULE OR SOMETHING LIKE THAT? IS THERE JOUSTING?
WHO ARE YOU?
OH, I'M SORRY. ARE YOU A GUEST HERE AS WELL? YOUR COSTUME IS VERY CONVINCING. WELL DONE. LOVELY PIGLET, BY THE WAY.
I DON'T KNOW YOU. WHERE DID YOU COME FROM?
THAT WAS WEIRD. ARE ALL HOLIDAY PLANETS THIS WELCOMING?
SOMETHING DOES SEEM A BIT OFF, DOESN'T IT?
AMY, LOOK THERE. THOSE BOYS DON'T LOOK LIKE THEY'RE HAVING MUCH OF A HOLIDAY, DO THEY?

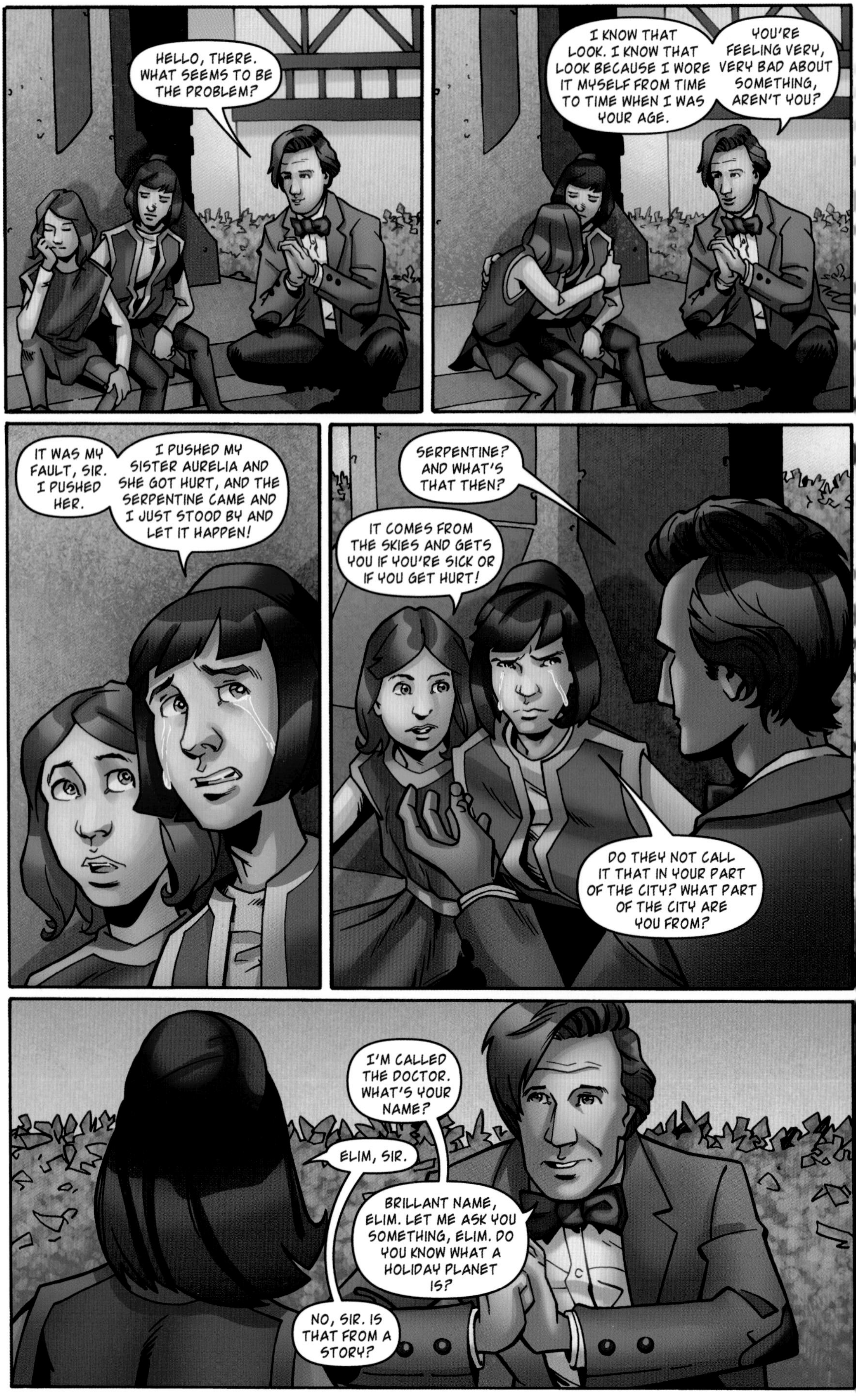
HELLO, THERE. WHAT SEEMS TO BE THE PROBLEM?
I KNOW THAT LOOK. I KNOW THAT LOOK BECAUSE I WORE IT MYSELF FROM TIME TO TIME WHEN I WAS YOUR AGE.
YOU'RE FEELING VERY, VERY BAD ABOUT SOMETHING, AREN'T YOU?
IT WAS MY FAULT, SIR. I PUSHED HER.
I PUSHED MY SISTER AURELIA AND SHE GOT HURT, AND THE SERPENTINE CAME AND I JUST STOOD BY AND LET IT HAPPEN!
SERPENTINE? AND WHAT'S THAT THEN?
IT COMES FROM THE SKIES AND GETS YOU IF YOU'RE SICK OR IF YOU GET HURT!
DO THEY NOT CALL IT THAT IN YOUR PART OF THE CITY? WHAT PART OF THE CITY ARE YOU FROM?
I'M CALLED THE DOCTOR. WHAT'S YOUR NAME?
ELIM, SIR.
BRILLANT NAME, ELIM. LET ME ASK YOU SOMETHING, ELIM. DO YOU KNOW WHAT A HOLIDAY PLANET IS?
NO, SIR. IS THAT FROM A STORY?

JUST OUT OF CURIOSITY, HAVE YOU LIVED HERE ALL YOUR LIFE?

YES, SIR. OF COURSE, SIR.

COME ON, JOON. WE SHOULD GO.

ELIM, WAIT. WHERE DID THESE SERPENTINES TAKE YOUR SISTER? I'D VERY MUCH LIKE TO KNOW THAT.

TO THE DREAD TOWER, OF COURSE. WHY ARE YOU ASKING ALL THESE QUESTIONS?

BECAUSE I AM VERY GOOD AT FINDING PEOPLE WHEN I PUT MY MIND TO IT.

PERHAPS I COULD FIND YOUR SISTER.

LET'S GO!

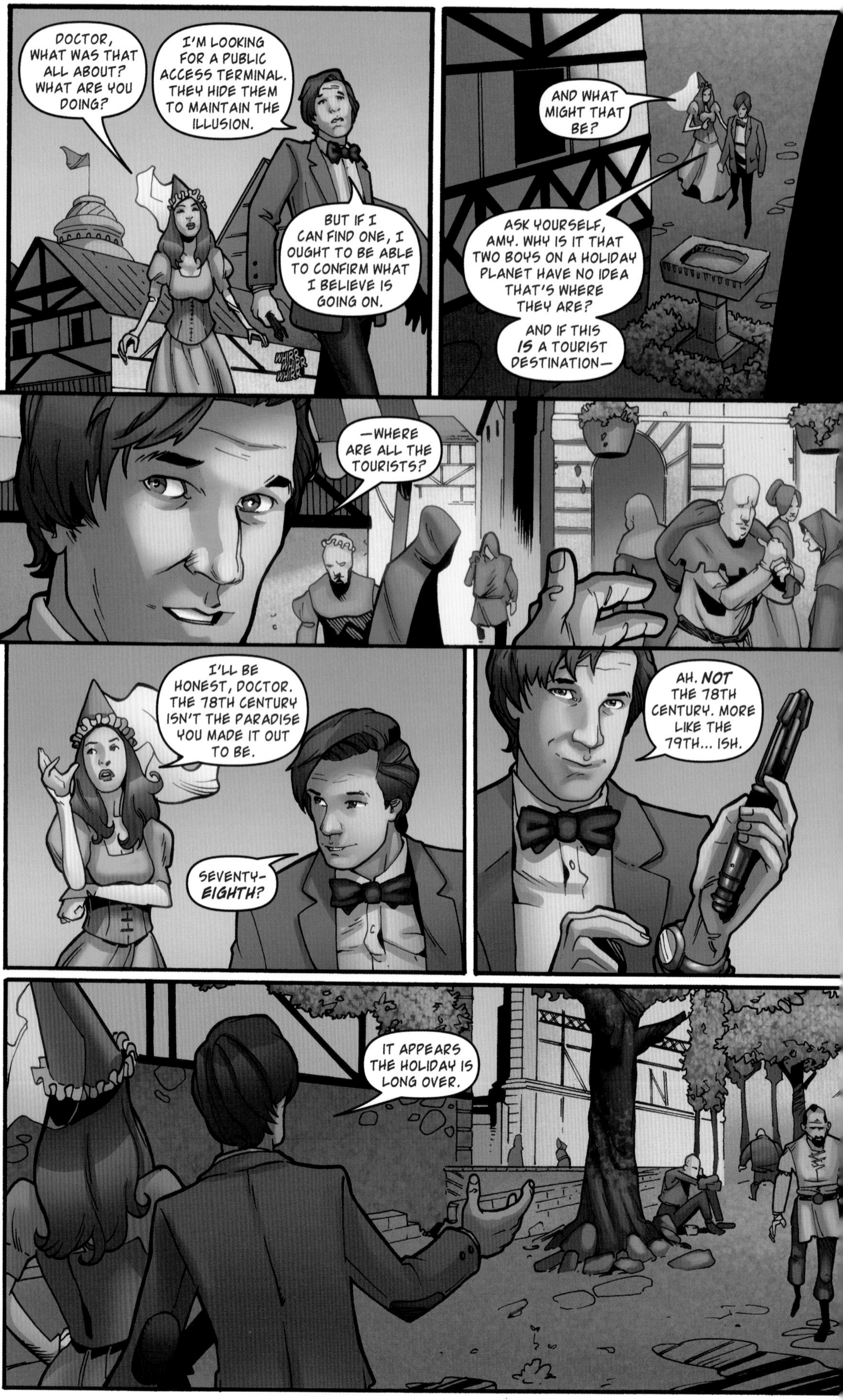
DOCTOR, WHAT WAS THAT ALL ABOUT? WHAT ARE YOU DOING?
I'M LOOKING FOR A PUBLIC ACCESS TERMINAL. THEY HIDE THEM TO MAINTAIN THE ILLUSION.
BUT IF I CAN FIND ONE, I OUGHT TO BE ABLE TO CONFIRM WHAT I BELIEVE IS GOING ON.
AND WHAT MIGHT THAT BE?
ASK YOURSELF, AMY. WHY IS IT THAT TWO BOYS ON A HOLIDAY PLANET HAVE NO IDEA THAT'S WHERE THEY ARE?
AND IF THIS IS A TOURIST DESTINATION—
—WHERE ARE ALL THE TOURISTS?
I'LL BE HONEST, DOCTOR. THE 78TH CENTURY ISN'T THE PARADISE YOU MADE IT OUT TO BE.
SEVENTY-EIGHTH?
AH. NOT THE 78TH CENTURY. MORE LIKE THE 79TH... ISH.
IT APPEARS THE HOLIDAY IS LONG OVER.

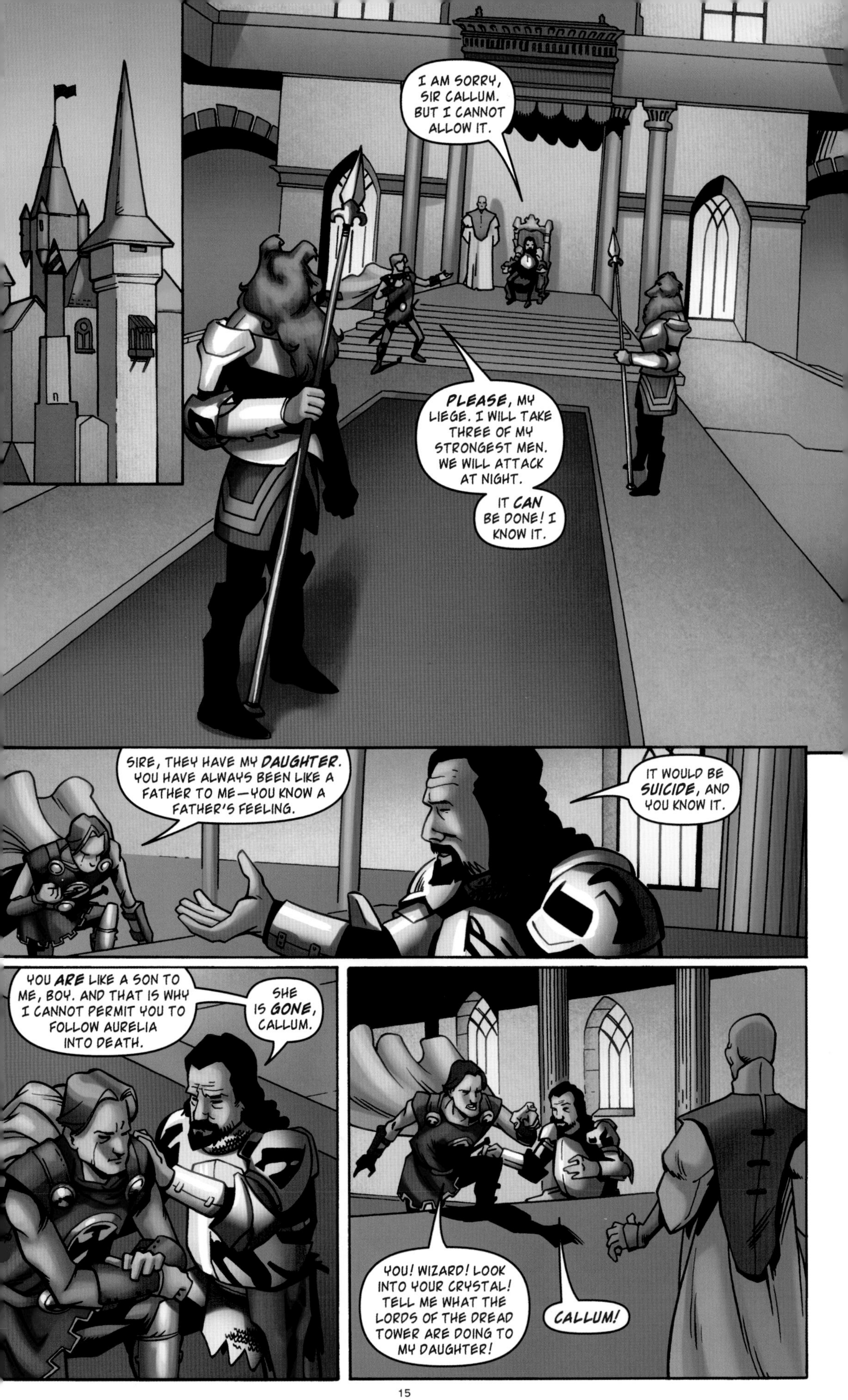
I AM SORRY, SIR CALLUM. BUT I CANNOT ALLOW IT.
PLEASE, MY LIEGE. I WILL TAKE THREE OF MY STRONGEST MEN. WE WILL ATTACK AT NIGHT.
IT CAN BE DONE! I KNOW IT.
SIRE, THEY HAVE MY DAUGHTER. YOU HAVE ALWAYS BEEN LIKE A FATHER TO ME—YOU KNOW A FATHER'S FEELING.
IT WOULD BE SUICIDE, AND YOU KNOW IT.
YOU ARE LIKE A SON TO ME, BOY. AND THAT IS WHY I CANNOT PERMIT YOU TO FOLLOW AURELIA INTO DEATH.
SHE IS GONE, CALLUM.
YOU! WIZARD! LOOK INTO YOUR CRYSTAL! TELL ME WHAT THE LORDS OF THE DREAD TOWER ARE DOING TO MY DAUGHTER!
CALLUM!

MY SCRYING CRYSTAL CANNOT PIERCE THE VEIL THAT SURROUNDS THAT PLACE, SIR CALLUM.

YOU KNOW THIS.

BUT SOMETHING *MUST* BE DONE! I CANNOT SIT BY AND DO NOTHING!

WHAT'S THIS?

WHAT DO YOU SEE, GWYDION?

A MAN AND A WOMAN I DO NOT KNOW. THEY ARE IN THE CITY. THEY HAVE BEEN TALKING WITH YOUR SON, SIR CALLUM.

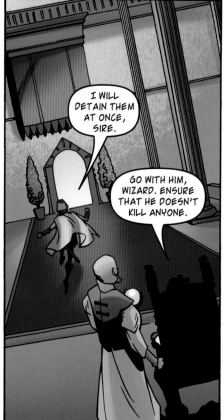

I WILL DETAIN THEM AT ONCE, SIRE.

GO WITH HIM, WIZARD. ENSURE THAT HE DOESN'T KILL ANYONE.

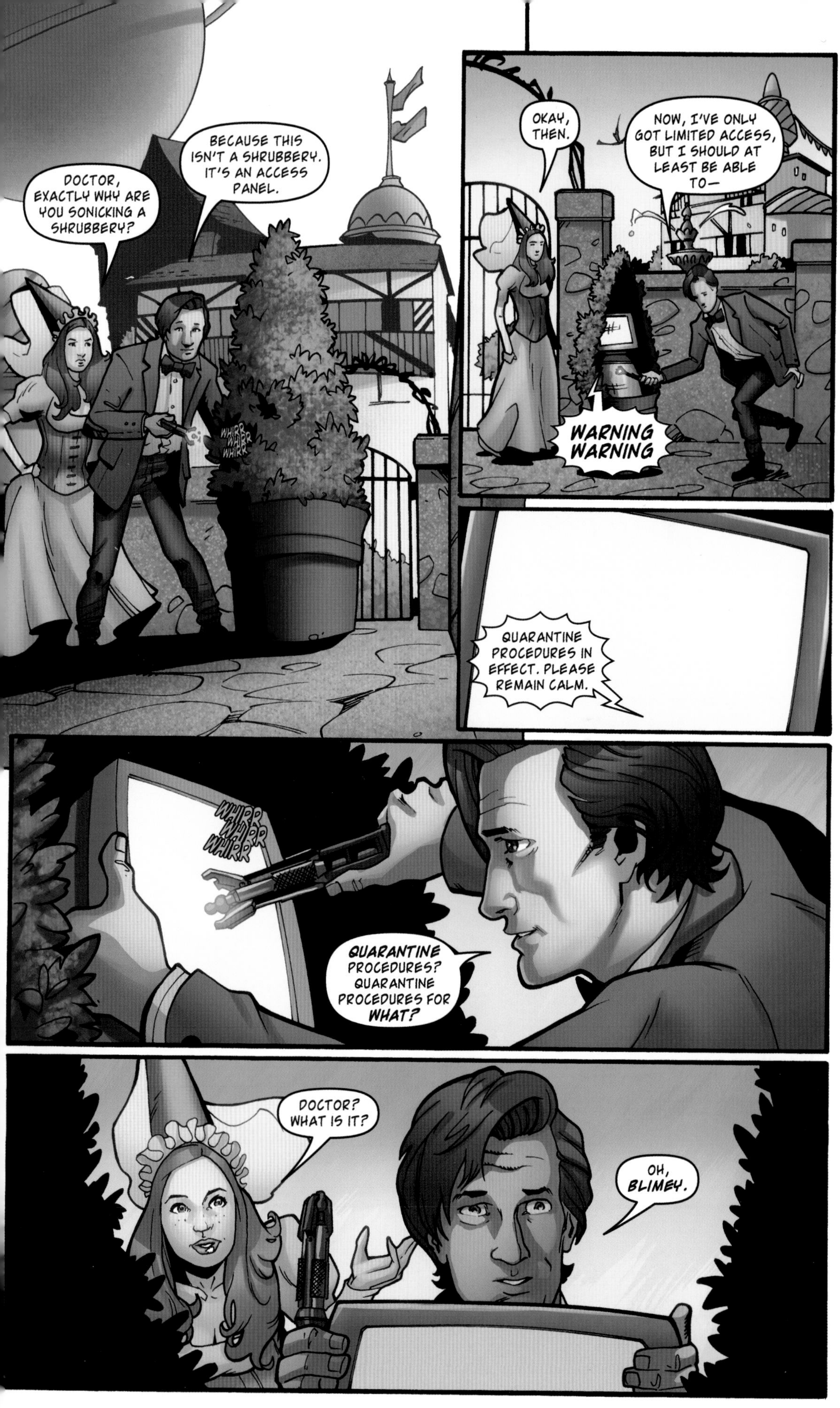
DOCTOR, EXACTLY WHY ARE YOU SONICKING A SHRUBBERY?
BECAUSE THIS ISN'T A SHRUBBERY. IT'S AN ACCESS PANEL.
WHIRR WHIRR WHIRR
OKAY, THEN.
NOW, I'VE ONLY GOT LIMITED ACCESS, BUT I SHOULD AT LEAST BE ABLE TO—
WARNING WARNING
QUARANTINE PROCEDURES IN EFFECT. PLEASE REMAIN CALM.
WHIRR WHIRR WHIRR
QUARANTINE PROCEDURES? QUARANTINE PROCEDURES FOR WHAT?
DOCTOR? WHAT IS IT?
OH, BLIMEY.

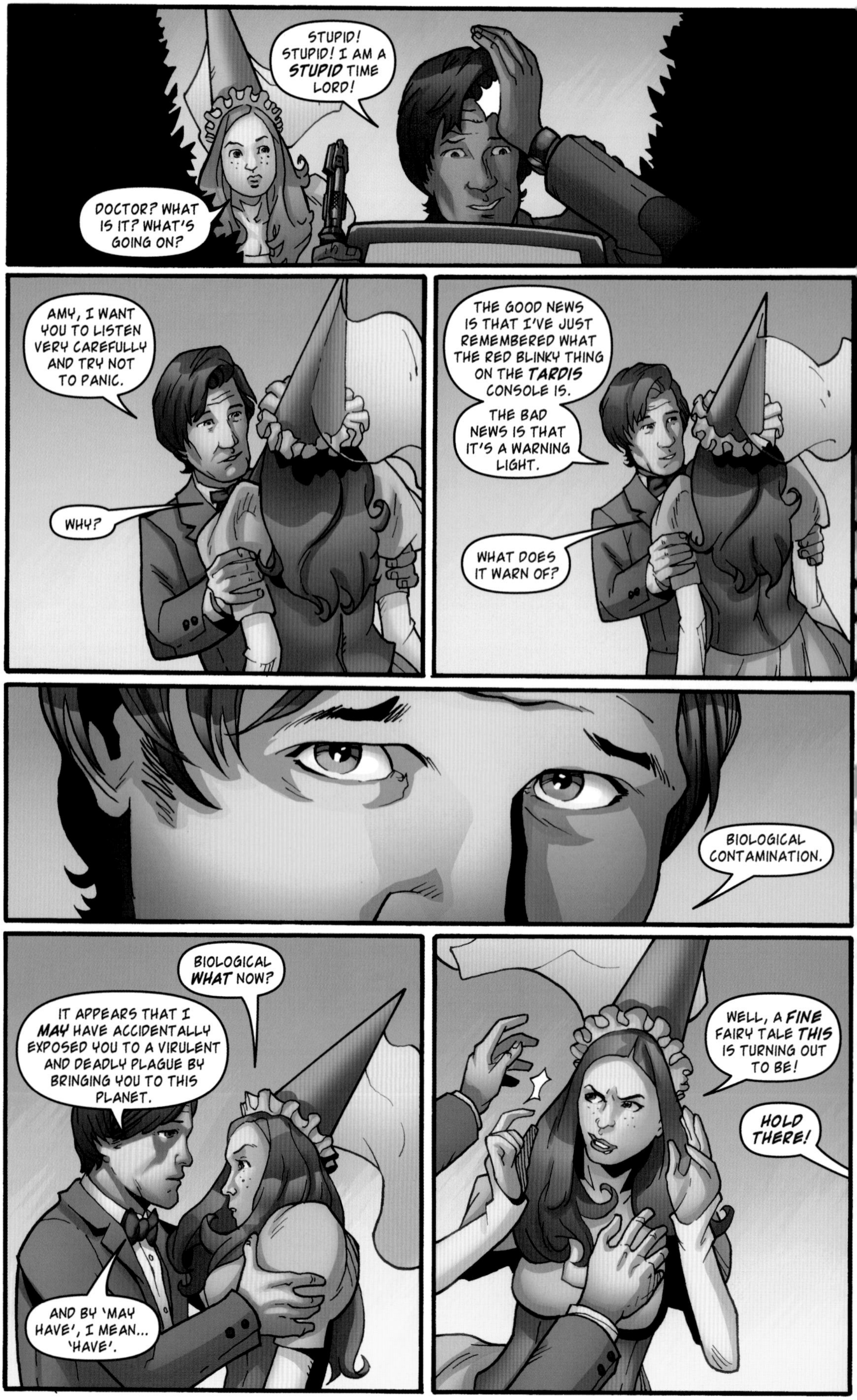
STUPID! STUPID! I AM A STUPID TIME LORD!
DOCTOR? WHAT IS IT? WHAT'S GOING ON?
AMY, I WANT YOU TO LISTEN VERY CAREFULLY AND TRY NOT TO PANIC.
WHY?
THE GOOD NEWS IS THAT I'VE JUST REMEMBERED WHAT THE RED BLINKY THING ON THE TARDIS CONSOLE IS.
THE BAD NEWS IS THAT IT'S A WARNING LIGHT.
WHAT DOES IT WARN OF?
BIOLOGICAL CONTAMINATION.
BIOLOGICAL WHAT NOW?
IT APPEARS THAT I MAY HAVE ACCIDENTALLY EXPOSED YOU TO A VIRULENT AND DEADLY PLAGUE BY BRINGING YOU TO THIS PLANET.
AND BY 'MAY HAVE', I MEAN... 'HAVE'.
WELL, A FINE FAIRY TALE THIS IS TURNING OUT TO BE!
HOLD THERE!

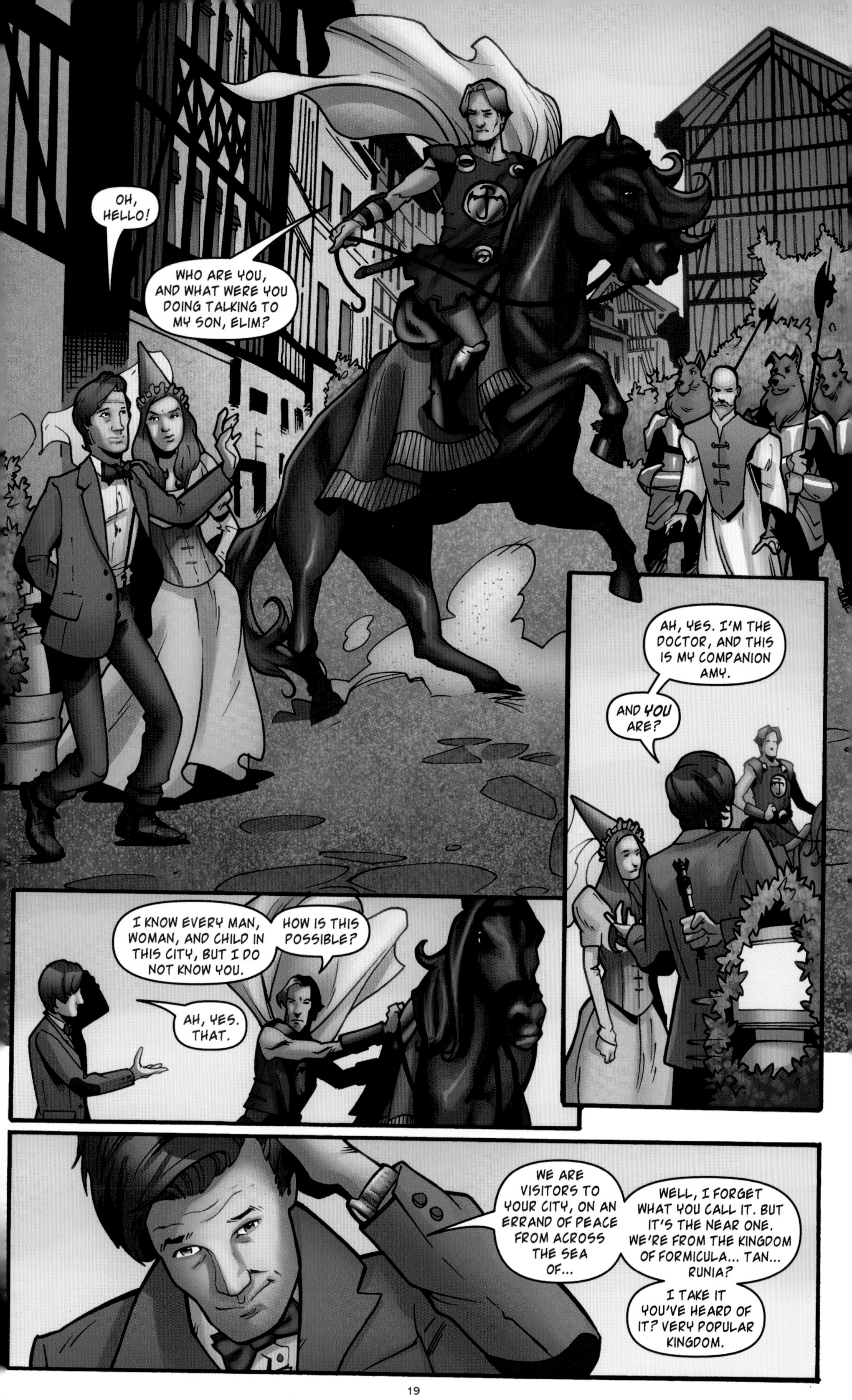
OH, HELLO!
WHO ARE YOU, AND WHAT WERE YOU DOING TALKING TO MY SON, ELIM?
AH, YES. I'M THE DOCTOR, AND THIS IS MY COMPANION AMY.
AND YOU ARE?
I KNOW EVERY MAN, WOMAN, AND CHILD IN THIS CITY, BUT I DO NOT KNOW YOU.
HOW IS THIS POSSIBLE?
AH, YES. THAT.
WE ARE VISITORS TO YOUR CITY, ON AN ERRAND OF PEACE FROM ACROSS THE SEA OF...
WELL, I FORGET WHAT YOU CALL IT. BUT IT'S THE NEAR ONE. WE'RE FROM THE KINGDOM OF FORMICULA... TAN... RUNIA?
I TAKE IT YOU'VE HEARD OF IT? VERY POPULAR KINGDOM.

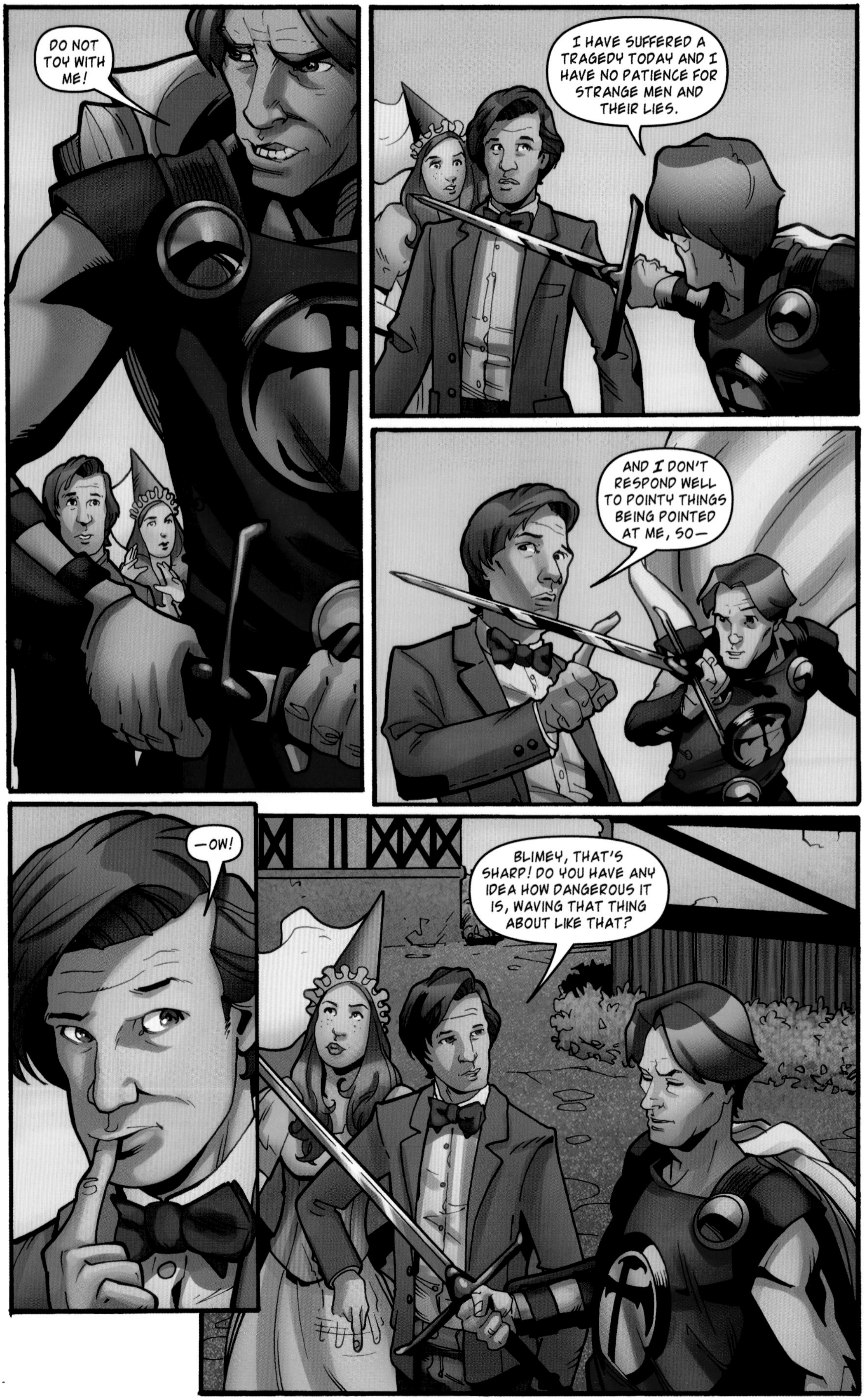
DO NOT TOY WITH ME!
I HAVE SUFFERED A TRAGEDY TODAY AND I HAVE NO PATIENCE FOR STRANGE MEN AND THEIR LIES.
AND I DON'T RESPOND WELL TO POINTY THINGS BEING POINTED AT ME, SO—
—OW!
BLIMEY, THAT'S SHARP! DO YOU HAVE ANY IDEA HOW DANGEROUS IT IS, WAVING THAT THING ABOUT LIKE THAT?

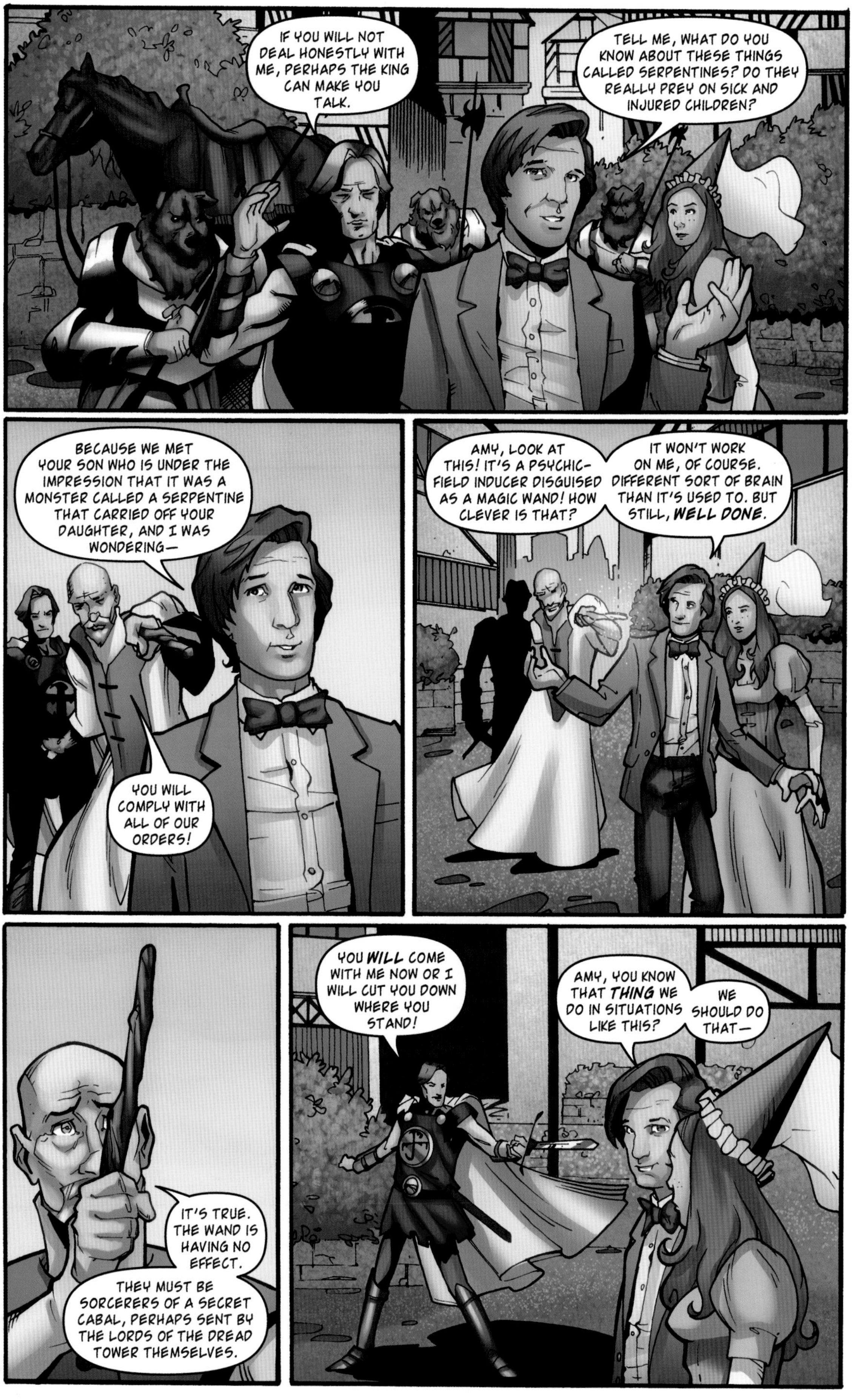
IF YOU WILL NOT DEAL HONESTLY WITH ME, PERHAPS THE KING CAN MAKE YOU TALK.
TELL ME, WHAT DO YOU KNOW ABOUT THESE THINGS CALLED SERPENTINES? DO THEY REALLY PREY ON SICK AND INJURED CHILDREN?
BECAUSE WE MET YOUR SON WHO IS UNDER THE IMPRESSION THAT IT WAS A MONSTER CALLED A SERPENTINE THAT CARRIED OFF YOUR DAUGHTER, AND I WAS WONDERING—
YOU WILL COMPLY WITH ALL OF OUR ORDERS!
AMY, LOOK AT THIS! IT'S A PSYCHIC-FIELD INDUCER DISGUISED AS A MAGIC WAND! HOW CLEVER IS THAT?
IT WON'T WORK ON ME, OF COURSE. DIFFERENT SORT OF BRAIN THAN IT'S USED TO. BUT STILL, *WELL DONE*.
IT'S TRUE. THE WAND IS HAVING NO EFFECT.
THEY MUST BE SORCERERS OF A SECRET CABAL, PERHAPS SENT BY THE LORDS OF THE DREAD TOWER THEMSELVES.
YOU *WILL* COME WITH ME NOW OR I WILL CUT YOU DOWN WHERE YOU STAND!
AMY, YOU KNOW THAT *THING* WE DO IN SITUATIONS LIKE THIS?
WE SHOULD DO THAT—

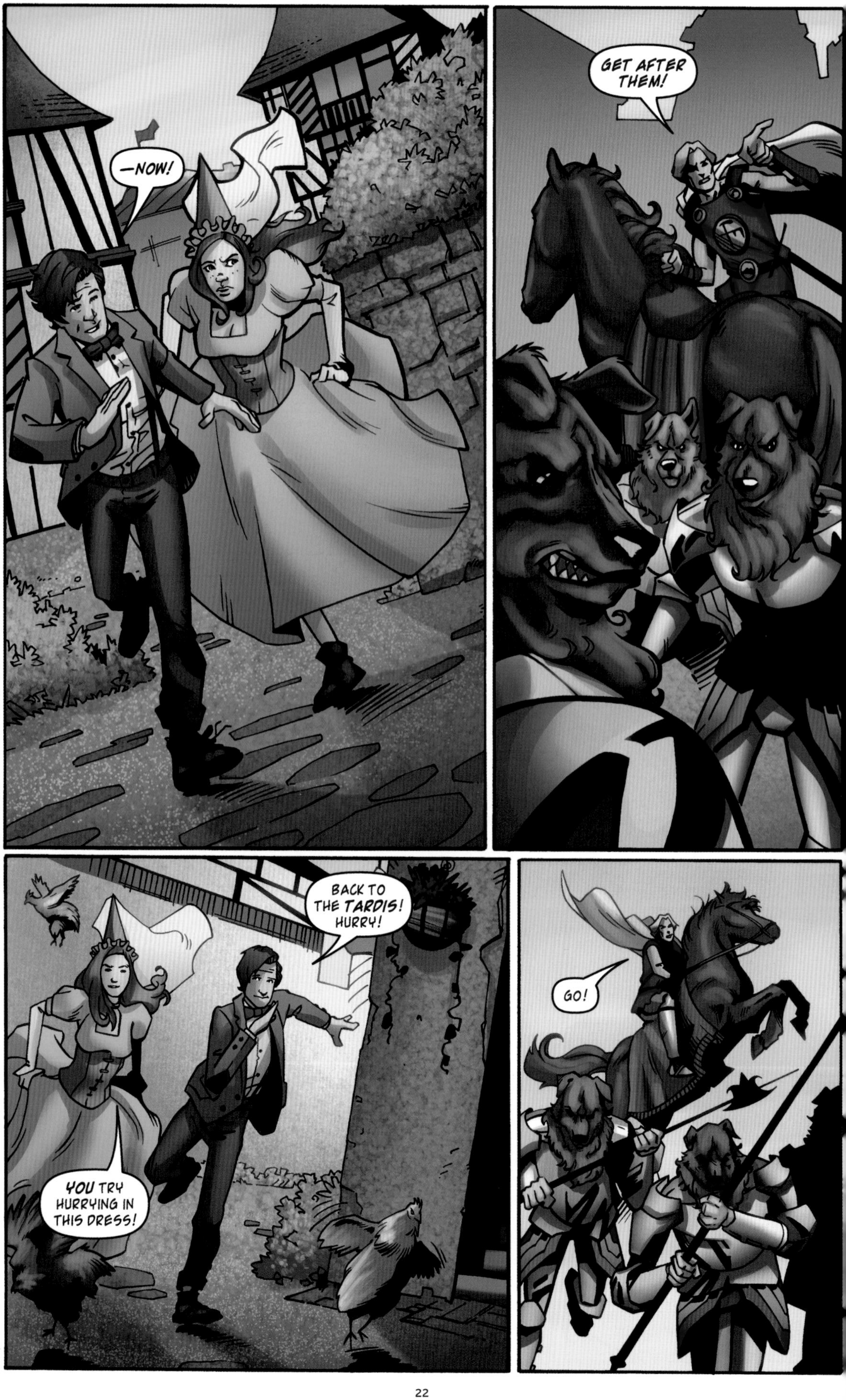

—NOW!
GET AFTER THEM!
BACK TO THE TARDIS! HURRY!
YOU TRY HURRYING IN THIS DRESS!
GO!

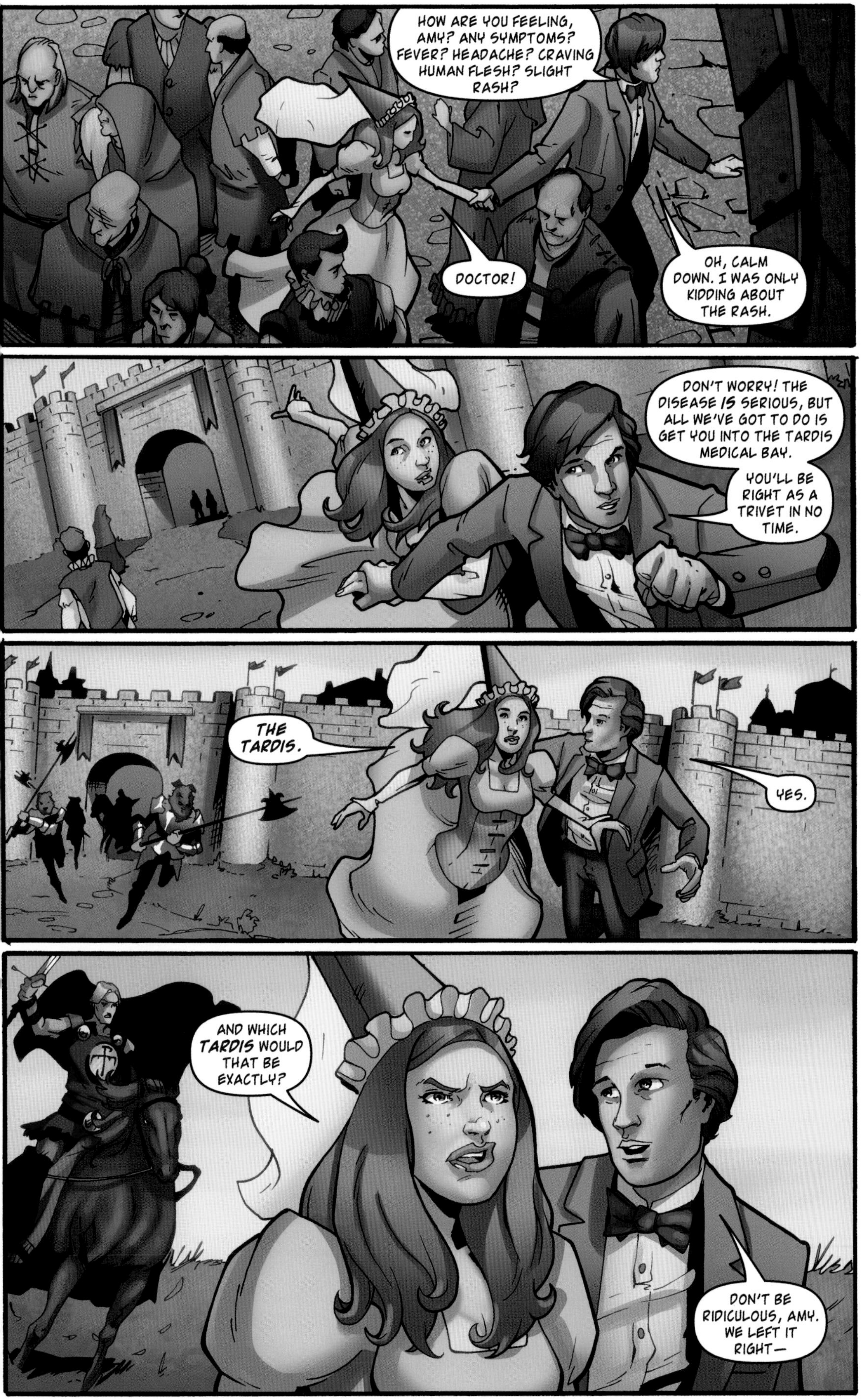
HOW ARE YOU FEELING, AMY? ANY SYMPTOMS? FEVER? HEADACHE? CRAVING HUMAN FLESH? SLIGHT RASH?
DOCTOR!
OH, CALM DOWN. I WAS ONLY KIDDING ABOUT THE RASH.
DON'T WORRY! THE DISEASE IS SERIOUS, BUT ALL WE'VE GOT TO DO IS GET YOU INTO THE TARDIS MEDICAL BAY.
YOU'LL BE RIGHT AS A TRIVET IN NO TIME.
THE TARDIS.
YES.
AND WHICH TARDIS WOULD THAT BE EXACTLY?
DON'T BE RIDICULOUS, AMY. WE LEFT IT RIGHT—

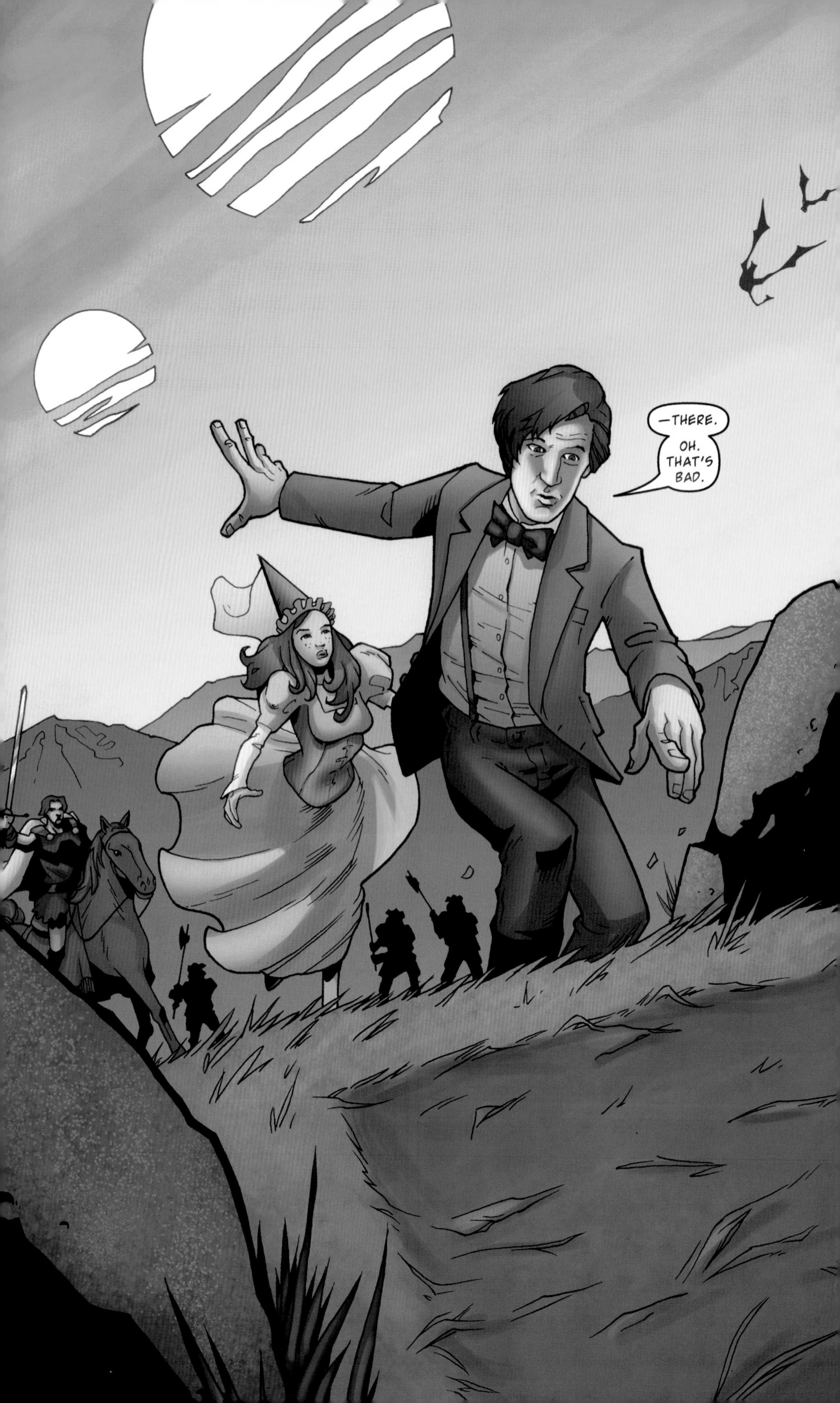
—THERE.
OH. THAT'S BAD.

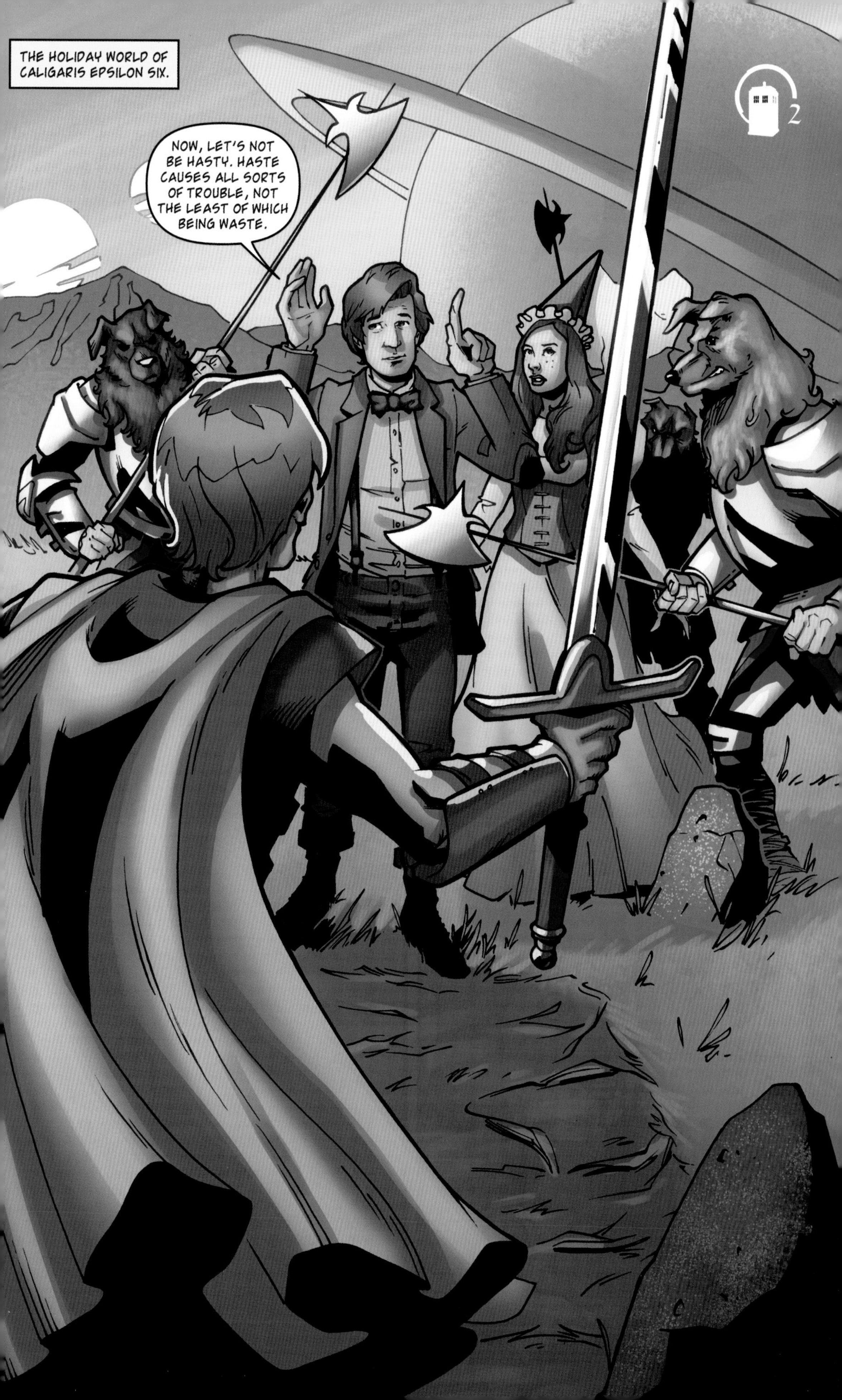
THE HOLIDAY WORLD OF CALIGARIS EPSILON SIX.
NOW, LET'S NOT BE HASTY. HASTE CAUSES ALL SORTS OF TROUBLE, NOT THE LEAST OF WHICH BEING WASTE.
2

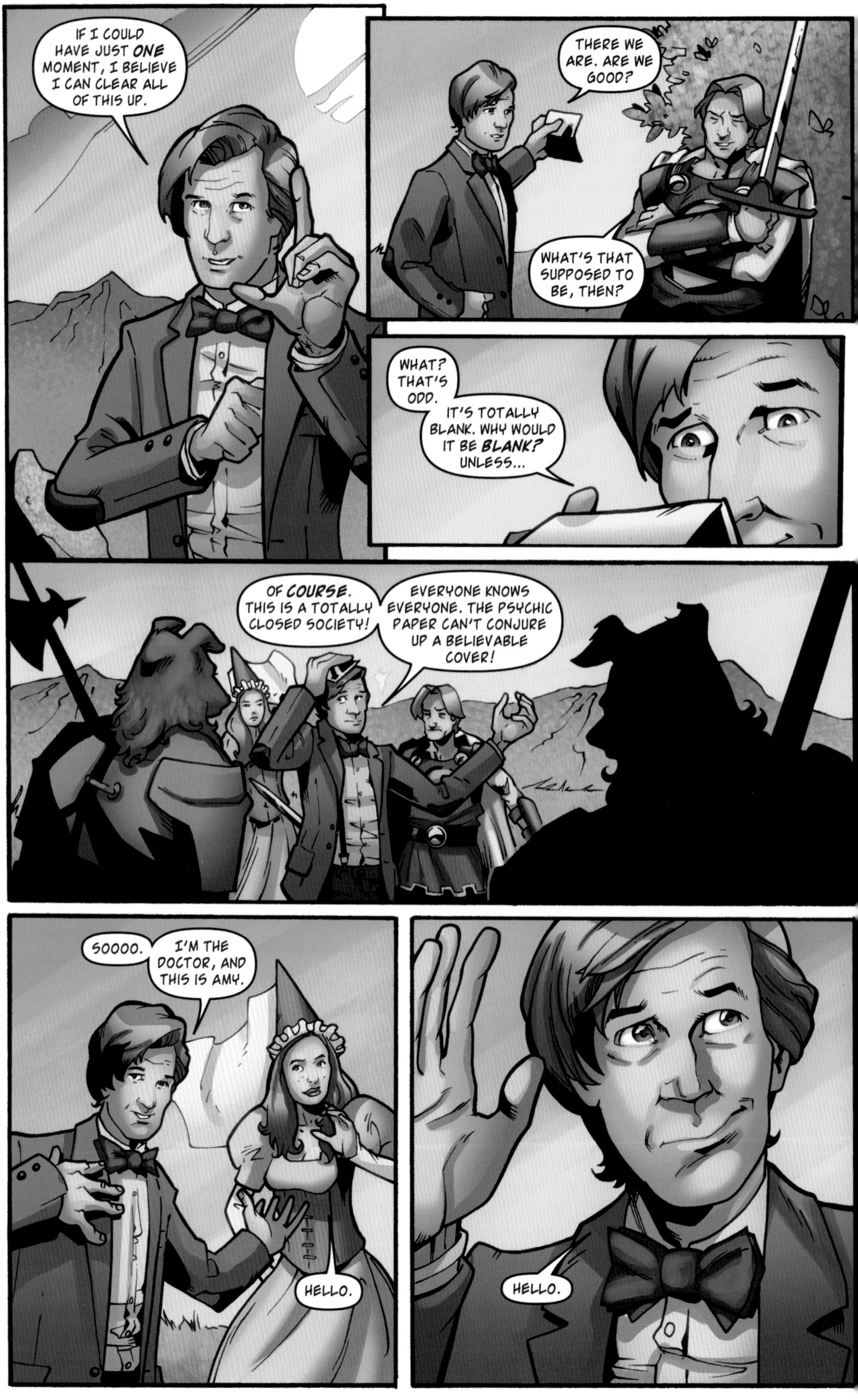
IF I COULD HAVE JUST ONE MOMENT, I BELIEVE I CAN CLEAR ALL OF THIS UP.
THERE WE ARE. ARE WE GOOD?
WHAT'S THAT SUPPOSED TO BE, THEN?
WHAT? THAT'S ODD.
IT'S TOTALLY BLANK. WHY WOULD IT BE BLANK? UNLESS...
OF COURSE. THIS IS A TOTALLY CLOSED SOCIETY!
EVERYONE KNOWS EVERYONE. THE PSYCHIC PAPER CAN'T CONJURE UP A BELIEVABLE COVER!
SOOOO.
I'M THE DOCTOR, AND THIS IS AMY.
HELLO.
HELLO.

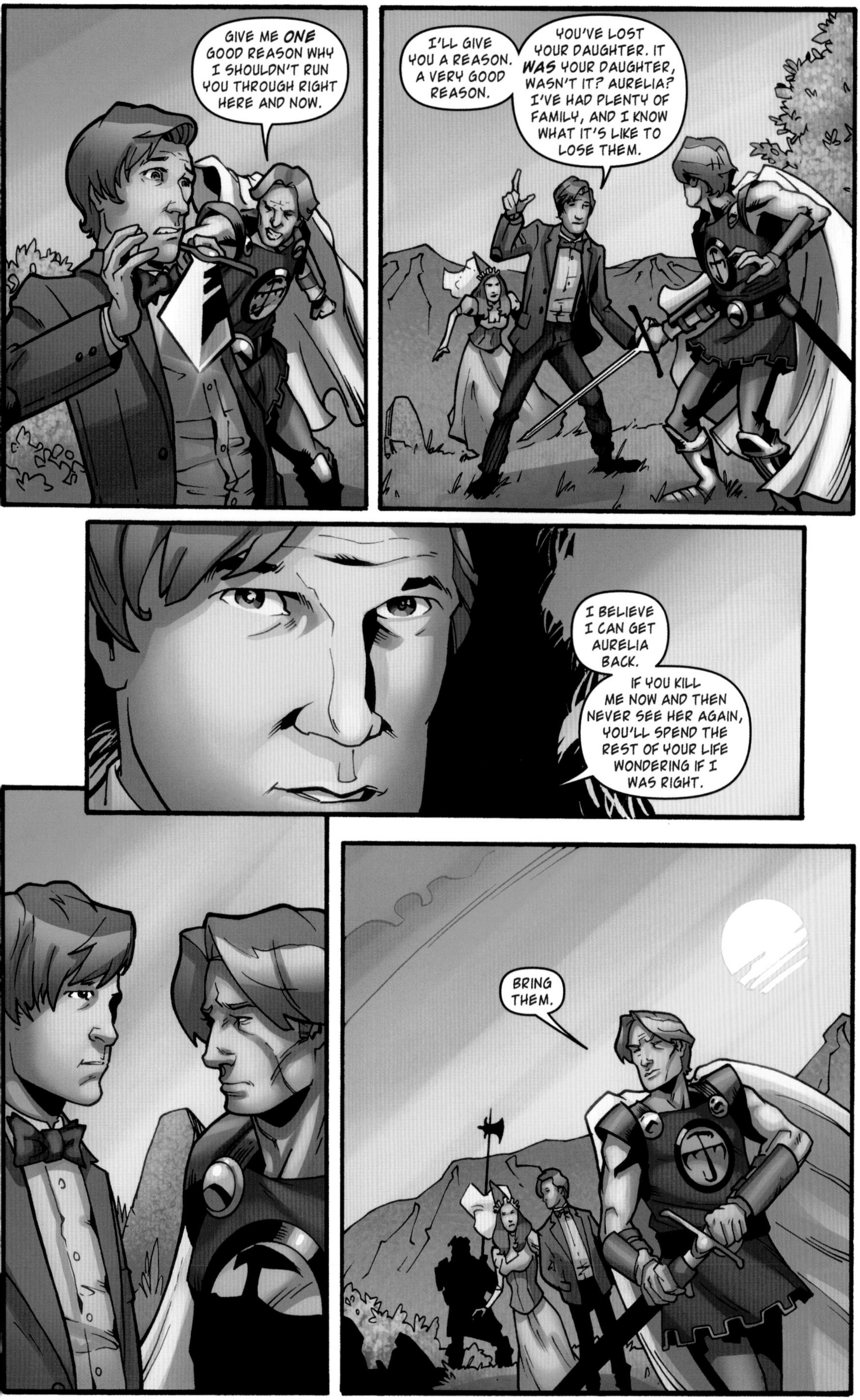
GIVE ME ONE GOOD REASON WHY I SHOULDN'T RUN YOU THROUGH RIGHT HERE AND NOW.
I'LL GIVE YOU A REASON. A VERY GOOD REASON.
YOU'VE LOST YOUR DAUGHTER. IT WAS YOUR DAUGHTER, WASN'T IT? AURELIA? I'VE HAD PLENTY OF FAMILY, AND I KNOW WHAT IT'S LIKE TO LOSE THEM.
I BELIEVE I CAN GET AURELIA BACK.
IF YOU KILL ME NOW AND THEN NEVER SEE HER AGAIN, YOU'LL SPEND THE REST OF YOUR LIFE WONDERING IF I WAS RIGHT.
BRING THEM.

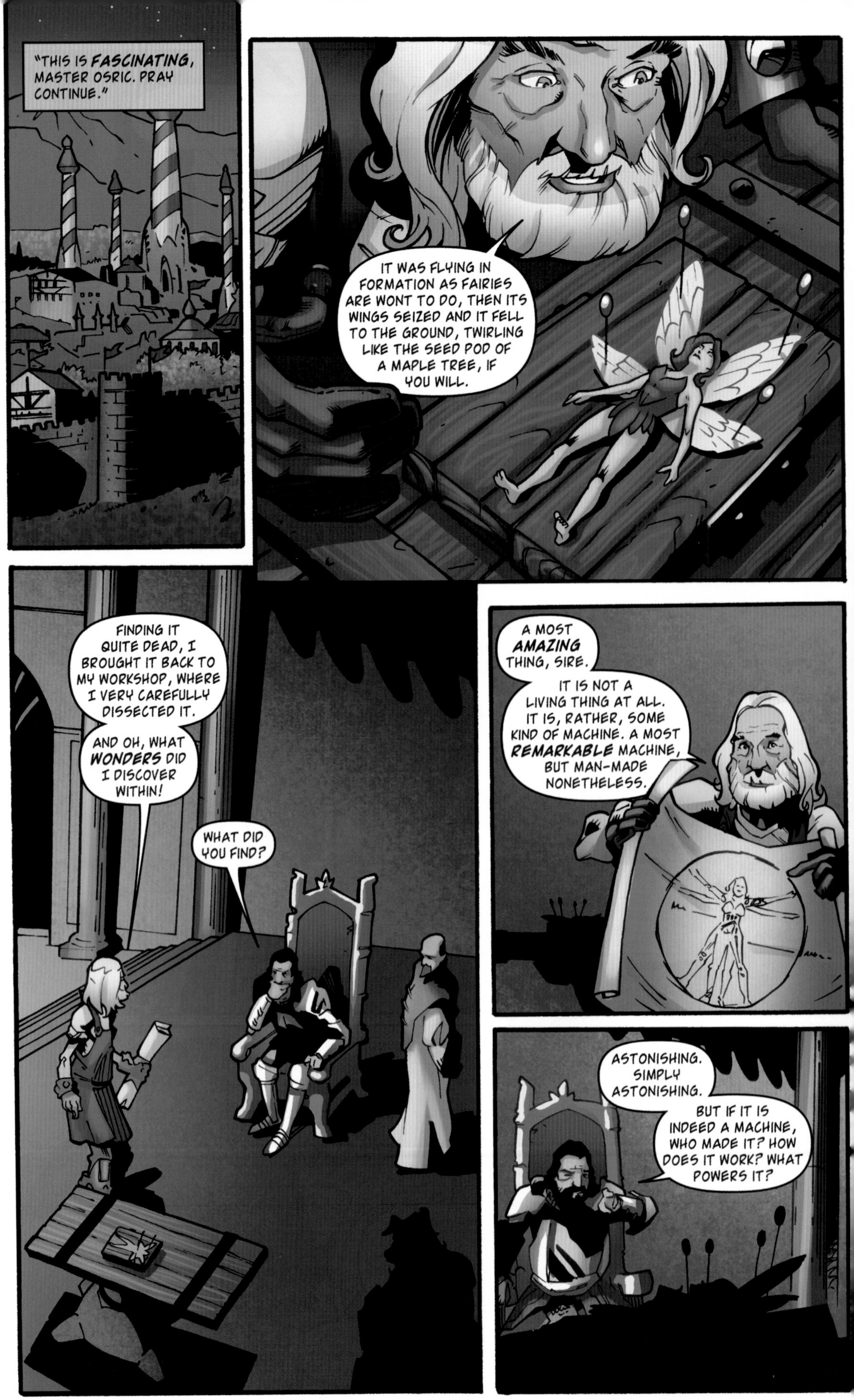
"THIS IS FASCINATING, MASTER OSRIC. PRAY CONTINUE."
IT WAS FLYING IN FORMATION AS FAIRIES ARE WONT TO DO, THEN ITS WINGS SEIZED AND IT FELL TO THE GROUND, TWIRLING LIKE THE SEED POD OF A MAPLE TREE, IF YOU WILL.
FINDING IT QUITE DEAD, I BROUGHT IT BACK TO MY WORKSHOP, WHERE I VERY CAREFULLY DISSECTED IT.
AND OH, WHAT WONDERS DID I DISCOVER WITHIN!
WHAT DID YOU FIND?
A MOST AMAZING THING, SIRE.
IT IS NOT A LIVING THING AT ALL. IT IS, RATHER, SOME KIND OF MACHINE. A MOST REMARKABLE MACHINE, BUT MAN-MADE NONETHELESS.
ASTONISHING. SIMPLY ASTONISHING.
BUT IF IT IS INDEED A MACHINE, WHO MADE IT? HOW DOES IT WORK? WHAT POWERS IT?

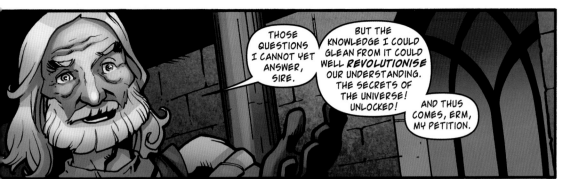

THOSE QUESTIONS I CANNOT YET ANSWER, SIRE.

BUT THE KNOWLEDGE I COULD GLEAN FROM IT COULD WELL *REVOLUTIONISE* OUR UNDERSTANDING. THE SECRETS OF THE UNIVERSE! UNLOCKED!

AND THUS COMES, ERM, MY PETITION.

I AM INTRIGUED BY WHAT YOU HAVE SHOWN ME. I GRANT YOUR REQUEST, A SUM OF GOLD WITH WHICH YOU MAY FORGO THE FORGE AND PURSUE YOUR STUDIES.

I AM DEEPLY HONORED, SIRE.

COME CLOSER, MASTER OSRIC. I HAVE WORDS FOR ONLY YOUR EARS.

DO YOU EVER SUSPECT, OSRIC, THAT OUR WORLD IS NOT ALL IT APPEARS TO BE?

WHATEVER DO YOU MEAN, SIRE?

YOU TELL ME.

I HAVE THEORIES, SIRE, BUT THEY SOUND MAD EVEN TO ME AT TIMES.

THAT THE MEN OF AGES PAST MIGHT HAVE HAD ACCESS TO LEARNING THAT HAS BEEN LOST. OR HIDDEN FROM US!

CONTINUE YOUR EFFORTS THEN, OSRIC. BUT DO IT DISCREETLY.

THERE ARE SOME WHO WOULD NOT WELCOME NEW IDEAS, DO YOU UNDERSTAND?

I DO, SIRE. I WILL TAKE CARE.

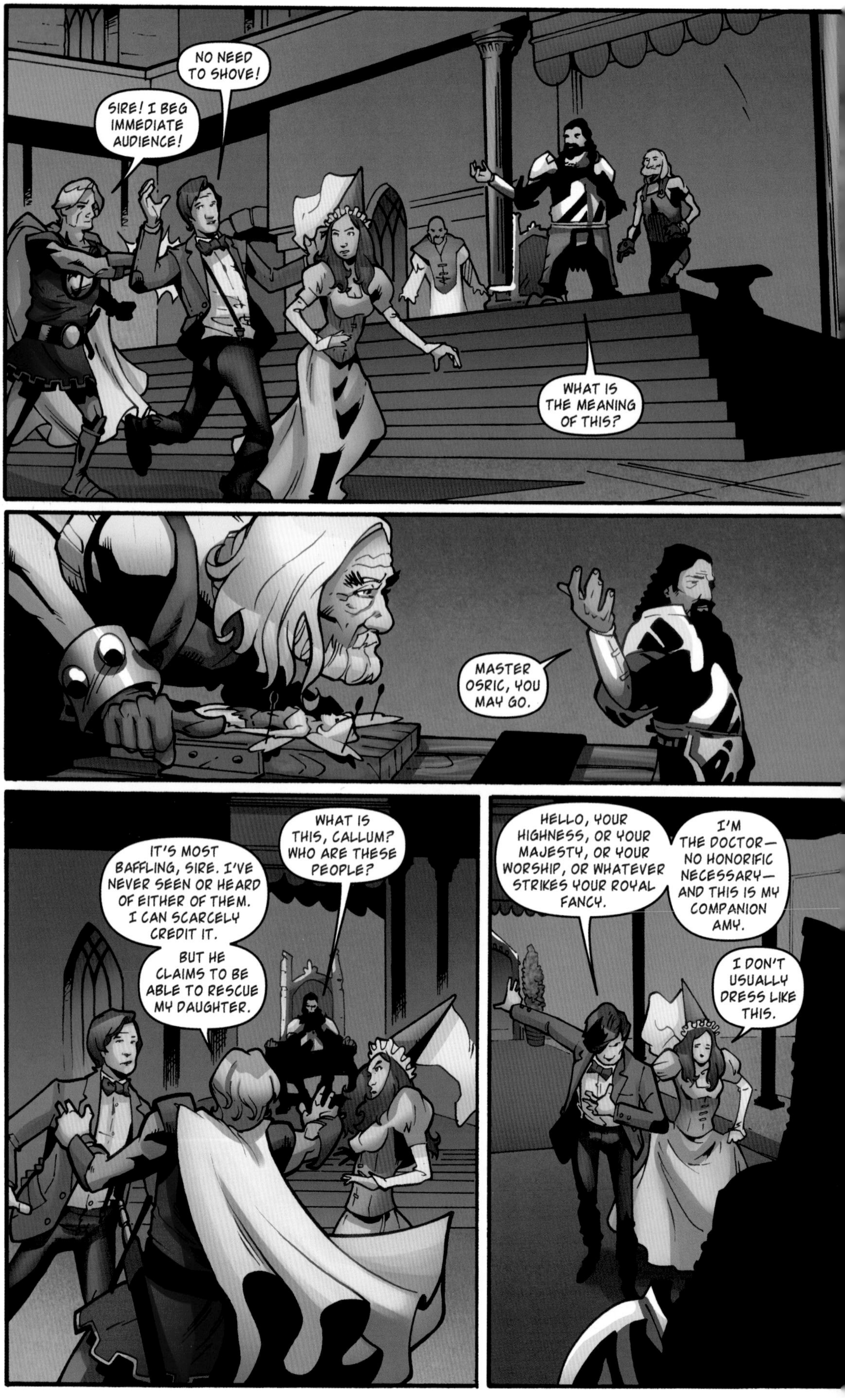

SIRE! I BEG IMMEDIATE AUDIENCE!
NO NEED TO SHOVE!
WHAT IS THE MEANING OF THIS?
MASTER OSRIC, YOU MAY GO.
IT'S MOST BAFFLING, SIRE. I'VE NEVER SEEN OR HEARD OF EITHER OF THEM. I CAN SCARCELY CREDIT IT.
BUT HE CLAIMS TO BE ABLE TO RESCUE MY DAUGHTER.
WHAT IS THIS, CALLUM? WHO ARE THESE PEOPLE?
HELLO, YOUR HIGHNESS, OR YOUR MAJESTY, OR YOUR WORSHIP, OR WHATEVER STRIKES YOUR ROYAL FANCY.
I'M THE DOCTOR— NO HONORIFIC NECESSARY— AND THIS IS MY COMPANION AMY.
I DON'T USUALLY DRESS LIKE THIS.

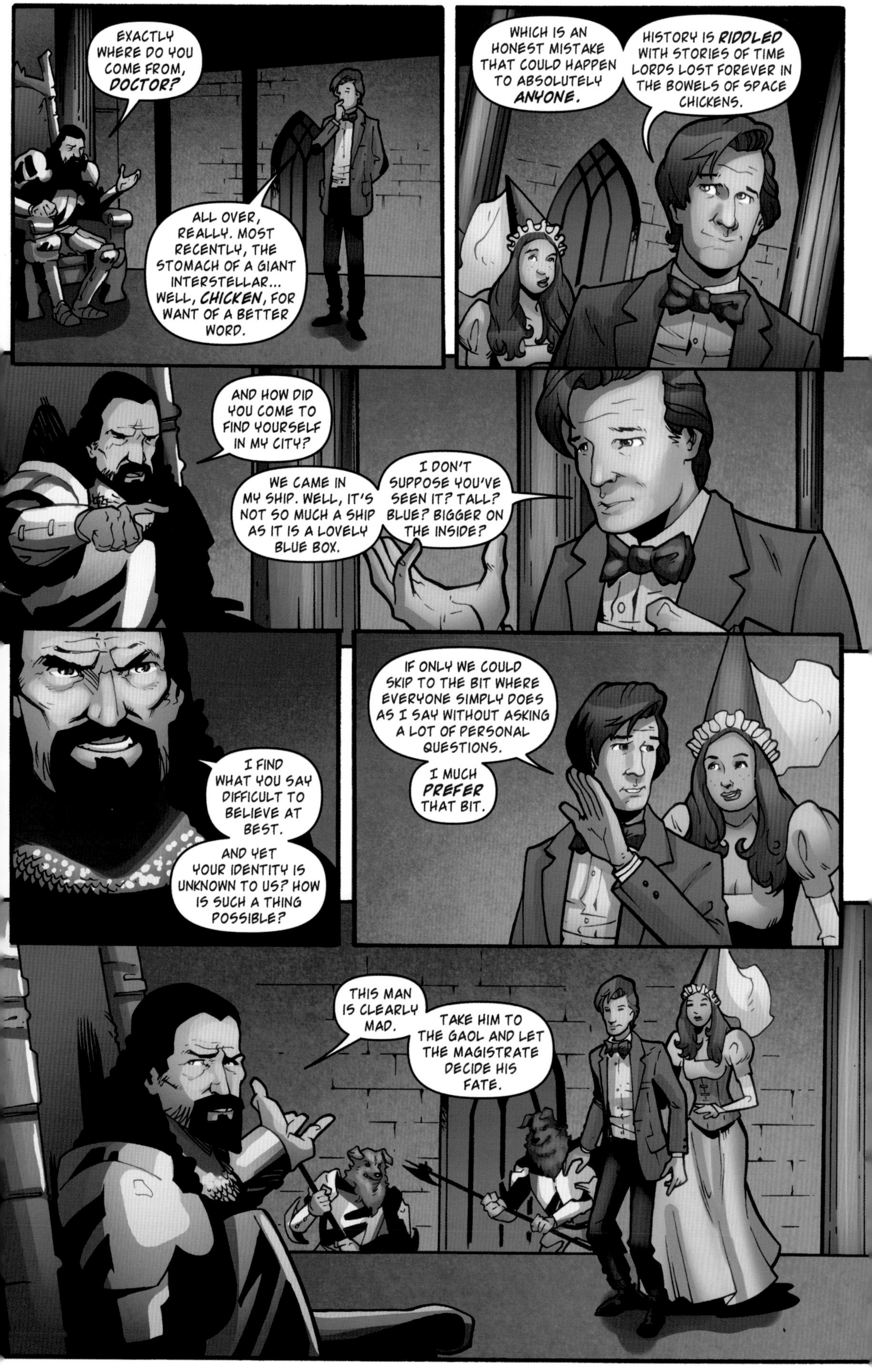
EXACTLY WHERE DO YOU COME FROM, DOCTOR?
ALL OVER, REALLY. MOST RECENTLY, THE STOMACH OF A GIANT INTERSTELLAR... WELL, CHICKEN, FOR WANT OF A BETTER WORD.
WHICH IS AN HONEST MISTAKE THAT COULD HAPPEN TO ABSOLUTELY ANYONE.
HISTORY IS RIDDLED WITH STORIES OF TIME LORDS LOST FOREVER IN THE BOWELS OF SPACE CHICKENS.
AND HOW DID YOU COME TO FIND YOURSELF IN MY CITY?
WE CAME IN MY SHIP. WELL, IT'S NOT SO MUCH A SHIP AS IT IS A LOVELY BLUE BOX.
I DON'T SUPPOSE YOU'VE SEEN IT? TALL? BLUE? BIGGER ON THE INSIDE?
I FIND WHAT YOU SAY DIFFICULT TO BELIEVE AT BEST.
AND YET YOUR IDENTITY IS UNKNOWN TO US? HOW IS SUCH A THING POSSIBLE?
IF ONLY WE COULD SKIP TO THE BIT WHERE EVERYONE SIMPLY DOES AS I SAY WITHOUT ASKING A LOT OF PERSONAL QUESTIONS.
I MUCH PREFER THAT BIT.
THIS MAN IS CLEARLY MAD.
TAKE HIM TO THE GAOL AND LET THE MAGISTRATE DECIDE HIS FATE.

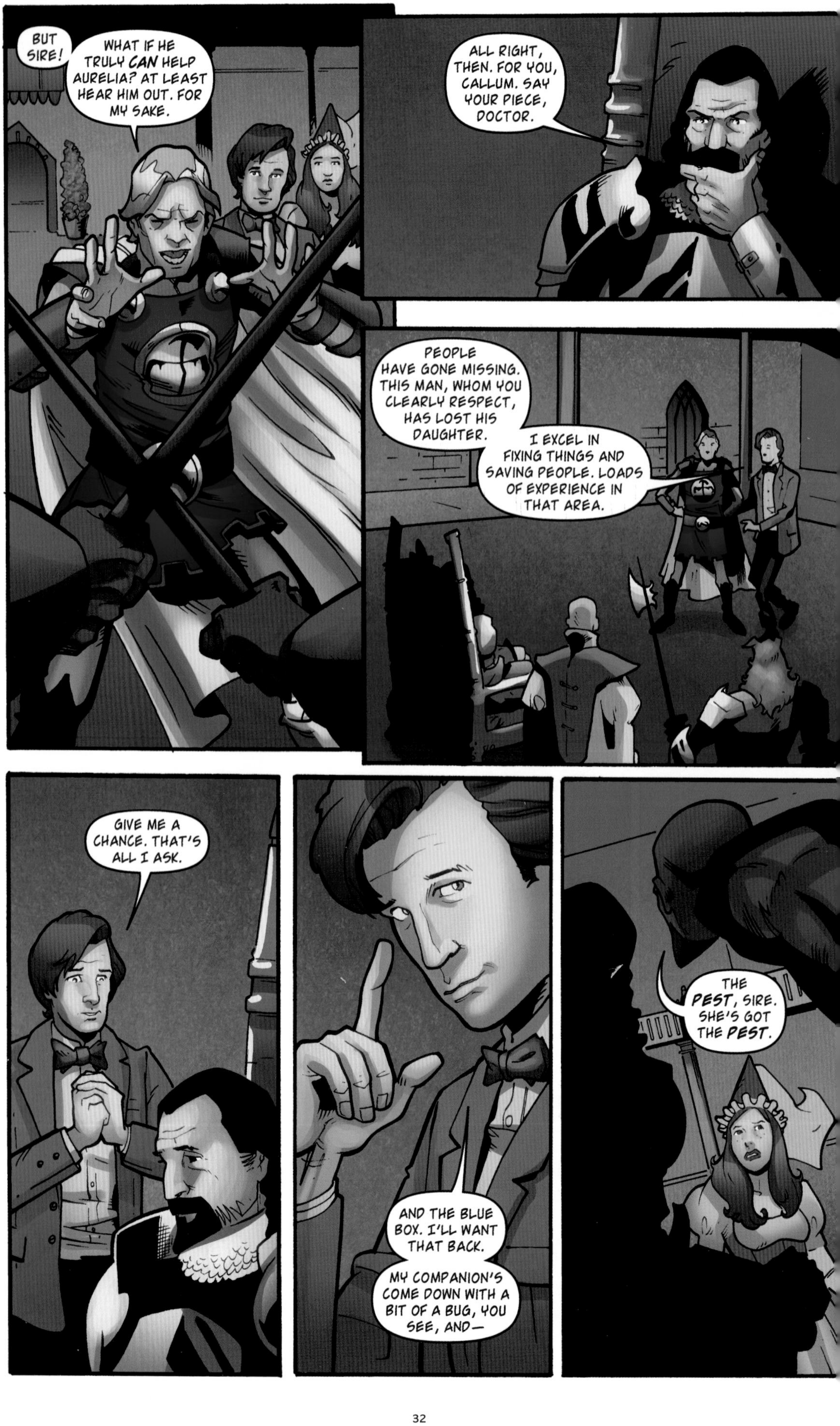
BUT SIRE!
WHAT IF HE TRULY CAN HELP AURELIA? AT LEAST HEAR HIM OUT. FOR MY SAKE.
ALL RIGHT, THEN. FOR YOU, CALLUM. SAY YOUR PIECE, DOCTOR.
PEOPLE HAVE GONE MISSING. THIS MAN, WHOM YOU CLEARLY RESPECT, HAS LOST HIS DAUGHTER.
I EXCEL IN FIXING THINGS AND SAVING PEOPLE. LOADS OF EXPERIENCE IN THAT AREA.
GIVE ME A CHANCE. THAT'S ALL I ASK.
AND THE BLUE BOX. I'LL WANT THAT BACK.
MY COMPANION'S COME DOWN WITH A BIT OF A BUG, YOU SEE, AND—
THE PEST, SIRE. SHE'S GOT THE PEST.

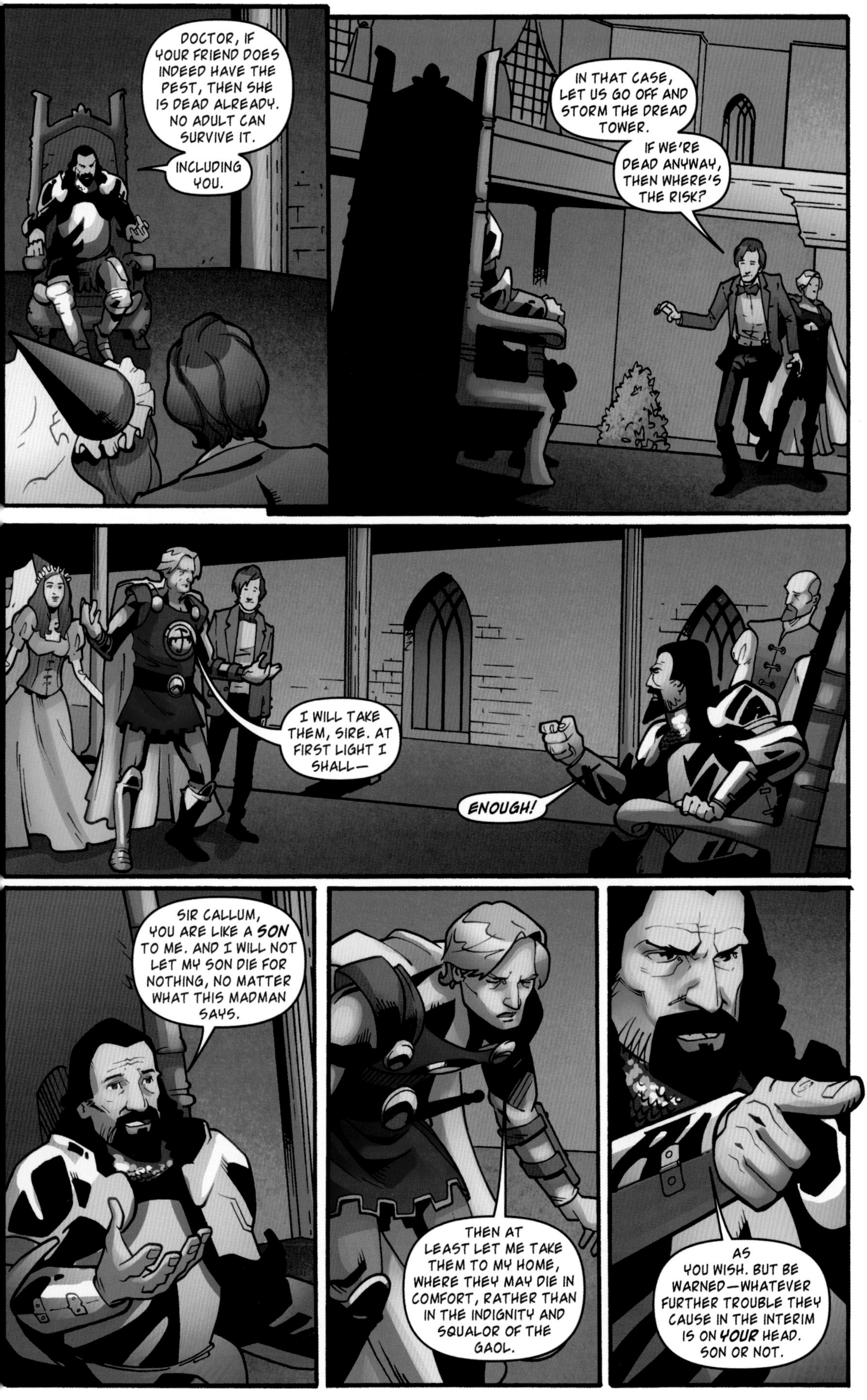
DOCTOR, IF YOUR FRIEND DOES INDEED HAVE THE PEST, THEN SHE IS DEAD ALREADY. NO ADULT CAN SURVIVE IT.
INCLUDING YOU.
IN THAT CASE, LET US GO OFF AND STORM THE DREAD TOWER.
IF WE'RE DEAD ANYWAY, THEN WHERE'S THE RISK?
I WILL TAKE THEM, SIRE. AT FIRST LIGHT I SHALL—
ENOUGH!
SIR CALLUM, YOU ARE LIKE A SON TO ME. AND I WILL NOT LET MY SON DIE FOR NOTHING, NO MATTER WHAT THIS MADMAN SAYS.
THEN AT LEAST LET ME TAKE THEM TO MY HOME, WHERE THEY MAY DIE IN COMFORT, RATHER THAN IN THE INDIGNITY AND SQUALOR OF THE GAOL.
AS YOU WISH. BUT BE WARNED—WHATEVER FURTHER TROUBLE THEY CAUSE IN THE INTERIM IS ON YOUR HEAD. SON OR NOT.

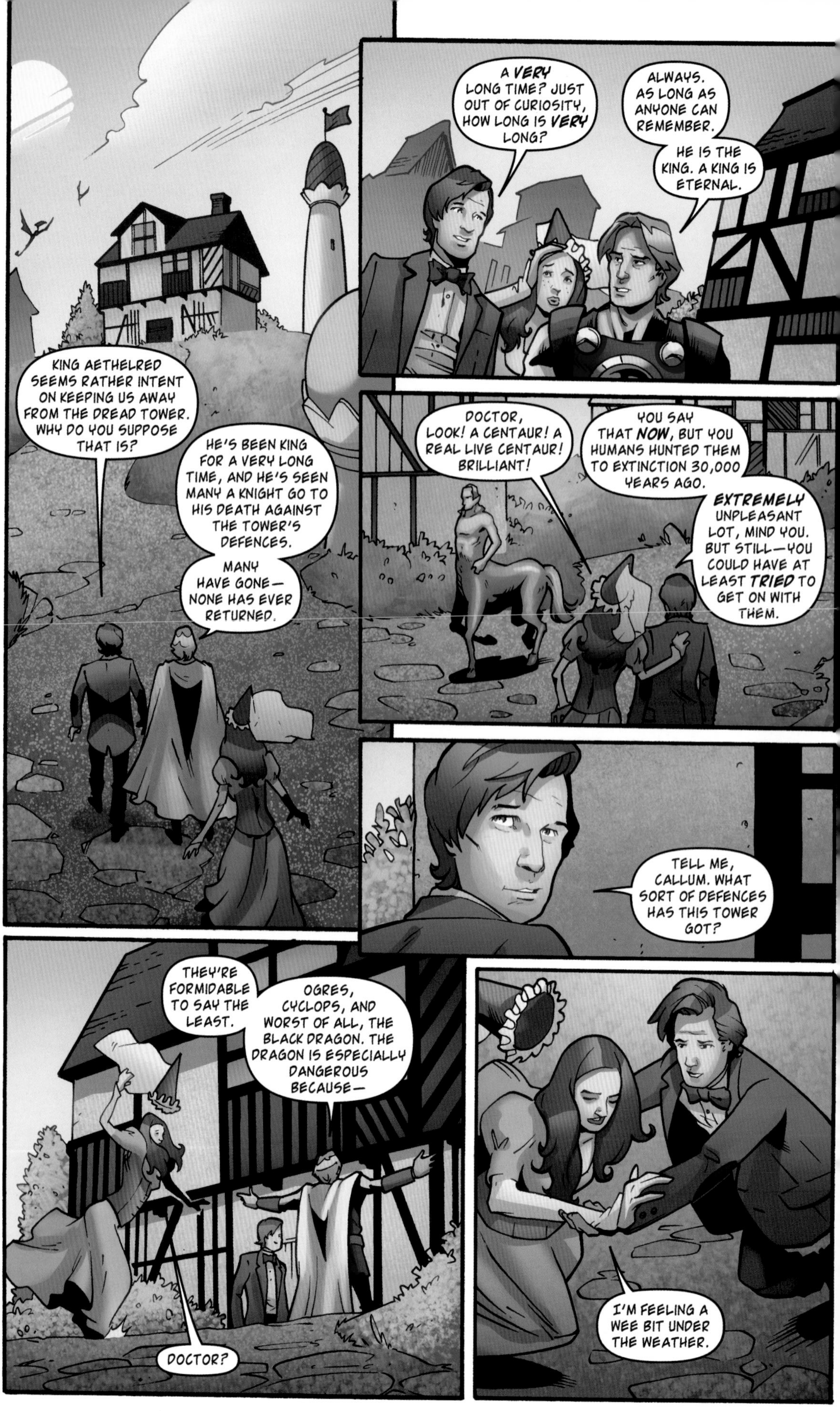

KING AETHELRED SEEMS RATHER INTENT ON KEEPING US AWAY FROM THE DREAD TOWER. WHY DO YOU SUPPOSE THAT IS?
HE'S BEEN KING FOR A VERY LONG TIME, AND HE'S SEEN MANY A KNIGHT GO TO HIS DEATH AGAINST THE TOWER'S DEFENCES.
MANY HAVE GONE—NONE HAS EVER RETURNED.
A VERY LONG TIME? JUST OUT OF CURIOSITY, HOW LONG IS VERY LONG?
ALWAYS. AS LONG AS ANYONE CAN REMEMBER.
HE IS THE KING. A KING IS ETERNAL.
DOCTOR, LOOK! A CENTAUR! A REAL LIVE CENTAUR! BRILLIANT!
YOU SAY THAT NOW, BUT YOU HUMANS HUNTED THEM TO EXTINCTION 30,000 YEARS AGO.
EXTREMELY UNPLEASANT LOT, MIND YOU. BUT STILL—YOU COULD HAVE AT LEAST TRIED TO GET ON WITH THEM.
TELL ME, CALLUM. WHAT SORT OF DEFENCES HAS THIS TOWER GOT?
THEY'RE FORMIDABLE TO SAY THE LEAST.
OGRES, CYCLOPS, AND WORST OF ALL, THE BLACK DRAGON. THE DRAGON IS ESPECIALLY DANGEROUS BECAUSE—
DOCTOR?
I'M FEELING A WEE BIT UNDER THE WEATHER.

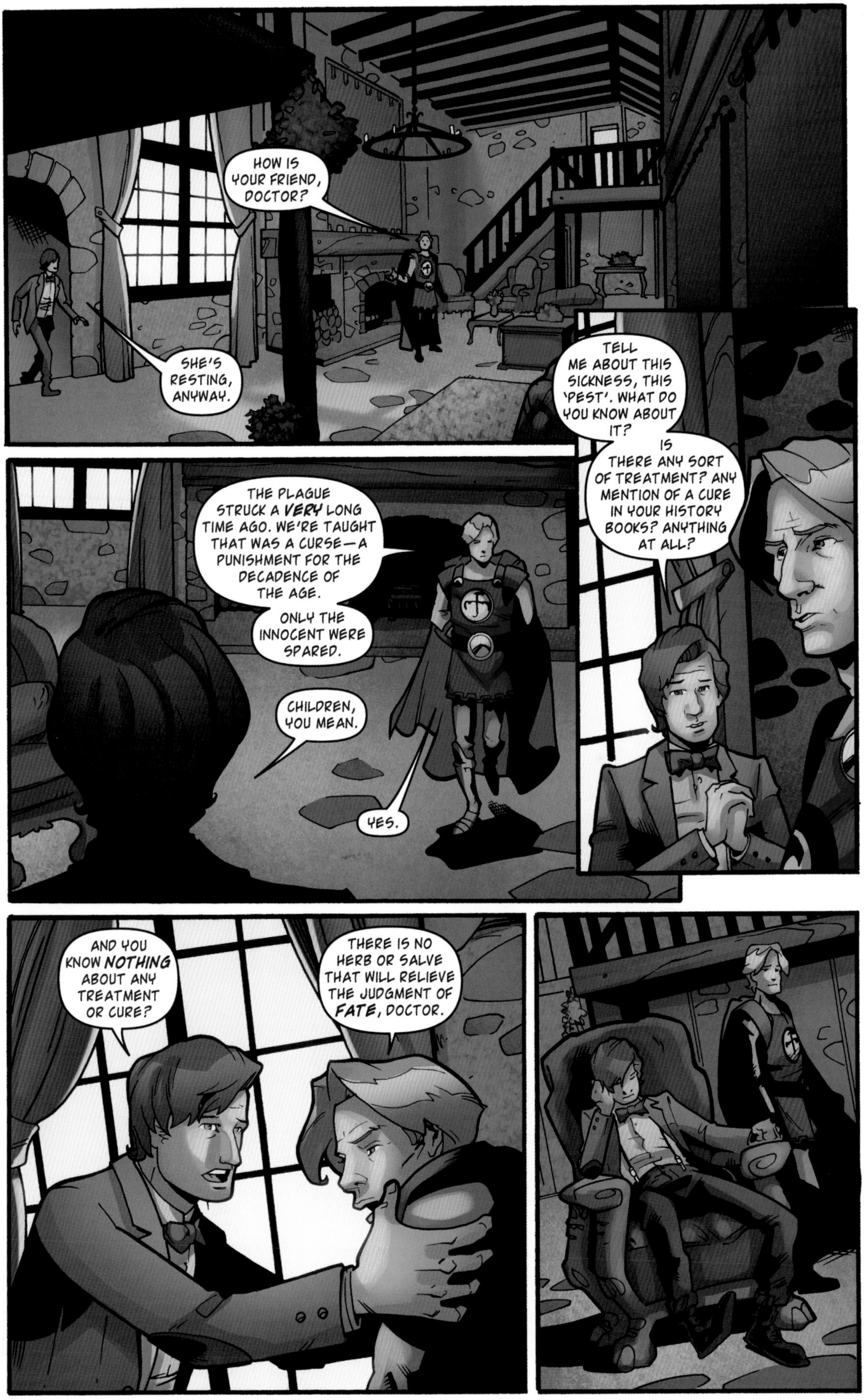
HOW IS YOUR FRIEND, DOCTOR?
SHE'S RESTING, ANYWAY.
TELL ME ABOUT THIS SICKNESS, THIS 'PEST'. WHAT DO YOU KNOW ABOUT IT?
IS THERE ANY SORT OF TREATMENT? ANY MENTION OF A CURE IN YOUR HISTORY BOOKS? ANYTHING AT ALL?
THE PLAGUE STRUCK A VERY LONG TIME AGO. WE'RE TAUGHT THAT WAS A CURSE—A PUNISHMENT FOR THE DECADENCE OF THE AGE.
ONLY THE INNOCENT WERE SPARED.
CHILDREN, YOU MEAN.
YES.
AND YOU KNOW NOTHING ABOUT ANY TREATMENT OR CURE?
THERE IS NO HERB OR SALVE THAT WILL RELIEVE THE JUDGMENT OF FATE, DOCTOR.

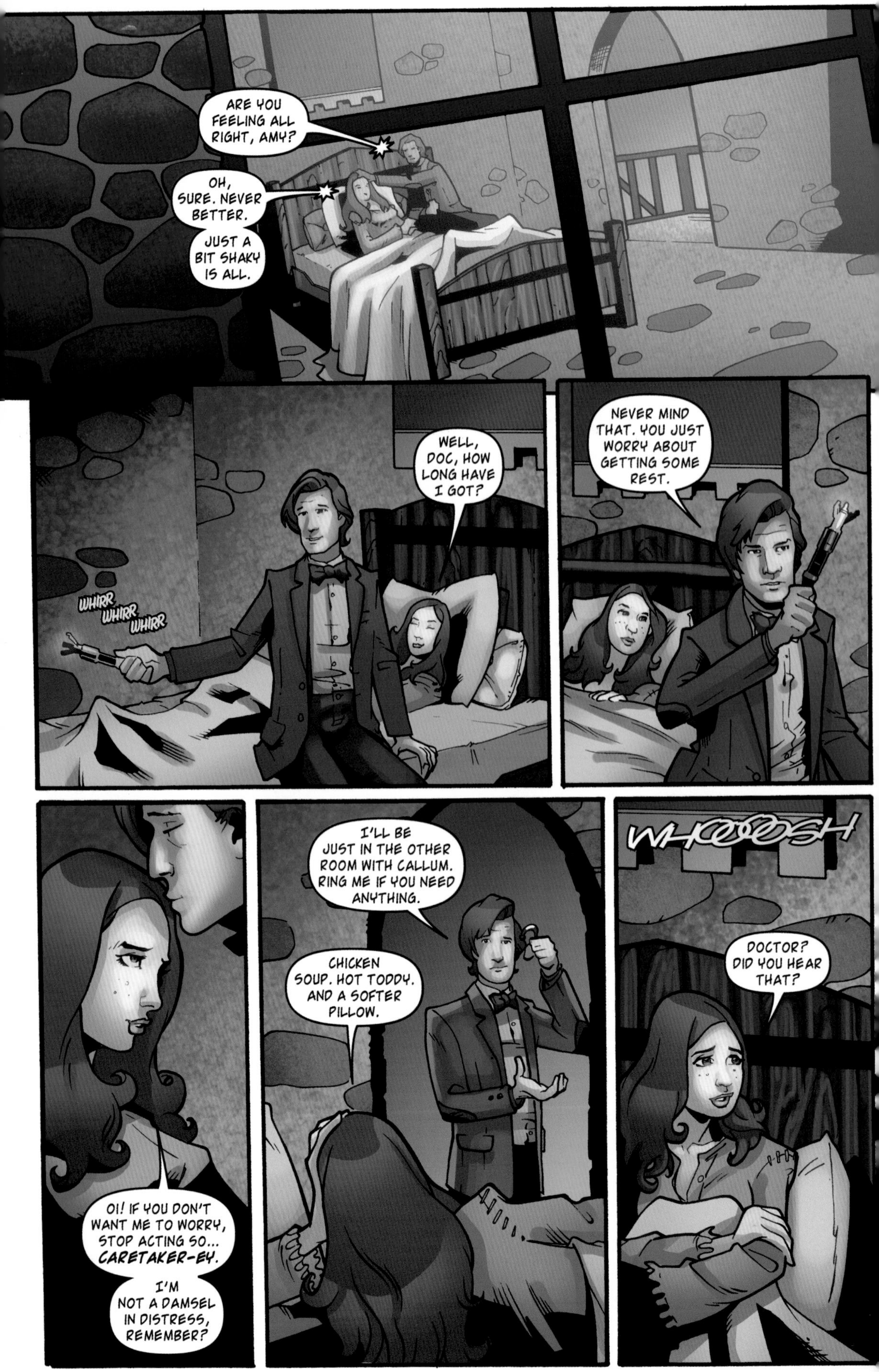

ARE YOU FEELING ALL RIGHT, AMY?
OH, SURE. NEVER BETTER.
JUST A BIT SHAKY IS ALL.
WHIRR WHIRR WHIRR
WELL, DOC, HOW LONG HAVE I GOT?
NEVER MIND THAT. YOU JUST WORRY ABOUT GETTING SOME REST.
OI! IF YOU DON'T WANT ME TO WORRY, STOP ACTING SO... CARETAKER-EY.
I'M NOT A DAMSEL IN DISTRESS, REMEMBER?
I'LL BE JUST IN THE OTHER ROOM WITH CALLUM. RING ME IF YOU NEED ANYTHING.
CHICKEN SOUP. HOT TODDY. AND A SOFTER PILLOW.
WHOOOSH
DOCTOR? DID YOU HEAR THAT?

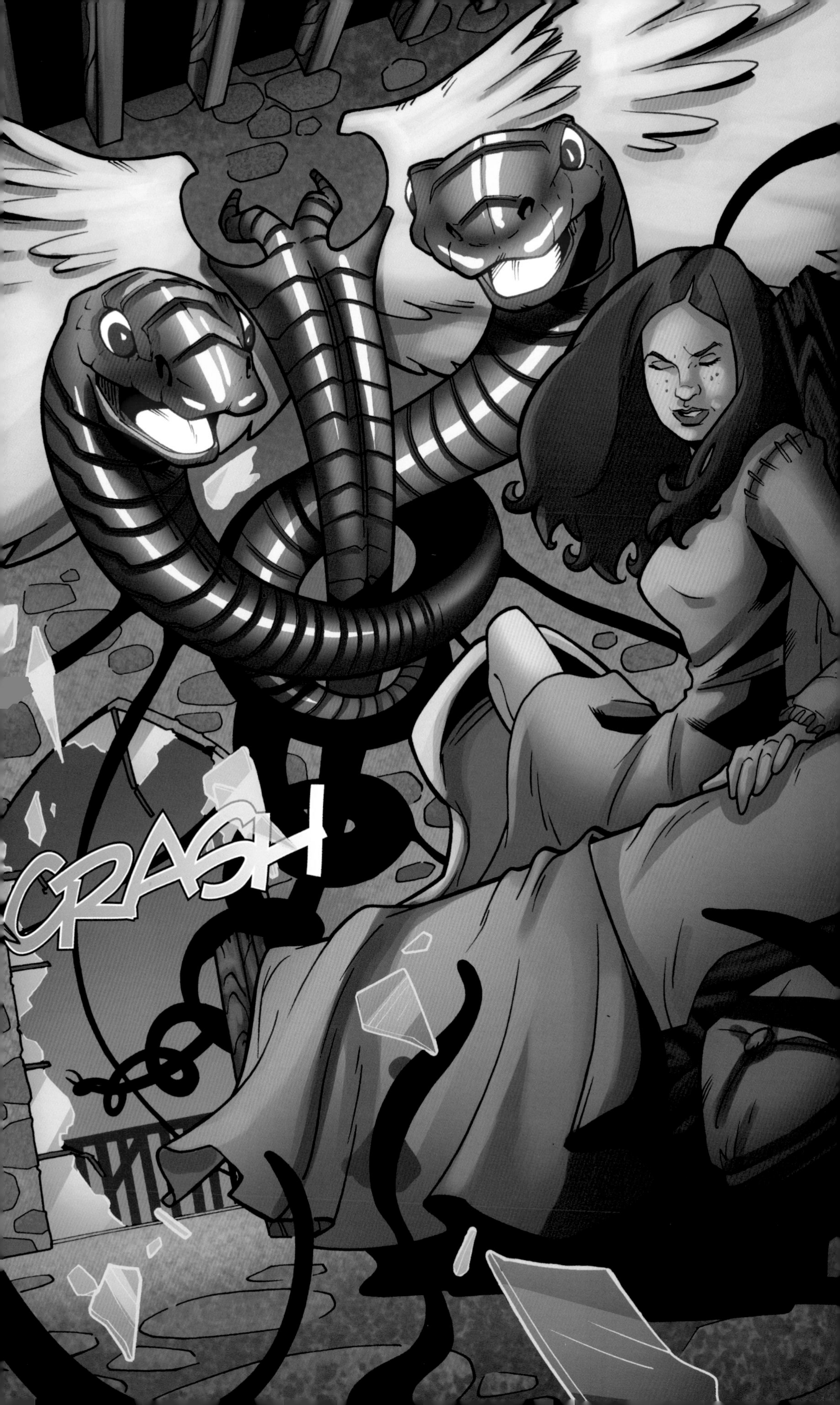
CRASH

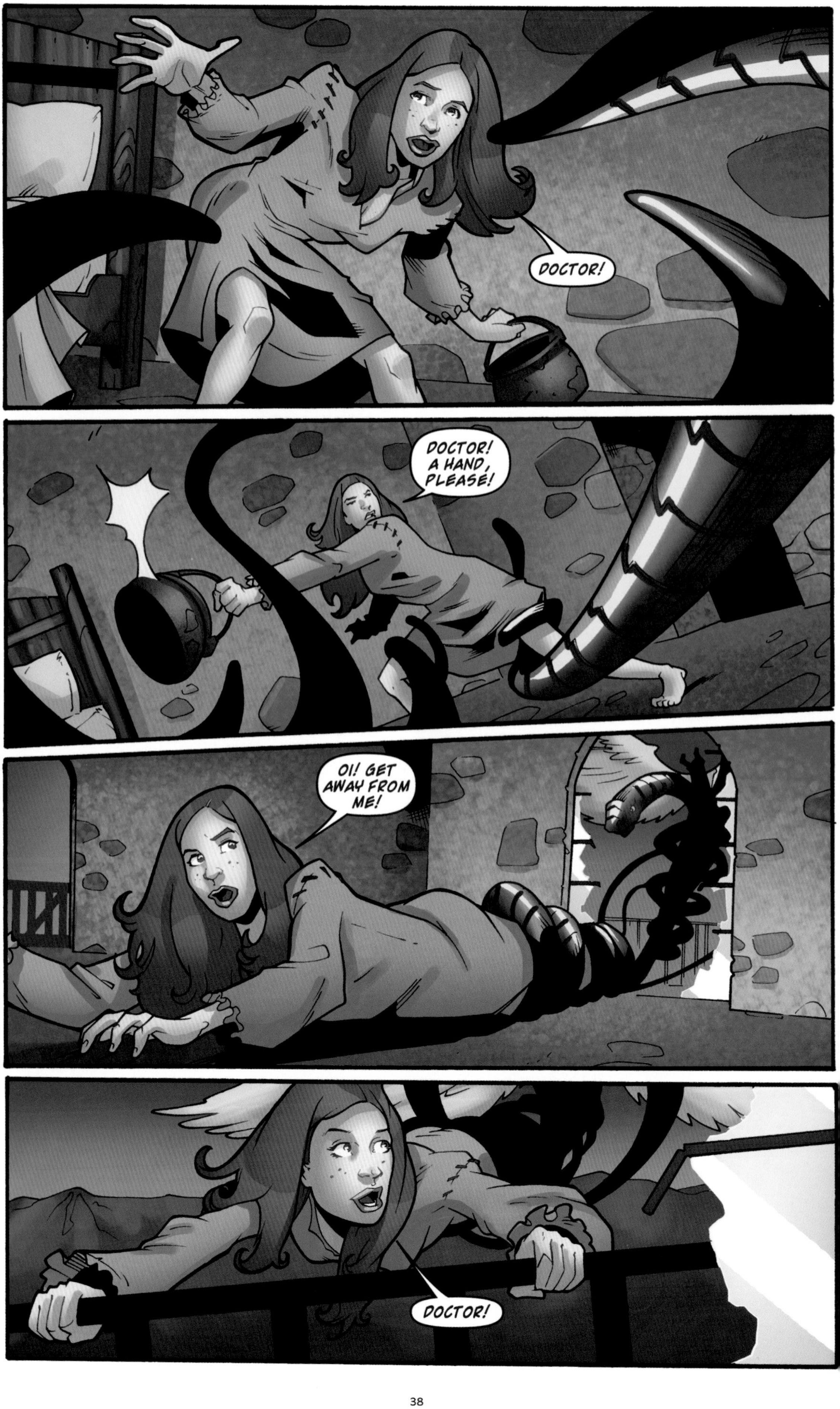
DOCTOR!
DOCTOR! A HAND, PLEASE!
OI! GET AWAY FROM ME!
DOCTOR!

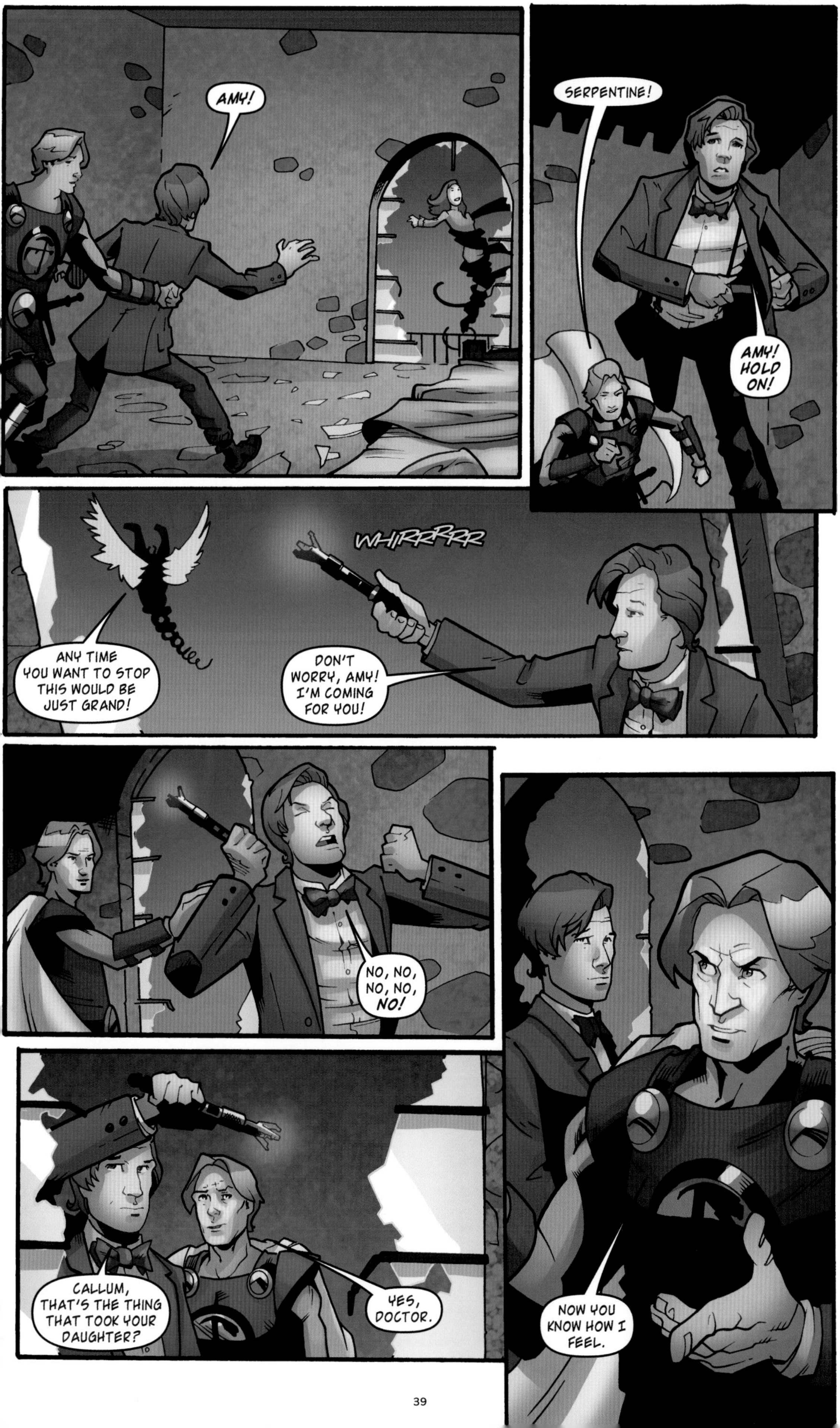
AMY!
SERPENTINE!
AMY! HOLD ON!
WHIRRRRR
ANY TIME YOU WANT TO STOP THIS WOULD BE JUST GRAND!
DON'T WORRY, AMY! I'M COMING FOR YOU!
NO, NO, NO, NO, NO!
CALLUM, THAT'S THE THING THAT TOOK YOUR DAUGHTER?
YES, DOCTOR.
NOW YOU KNOW HOW I FEEL.

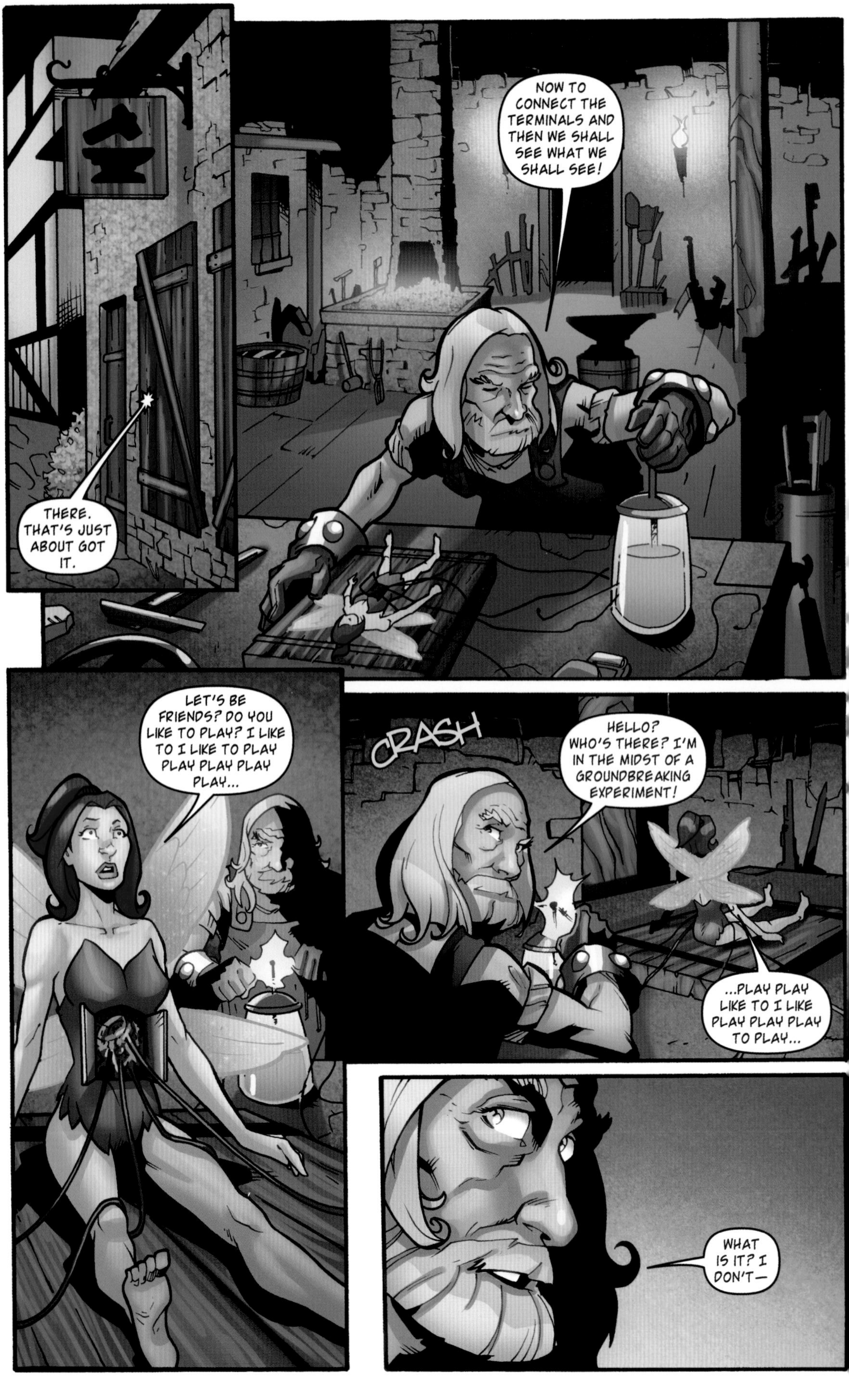
THERE. THAT'S JUST ABOUT GOT IT.
NOW TO CONNECT THE TERMINALS AND THEN WE SHALL SEE WHAT WE SHALL SEE!
LET'S BE FRIENDS? DO YOU LIKE TO PLAY? I LIKE TO I LIKE TO PLAY PLAY PLAY PLAY PLAY...
CRASH
HELLO? WHO'S THERE? I'M IN THE MIDST OF A GROUNDBREAKING EXPERIMENT!
...PLAY PLAY LIKE TO I LIKE PLAY PLAY PLAY TO PLAY...
WHAT IS IT? I DON'T—

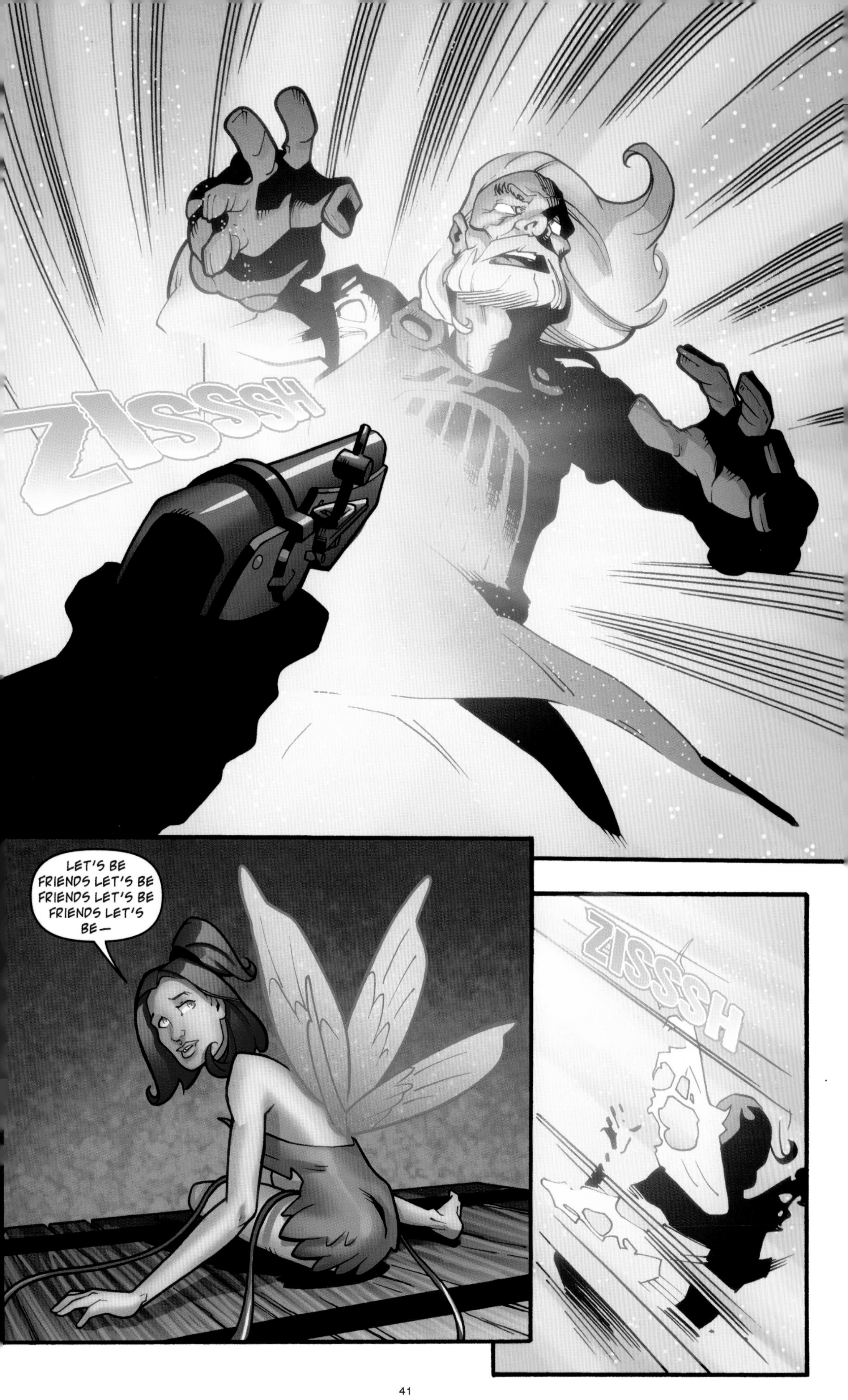
ZISSSH
LET'S BE FRIENDS LET'S BE FRIENDS LET'S BE FRIENDS LET'S BE—
ZISSSH

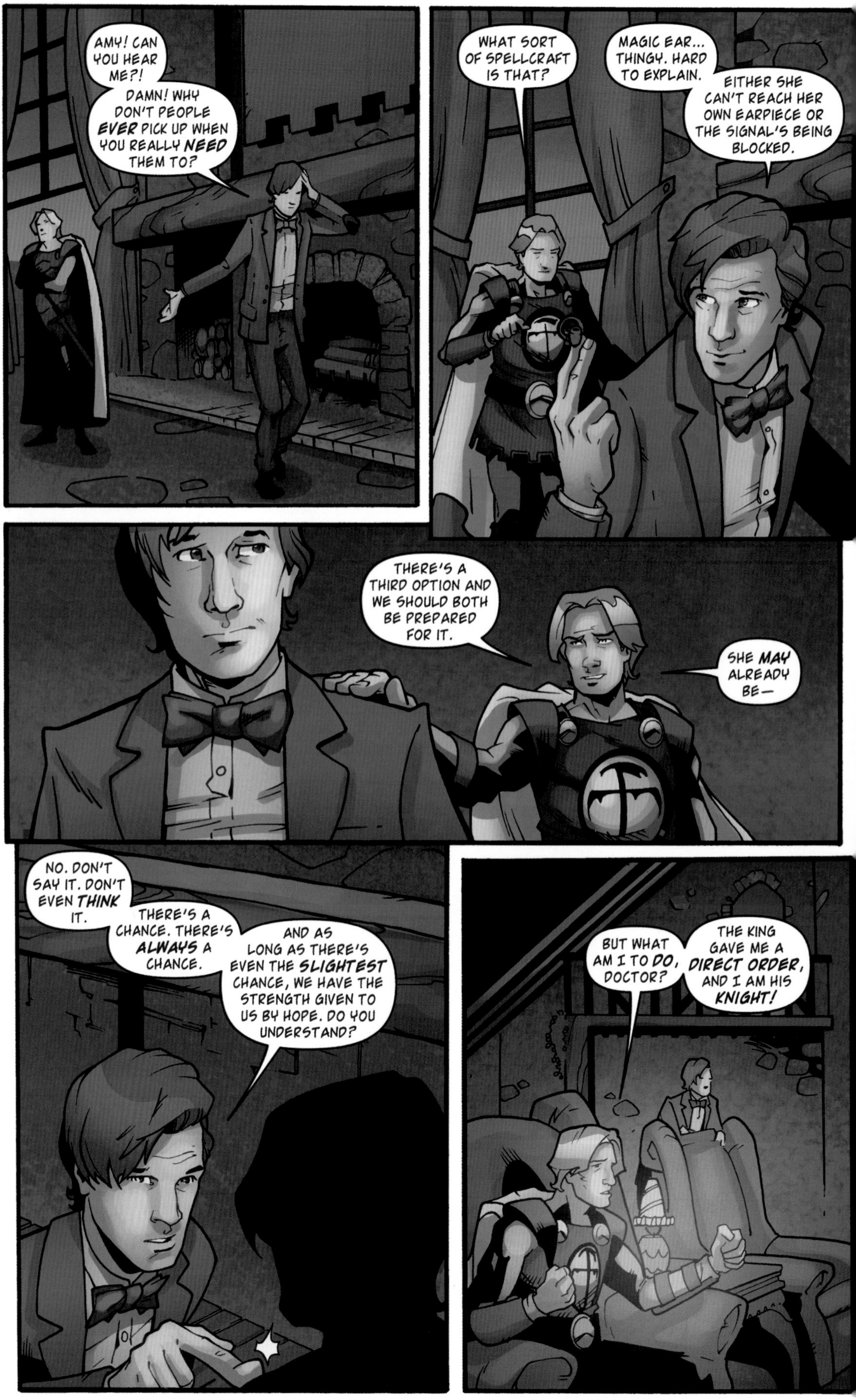
AMY! CAN YOU HEAR ME?!
DAMN! WHY DON'T PEOPLE **EVER** PICK UP WHEN YOU REALLY **NEED** THEM TO?
WHAT SORT OF SPELLCRAFT IS THAT?
MAGIC EAR... THINGY. HARD TO EXPLAIN.
EITHER SHE CAN'T REACH HER OWN EARPIECE OR THE SIGNAL'S BEING BLOCKED.
THERE'S A THIRD OPTION AND WE SHOULD BOTH BE PREPARED FOR IT.
SHE **MAY** ALREADY BE—
NO. DON'T SAY IT. DON'T EVEN **THINK** IT.
THERE'S A CHANCE. THERE'S **ALWAYS** A CHANCE.
AND AS LONG AS THERE'S EVEN THE **SLIGHTEST** CHANCE, WE HAVE THE STRENGTH GIVEN TO US BY HOPE. DO YOU UNDERSTAND?
BUT WHAT AM I TO **DO**, DOCTOR?
THE KING GAVE ME A **DIRECT ORDER**, AND I AM HIS **KNIGHT**!

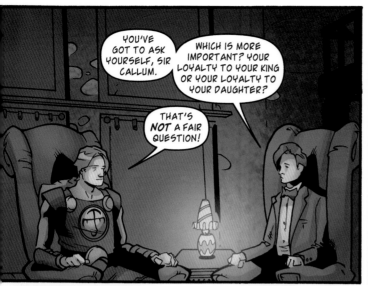

YOU'VE GOT TO ASK YOURSELF, SIR CALLUM.

WHICH IS MORE IMPORTANT? YOUR LOYALTY TO YOUR KING OR YOUR LOYALTY TO YOUR DAUGHTER?

THAT'S **NOT** A FAIR QUESTION!

MAYBE NOT, BUT IT'S THE QUESTION YOU'VE GOT TO ASK. DECIDE, CALLUM.

BECAUSE I'M **GOING** TO THE DREAD TOWER AND I'M **GOING** TO RESCUE AMY, AND I WOULD VERY MUCH LIKE YOUR HELP.

THEN I WILL GO WITH YOU. I'D RATHER DIE A TRAITOR WITH A DAUGHTER THAN AN HONORABLE MAN ALONE.

BRILLIANT. THAT'S. SORTED.

OF COURSE, TO PROVE YOURSELF WORTHY OF QUESTING WITH ME, YOU'LL HAVE TO DEFEAT ME IN SINGLE COMBAT FIRST.

WHAT? SERIOUSLY?

NO, OF COURSE NOT. BUT YOU SHOULD SEE THE LOOK ON YOUR FACE!

I LIKE YOU, CALLUM. A MAN WHO LAUGHS IN THE FACE OF DEATH IS EITHER A VERY **BRAVE** MAN, OR A LUNATIC.

JUST LIKE ME.

LIKE YOU **HOW?** DO YOU MEAN YOU'RE A BRAVE MAN OR THAT YOU'RE A LUNATIC?

EXACTLY.

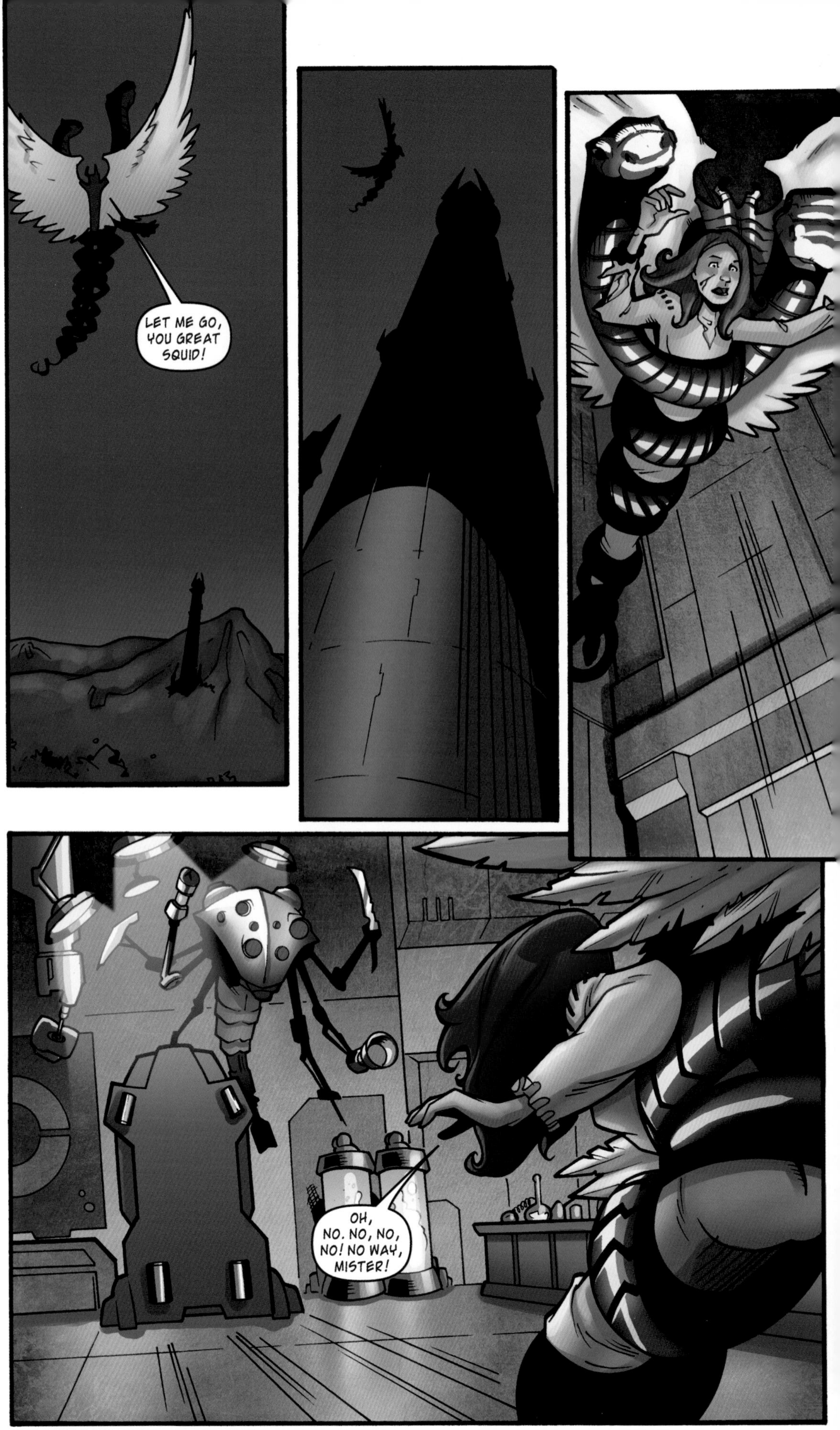
LET ME GO, YOU GREAT SQUID!
OH, NO. NO, NO, NO! NO WAY, MISTER!

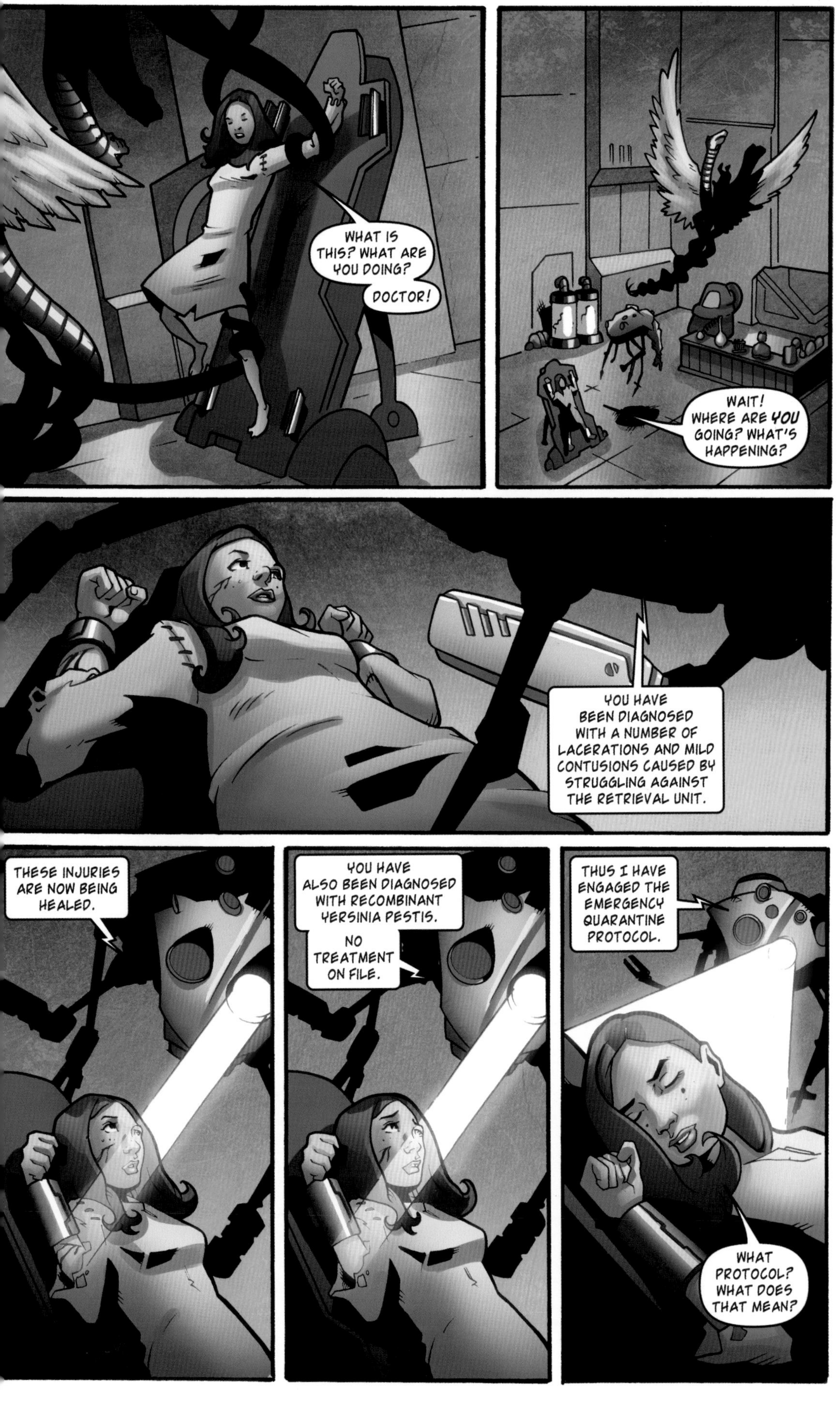
WHAT IS THIS? WHAT ARE YOU DOING?
DOCTOR!
WAIT! WHERE ARE YOU GOING? WHAT'S HAPPENING?
YOU HAVE BEEN DIAGNOSED WITH A NUMBER OF LACERATIONS AND MILD CONTUSIONS CAUSED BY STRUGGLING AGAINST THE RETRIEVAL UNIT.
THESE INJURIES ARE NOW BEING HEALED.
YOU HAVE ALSO BEEN DIAGNOSED WITH RECOMBINANT YERSINIA PESTIS.
NO TREATMENT ON FILE.
THUS I HAVE ENGAGED THE EMERGENCY QUARANTINE PROTOCOL.
WHAT PROTOCOL? WHAT DOES THAT MEAN?

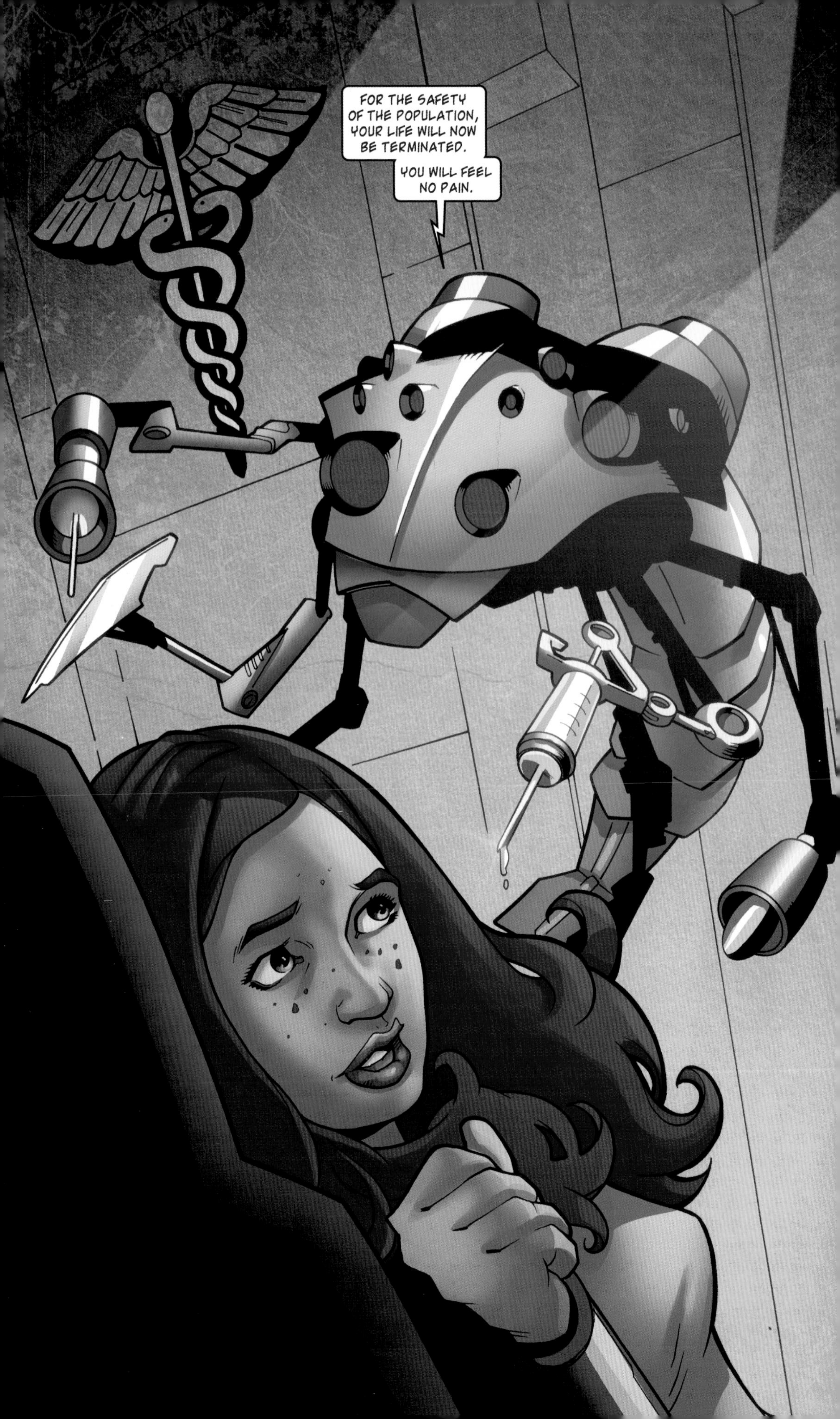
FOR THE SAFETY OF THE POPULATION, YOUR LIFE WILL NOW BE TERMINATED.
YOU WILL FEEL NO PAIN.

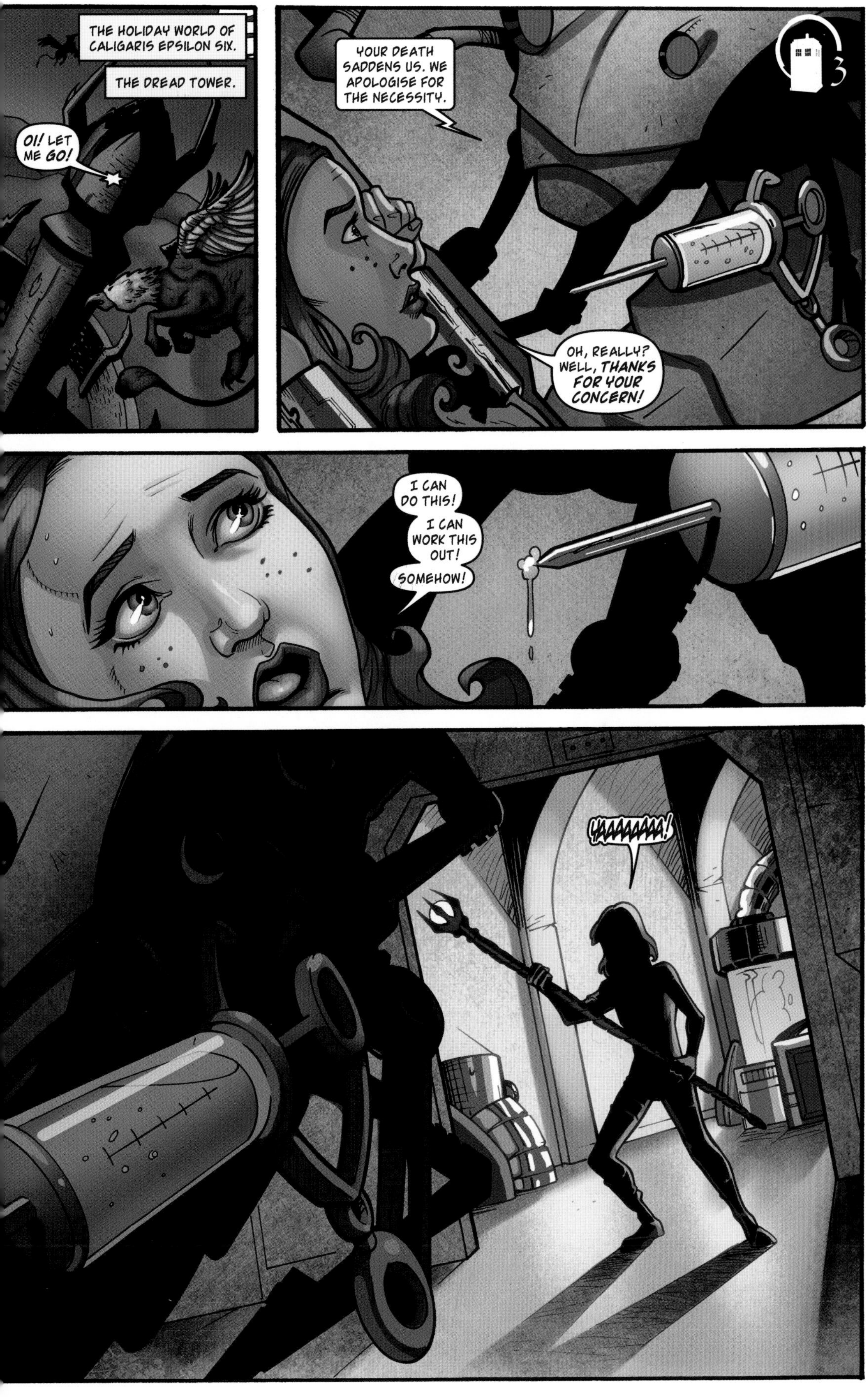

THE HOLIDAY WORLD OF CALIGARIS EPSILON SIX.
THE DREAD TOWER.
OI! LET ME GO!
YOUR DEATH SADDENS US. WE APOLOGISE FOR THE NECESSITY.
OH, REALLY? WELL, THANKS FOR YOUR CONCERN!
I CAN DO THIS!
I CAN WORK THIS OUT!
SOMEHOW!
YAAAAAAAA!

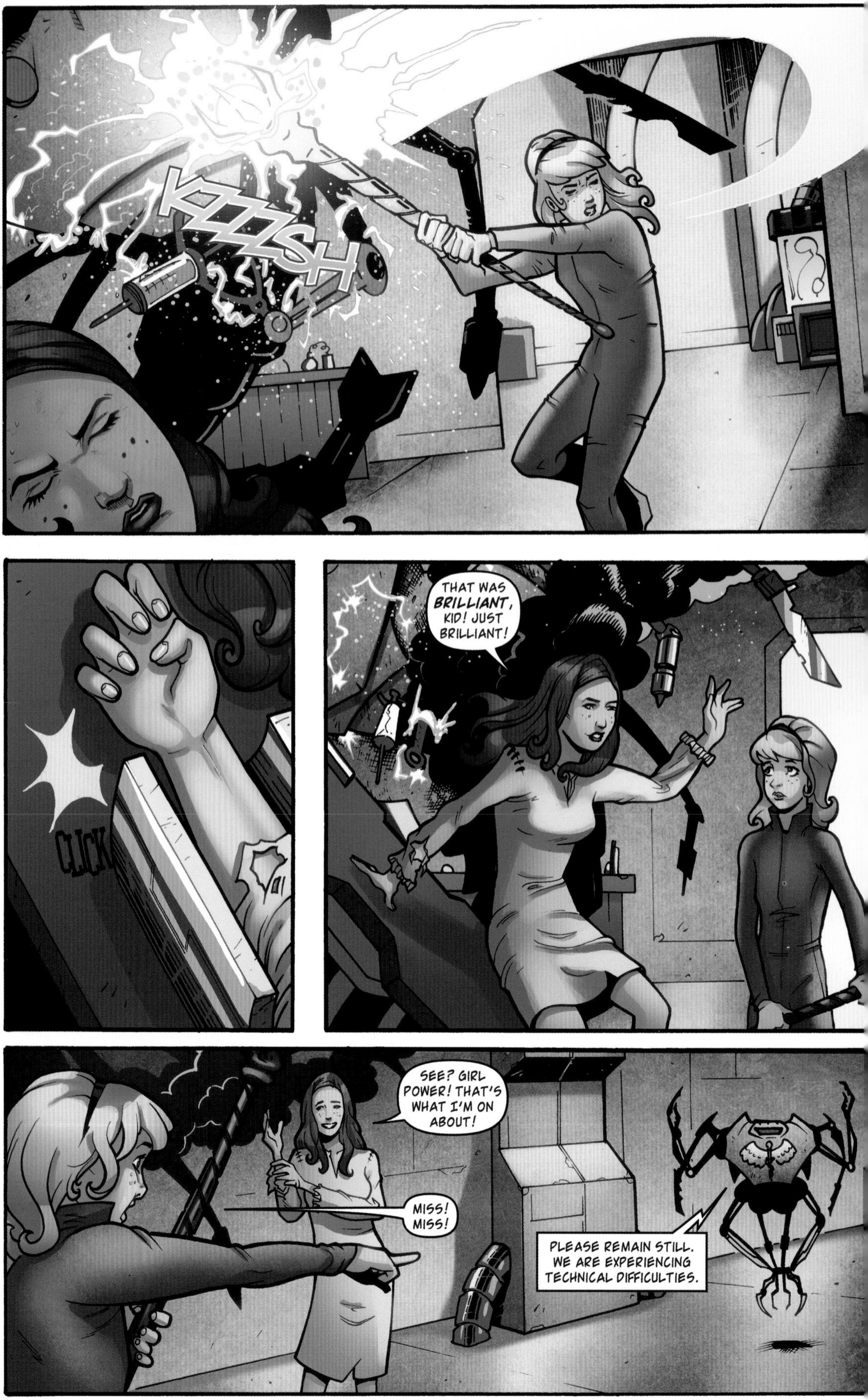
KZZZSH
CLICK
THAT WAS BRILLIANT, KID! JUST BRILLIANT!
SEE? GIRL POWER! THAT'S WHAT I'M ON ABOUT!
MISS! MISS!
PLEASE REMAIN STILL. WE ARE EXPERIENCING TECHNICAL DIFFICULTIES.

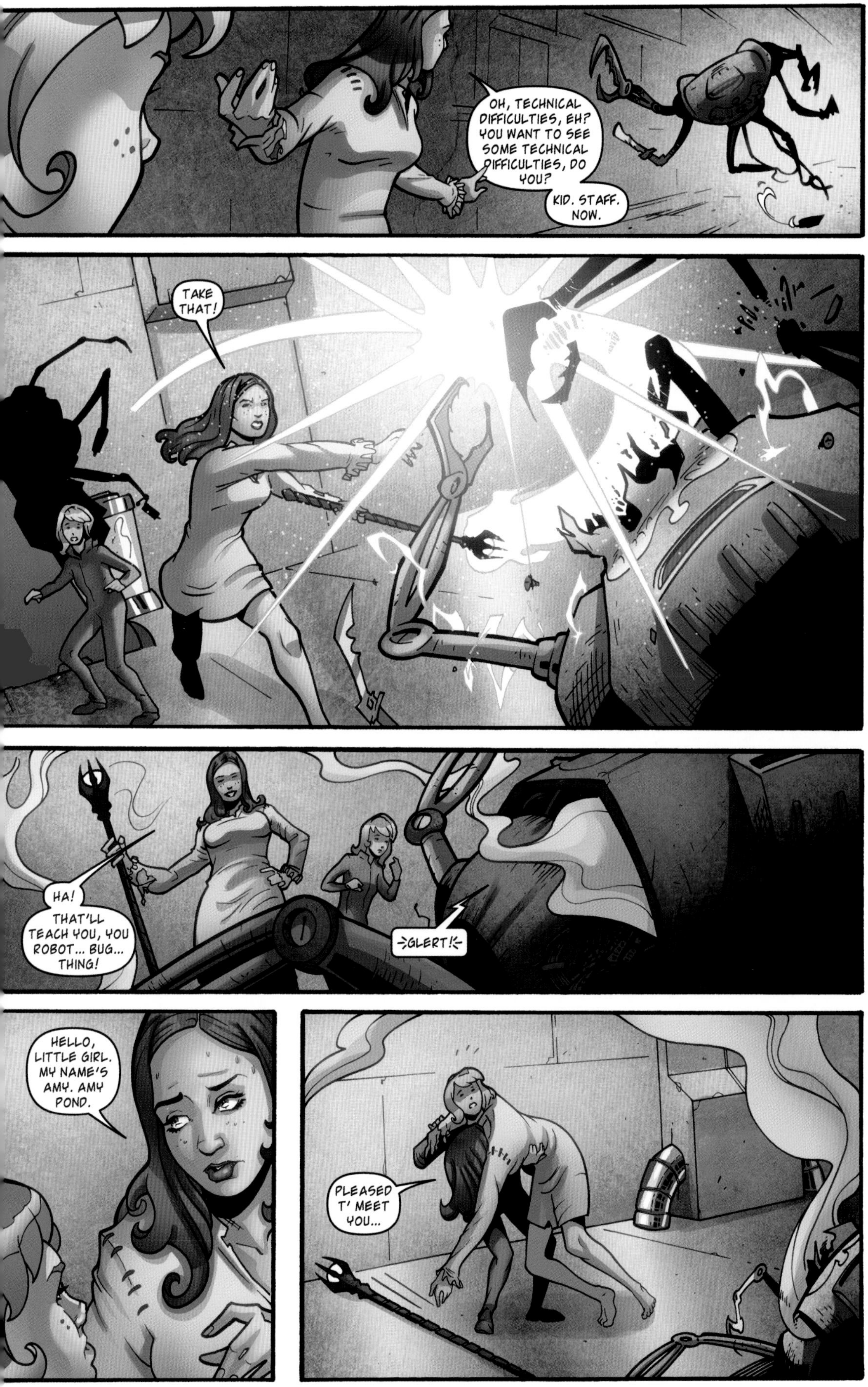
OH, TECHNICAL DIFFICULTIES, EH? YOU WANT TO SEE SOME TECHNICAL DIFFICULTIES, DO YOU?
KID. STAFF. NOW.
TAKE THAT!
HA! THAT'LL TEACH YOU, YOU ROBOT... BUG... THING!
GLERT!
HELLO, LITTLE GIRL. MY NAME'S AMY. AMY POND.
PLEASED T' MEET YOU...

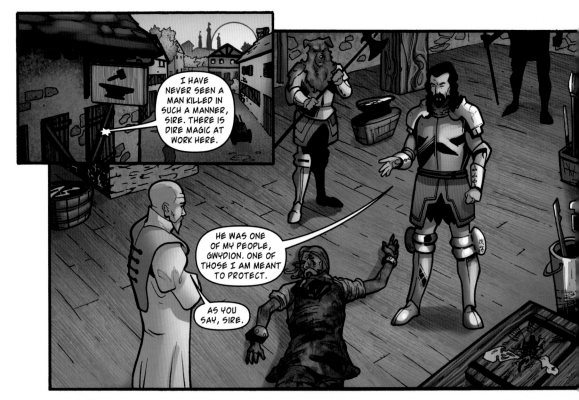

I HAVE NEVER SEEN A MAN KILLED IN SUCH A MANNER, SIRE. THERE IS DIRE MAGIC AT WORK HERE.

HE WAS ONE OF MY PEOPLE, GWYDION. ONE OF THOSE I AM MEANT TO PROTECT.

AS YOU SAY, SIRE.

HE WAS A GOOD MAN. WITH A BRILLIANT, INQUISITIVE MIND.

HE DID NOT DESERVE SUCH AN END.

HE WAS ONE OF MY PEOPLE!

HAVE THE DOCTOR ARRESTED. HE WILL PAY FOR THIS.

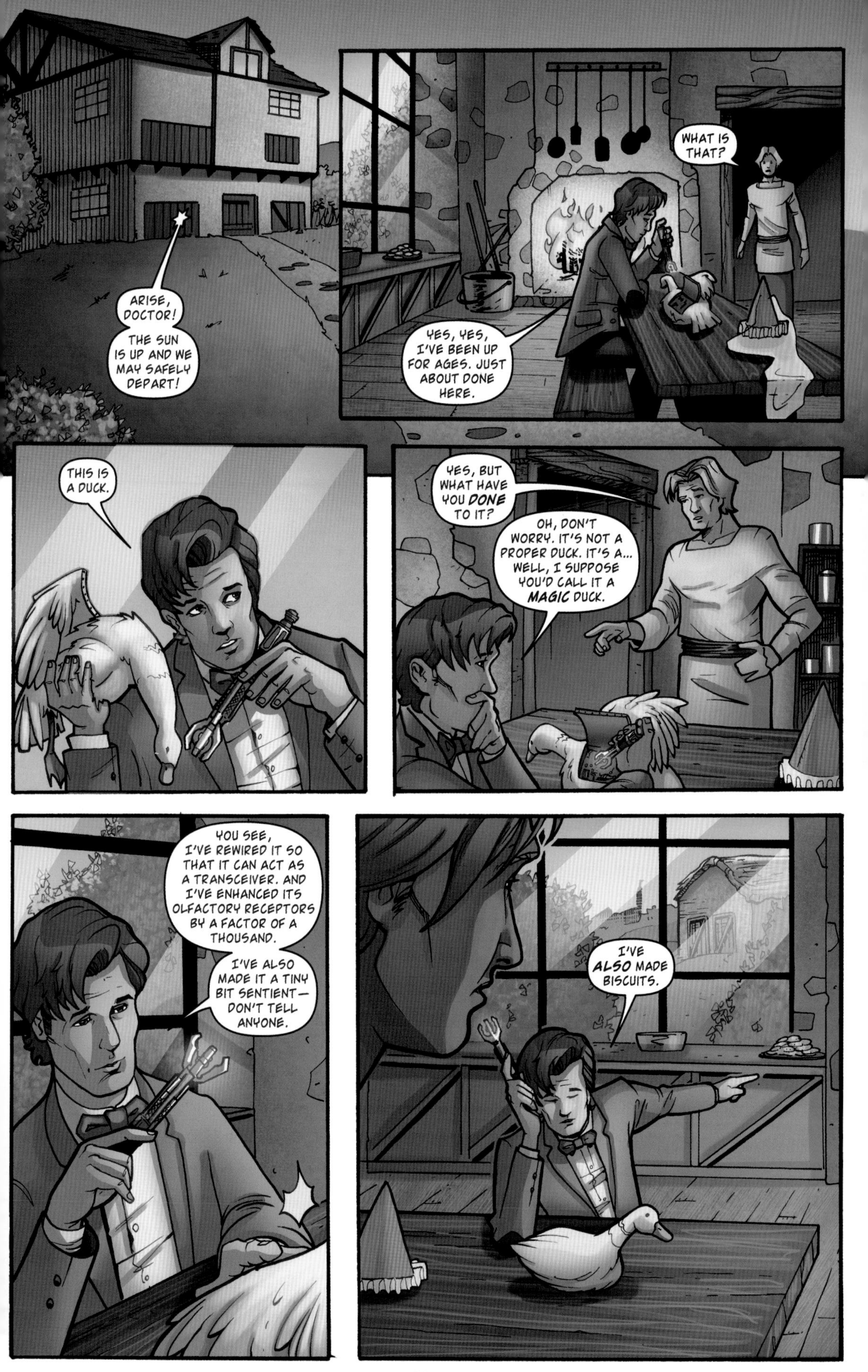
ARISE, DOCTOR!
THE SUN IS UP AND WE MAY SAFELY DEPART!
WHAT IS THAT?
YES, YES, I'VE BEEN UP FOR AGES. JUST ABOUT DONE HERE.
THIS IS A DUCK.
YES, BUT WHAT HAVE YOU DONE TO IT?
OH, DON'T WORRY. IT'S NOT A PROPER DUCK. IT'S A... WELL, I SUPPOSE YOU'D CALL IT A MAGIC DUCK.
YOU SEE, I'VE REWIRED IT SO THAT IT CAN ACT AS A TRANSCEIVER. AND I'VE ENHANCED ITS OLFACTORY RECEPTORS BY A FACTOR OF A THOUSAND.
I'VE ALSO MADE IT A TINY BIT SENTIENT— DON'T TELL ANYONE.
I'VE ALSO MADE BISCUITS.

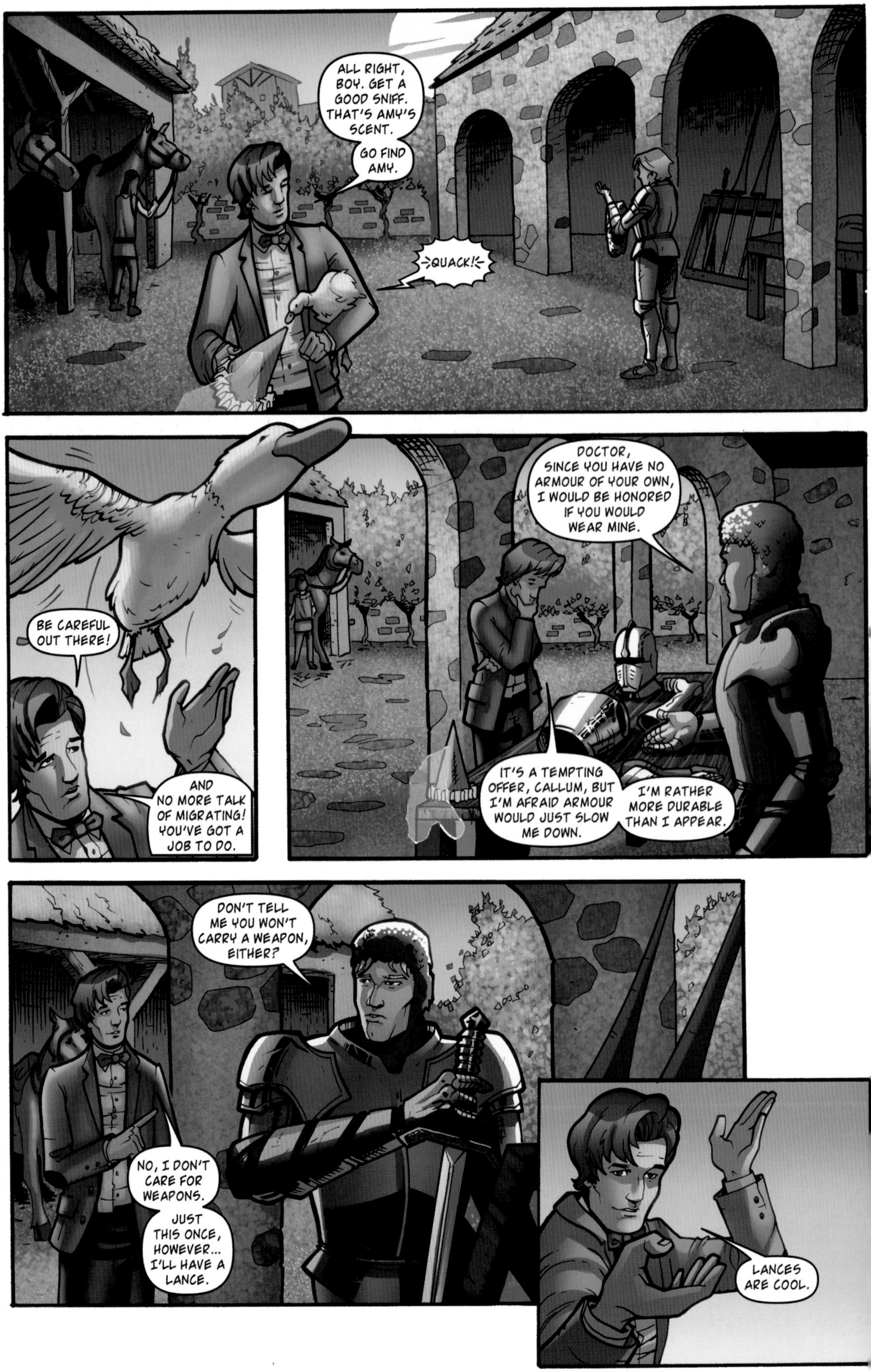
ALL RIGHT, BOY. GET A GOOD SNIFF. THAT'S AMY'S SCENT.
GO FIND AMY.
QUACK!
BE CAREFUL OUT THERE!
AND NO MORE TALK OF MIGRATING! YOU'VE GOT A JOB TO DO.
DOCTOR, SINCE YOU HAVE NO ARMOUR OF YOUR OWN, I WOULD BE HONORED IF YOU WOULD WEAR MINE.
IT'S A TEMPTING OFFER, CALLUM, BUT I'M AFRAID ARMOUR WOULD JUST SLOW ME DOWN.
I'M RATHER MORE DURABLE THAN I APPEAR.
DON'T TELL ME YOU WON'T CARRY A WEAPON, EITHER?
NO, I DON'T CARE FOR WEAPONS.
JUST THIS ONCE, HOWEVER... I'LL HAVE A LANCE.
LANCES ARE COOL.

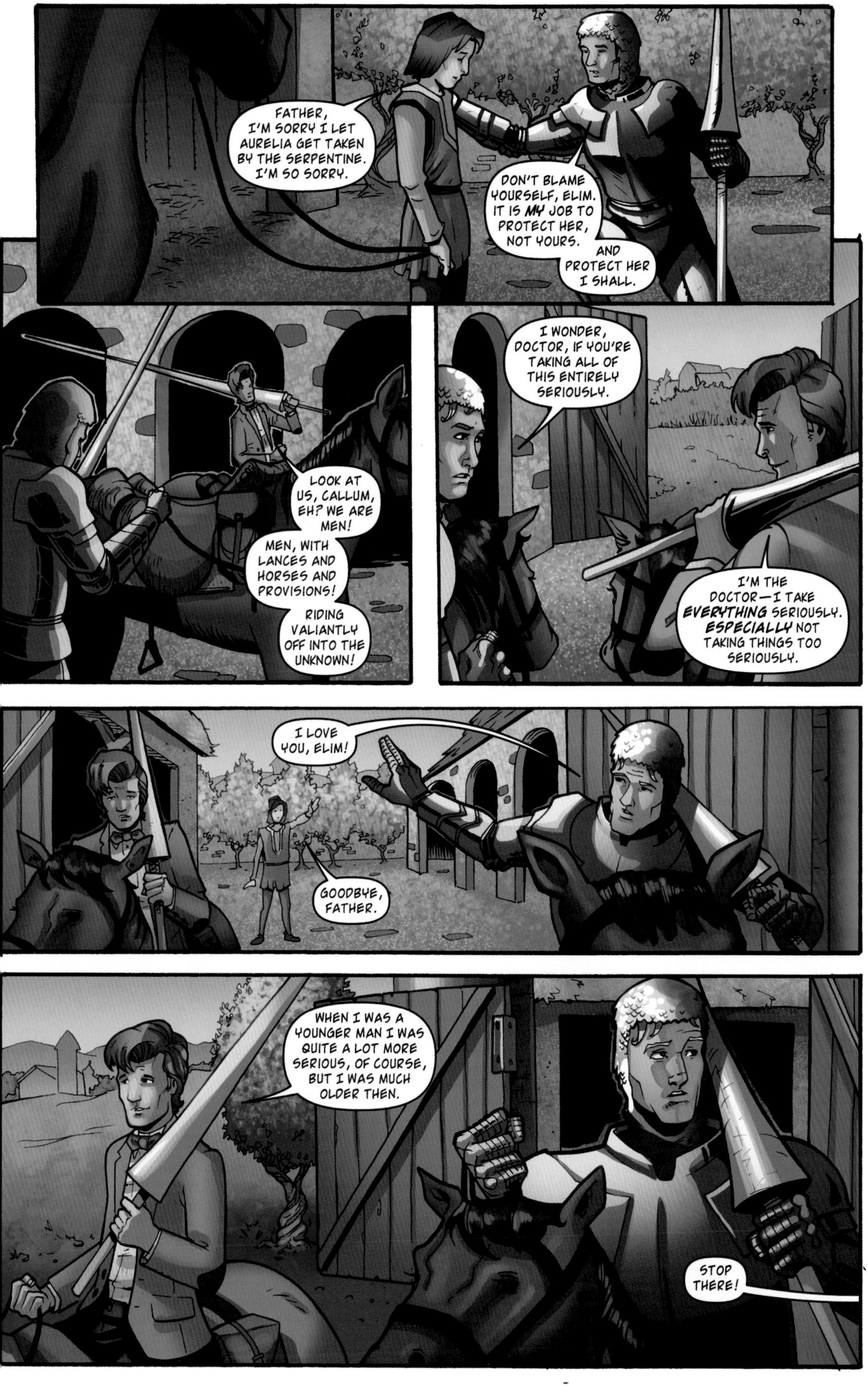
FATHER, I'M SORRY I LET AURELIA GET TAKEN BY THE SERPENTINE. I'M SO SORRY.
DON'T BLAME YOURSELF, ELIM. IT IS MY JOB TO PROTECT HER, NOT YOURS.
AND PROTECT HER I SHALL.
LOOK AT US, CALLUM, EH? WE ARE MEN!
MEN, WITH LANCES AND HORSES AND PROVISIONS!
RIDING VALIANTLY OFF INTO THE UNKNOWN!
I WONDER, DOCTOR, IF YOU'RE TAKING ALL OF THIS ENTIRELY SERIOUSLY.
I'M THE DOCTOR—I TAKE EVERYTHING SERIOUSLY. ESPECIALLY NOT TAKING THINGS TOO SERIOUSLY.
I LOVE YOU, ELIM!
GOODBYE, FATHER.
WHEN I WAS A YOUNGER MAN I WAS QUITE A LOT MORE SERIOUS, OF COURSE, BUT I WAS MUCH OLDER THEN.
STOP THERE!

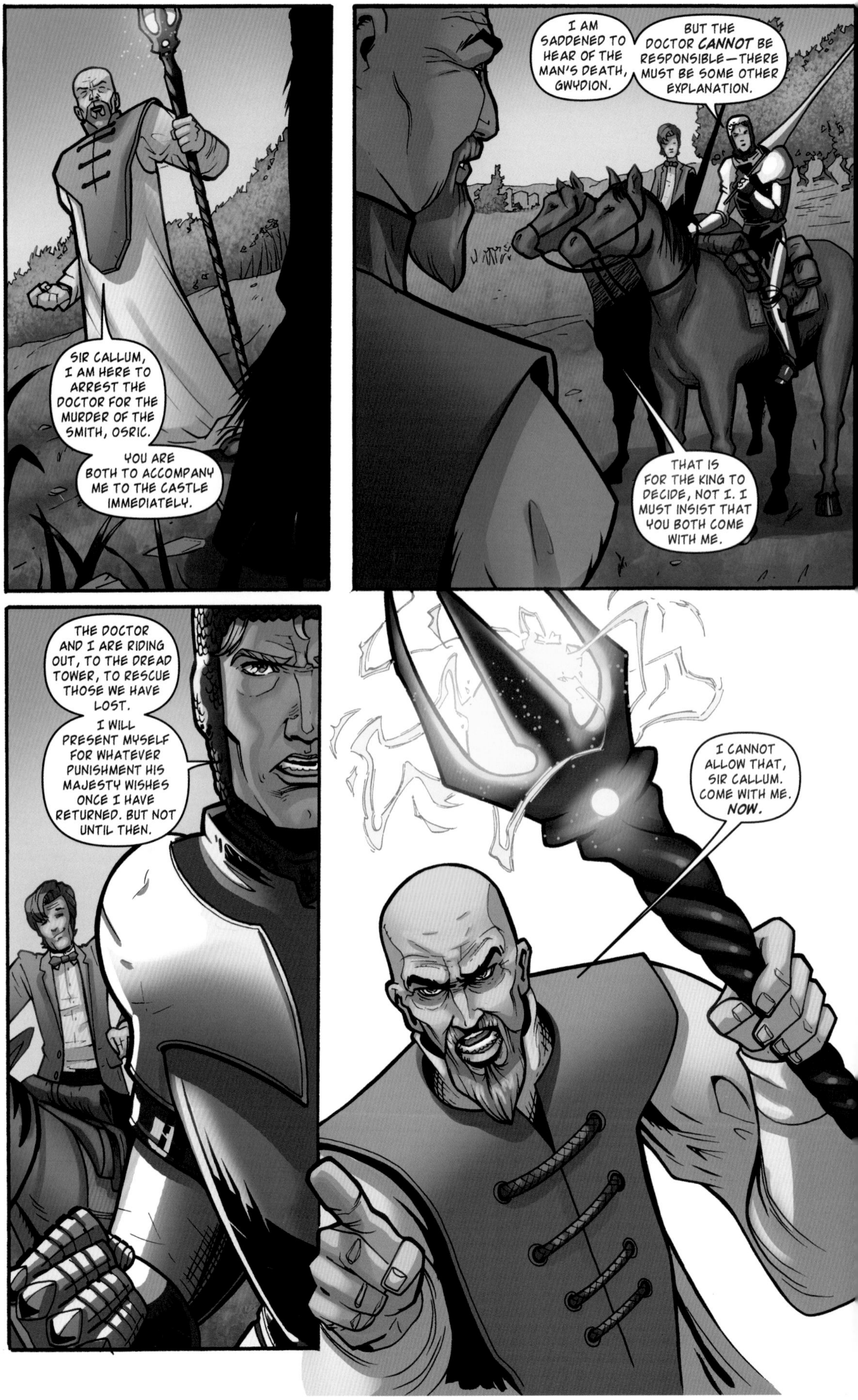
SIR CALLUM, I AM HERE TO ARREST THE DOCTOR FOR THE MURDER OF THE SMITH, OSRIC.
YOU ARE BOTH TO ACCOMPANY ME TO THE CASTLE IMMEDIATELY.
I AM SADDENED TO HEAR OF THE MAN'S DEATH, GWYDION.
BUT THE DOCTOR **CANNOT** BE RESPONSIBLE—THERE MUST BE SOME OTHER EXPLANATION.
THAT IS FOR THE KING TO DECIDE, NOT I. I MUST INSIST THAT YOU BOTH COME WITH ME.
THE DOCTOR AND I ARE RIDING OUT, TO THE DREAD TOWER, TO RESCUE THOSE WE HAVE LOST.
I WILL PRESENT MYSELF FOR WHATEVER PUNISHMENT HIS MAJESTY WISHES ONCE I HAVE RETURNED. BUT NOT UNTIL THEN.
I CANNOT ALLOW THAT, SIR CALLUM. COME WITH ME. **NOW.**

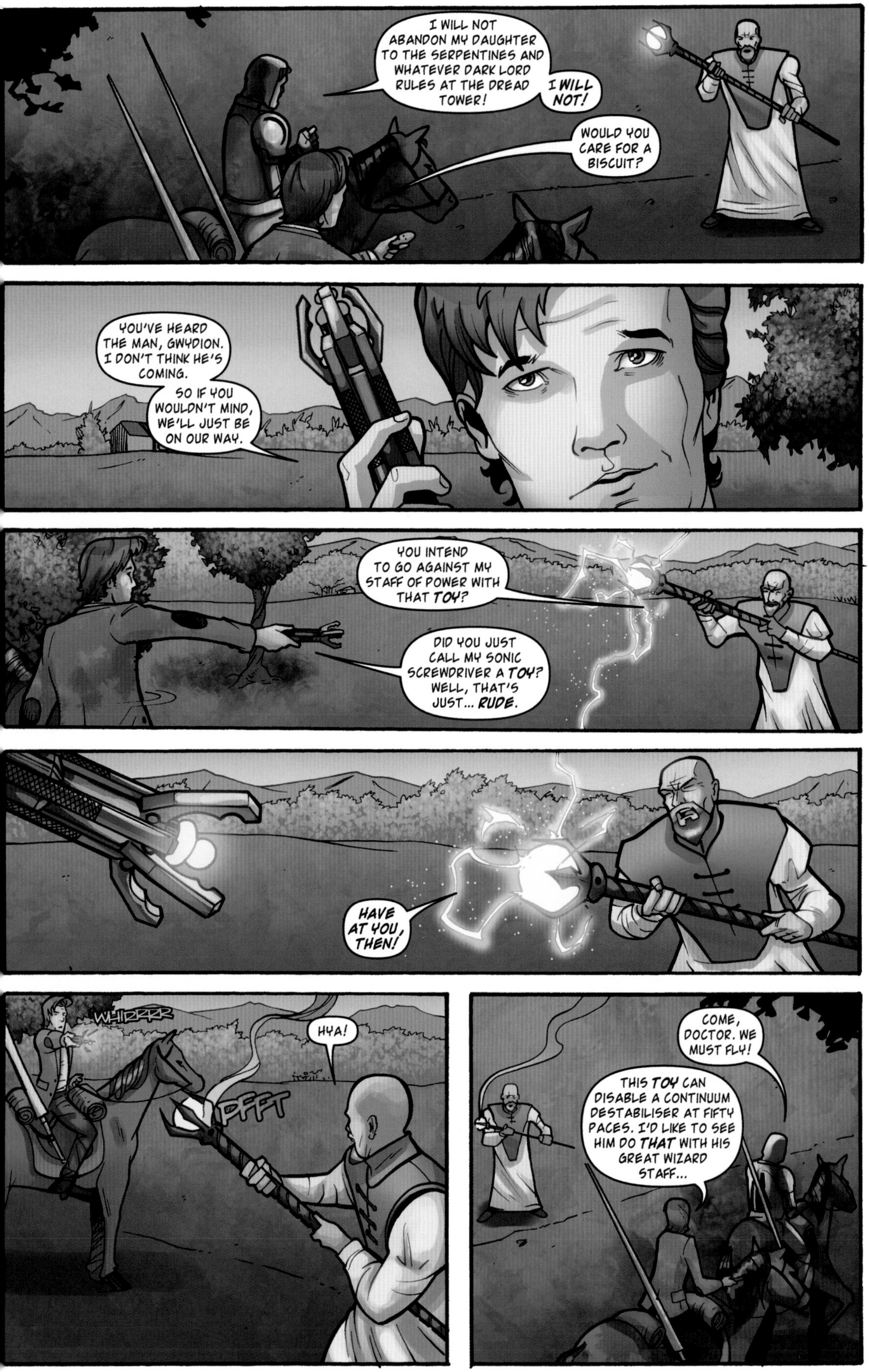
I WILL NOT ABANDON MY DAUGHTER TO THE SERPENTINES AND WHATEVER DARK LORD RULES AT THE DREAD TOWER!
I WILL NOT!
WOULD YOU CARE FOR A BISCUIT?
YOU'VE HEARD THE MAN, GWYDION. I DON'T THINK HE'S COMING.
SO IF YOU WOULDN'T MIND, WE'LL JUST BE ON OUR WAY.
YOU INTEND TO GO AGAINST MY STAFF OF POWER WITH THAT TOY?
DID YOU JUST CALL MY SONIC SCREWDRIVER A TOY? WELL, THAT'S JUST... RUDE.
HAVE AT YOU, THEN!
WHIRRRR
HYA!
PFFT
COME, DOCTOR. WE MUST FLY!
THIS TOY CAN DISABLE A CONTINUUM DESTABILISER AT FIFTY PACES. I'D LIKE TO SEE HIM DO THAT WITH HIS GREAT WIZARD STAFF...

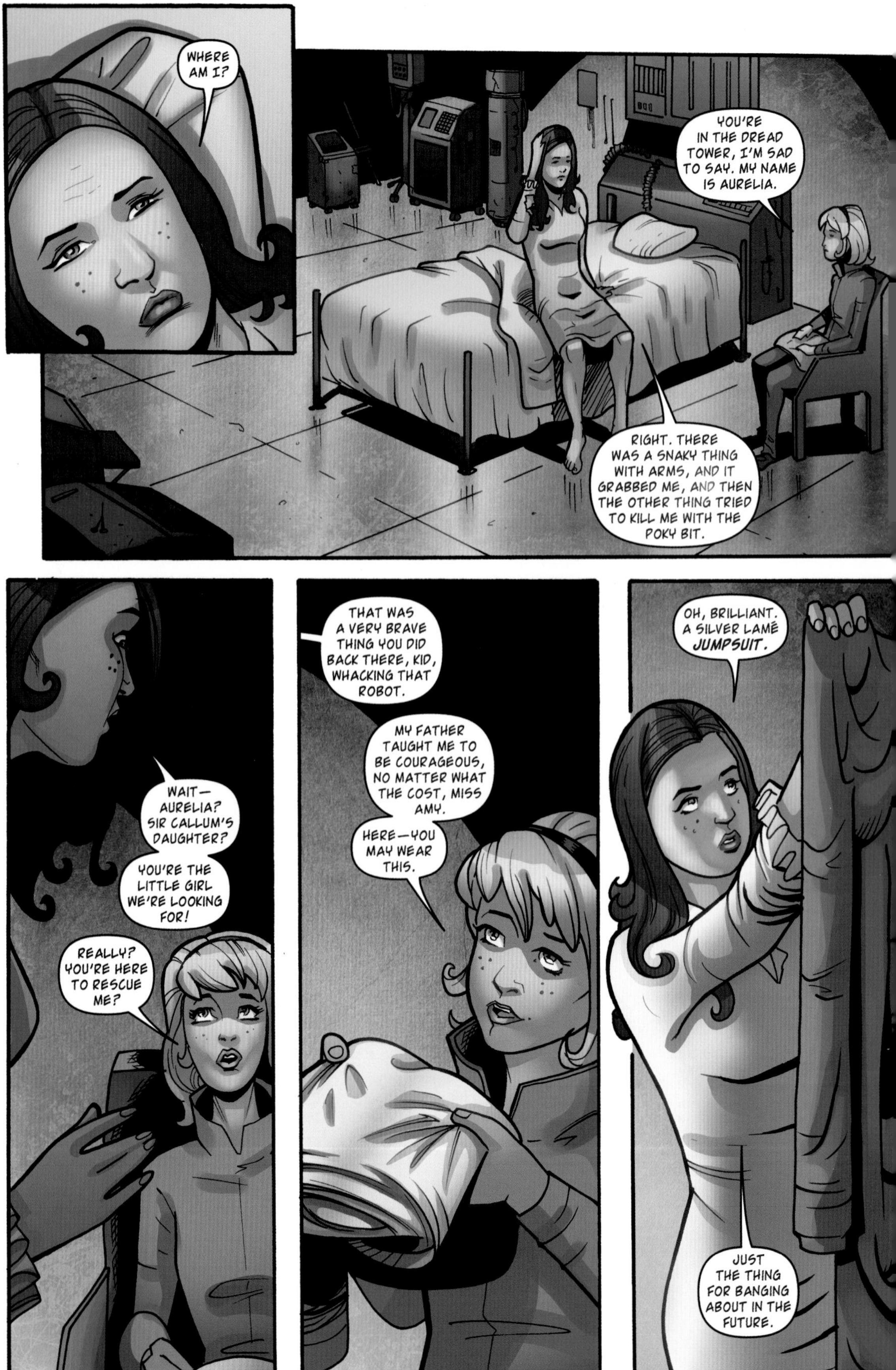

WHERE AM I?
YOU'RE IN THE DREAD TOWER, I'M SAD TO SAY. MY NAME IS AURELIA.
RIGHT. THERE WAS A SNAKY THING WITH ARMS, AND IT GRABBED ME, AND THEN THE OTHER THING TRIED TO KILL ME WITH THE POKY BIT.
WAIT— AURELIA? SIR CALLUM'S DAUGHTER?
YOU'RE THE LITTLE GIRL WE'RE LOOKING FOR!
REALLY? YOU'RE HERE TO RESCUE ME?
THAT WAS A VERY BRAVE THING YOU DID BACK THERE, KID, WHACKING THAT ROBOT.
MY FATHER TAUGHT ME TO BE COURAGEOUS, NO MATTER WHAT THE COST, MISS AMY.
HERE—YOU MAY WEAR THIS.
OH, BRILLIANT. A SILVER LAMÉ JUMPSUIT.
JUST THE THING FOR BANGING ABOUT IN THE FUTURE.

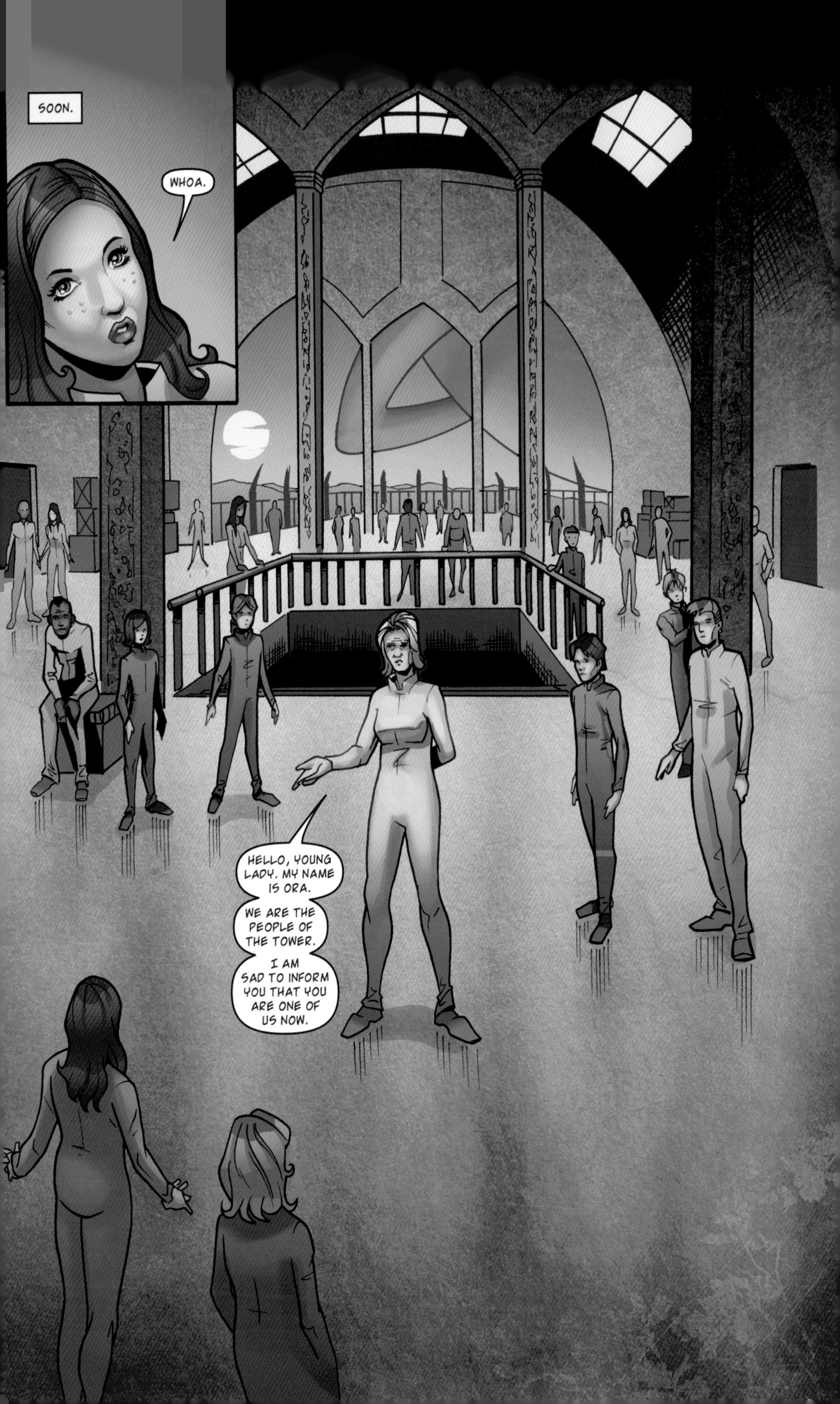
SOON.
WHOA.
HELLO, YOUNG LADY. MY NAME IS ORA.
WE ARE THE PEOPLE OF THE TOWER.
I AM SAD TO INFORM YOU THAT YOU ARE ONE OF US NOW.

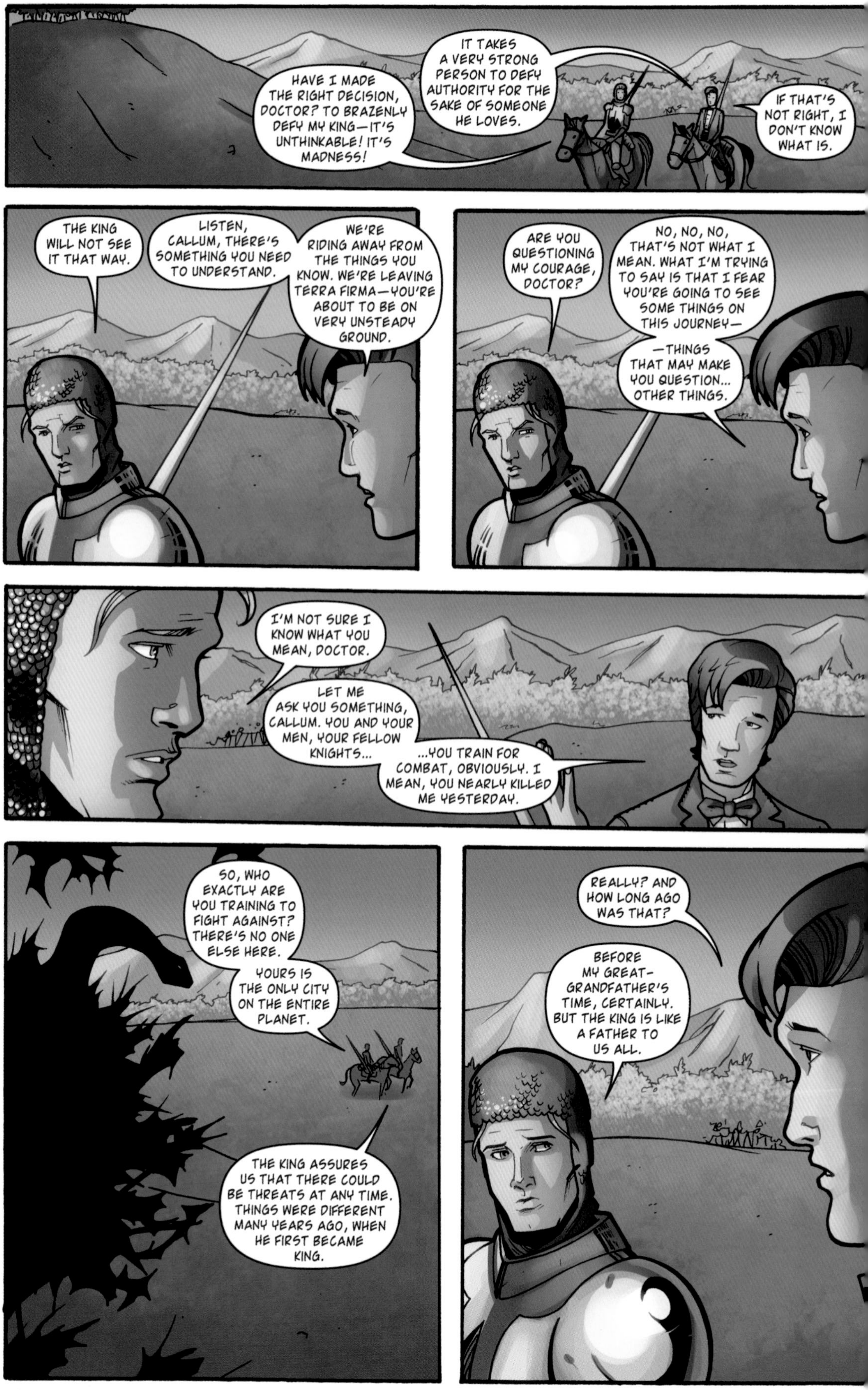

HAVE I MADE THE RIGHT DECISION, DOCTOR? TO BRAZENLY DEFY MY KING—IT'S UNTHINKABLE! IT'S MADNESS!
IT TAKES A VERY STRONG PERSON TO DEFY AUTHORITY FOR THE SAKE OF SOMEONE HE LOVES.
IF THAT'S NOT RIGHT, I DON'T KNOW WHAT IS.
THE KING WILL NOT SEE IT THAT WAY.
LISTEN, CALLUM, THERE'S SOMETHING YOU NEED TO UNDERSTAND.
WE'RE RIDING AWAY FROM THE THINGS YOU KNOW. WE'RE LEAVING TERRA FIRMA—YOU'RE ABOUT TO BE ON VERY UNSTEADY GROUND.
ARE YOU QUESTIONING MY COURAGE, DOCTOR?
NO, NO, NO, THAT'S NOT WHAT I MEAN. WHAT I'M TRYING TO SAY IS THAT I FEAR YOU'RE GOING TO SEE SOME THINGS ON THIS JOURNEY—
—THINGS THAT MAY MAKE YOU QUESTION... OTHER THINGS.
I'M NOT SURE I KNOW WHAT YOU MEAN, DOCTOR.
LET ME ASK YOU SOMETHING, CALLUM. YOU AND YOUR MEN, YOUR FELLOW KNIGHTS...
...YOU TRAIN FOR COMBAT, OBVIOUSLY. I MEAN, YOU NEARLY KILLED ME YESTERDAY.
SO, WHO EXACTLY ARE YOU TRAINING TO FIGHT AGAINST? THERE'S NO ONE ELSE HERE.
YOURS IS THE ONLY CITY ON THE ENTIRE PLANET.
THE KING ASSURES US THAT THERE COULD BE THREATS AT ANY TIME. THINGS WERE DIFFERENT MANY YEARS AGO, WHEN HE FIRST BECAME KING.
REALLY? AND HOW LONG AGO WAS THAT?
BEFORE MY GREAT-GRANDFATHER'S TIME, CERTAINLY. BUT THE KING IS LIKE A FATHER TO US ALL.

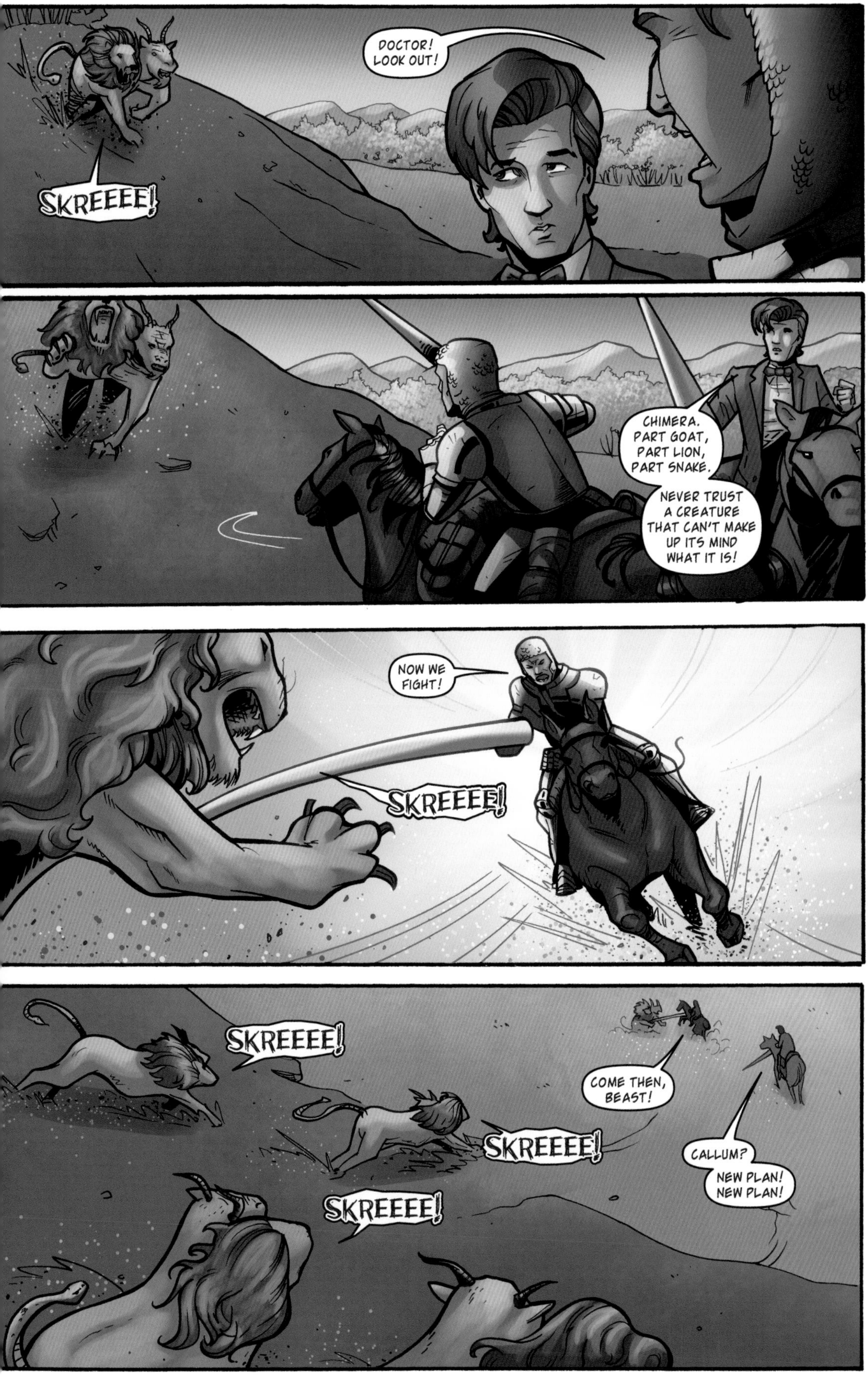
DOCTOR! LOOK OUT!
SKREEEE!
CHIMERA. PART GOAT, PART LION, PART SNAKE.
NEVER TRUST A CREATURE THAT CAN'T MAKE UP ITS MIND WHAT IT IS!
NOW WE FIGHT!
SKREEEE!
SKREEEE!
COME THEN, BEAST!
SKREEEE!
CALLUM?
NEW PLAN! NEW PLAN!
SKREEEE!

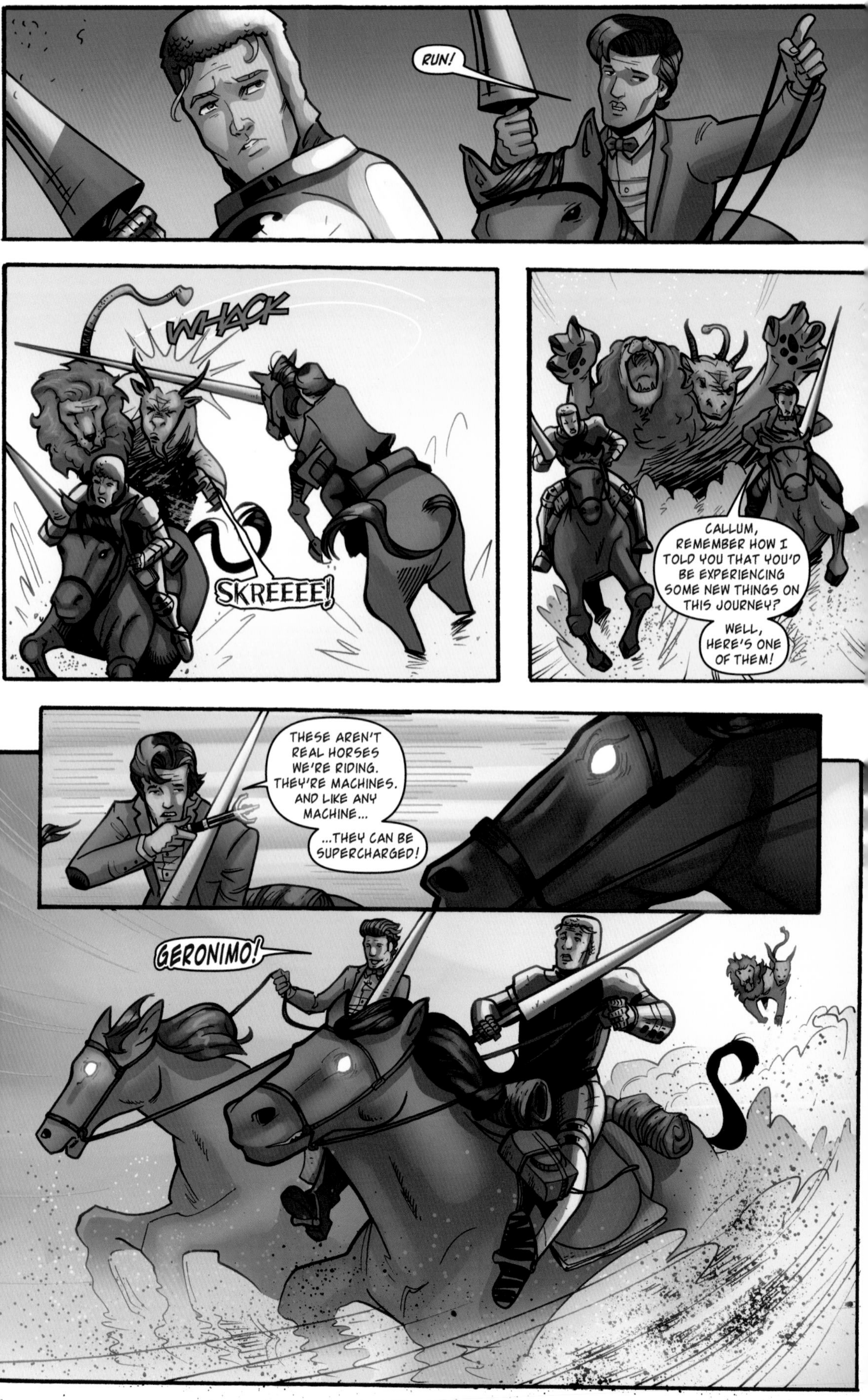
RUN!
WHACK
SKREEEE!
CALLUM, REMEMBER HOW I TOLD YOU THAT YOU'D BE EXPERIENCING SOME NEW THINGS ON THIS JOURNEY?
WELL, HERE'S ONE OF THEM!
THESE AREN'T REAL HORSES WE'RE RIDING. THEY'RE MACHINES. AND LIKE ANY MACHINE...
...THEY CAN BE SUPERCHARGED!
GERONIMO!

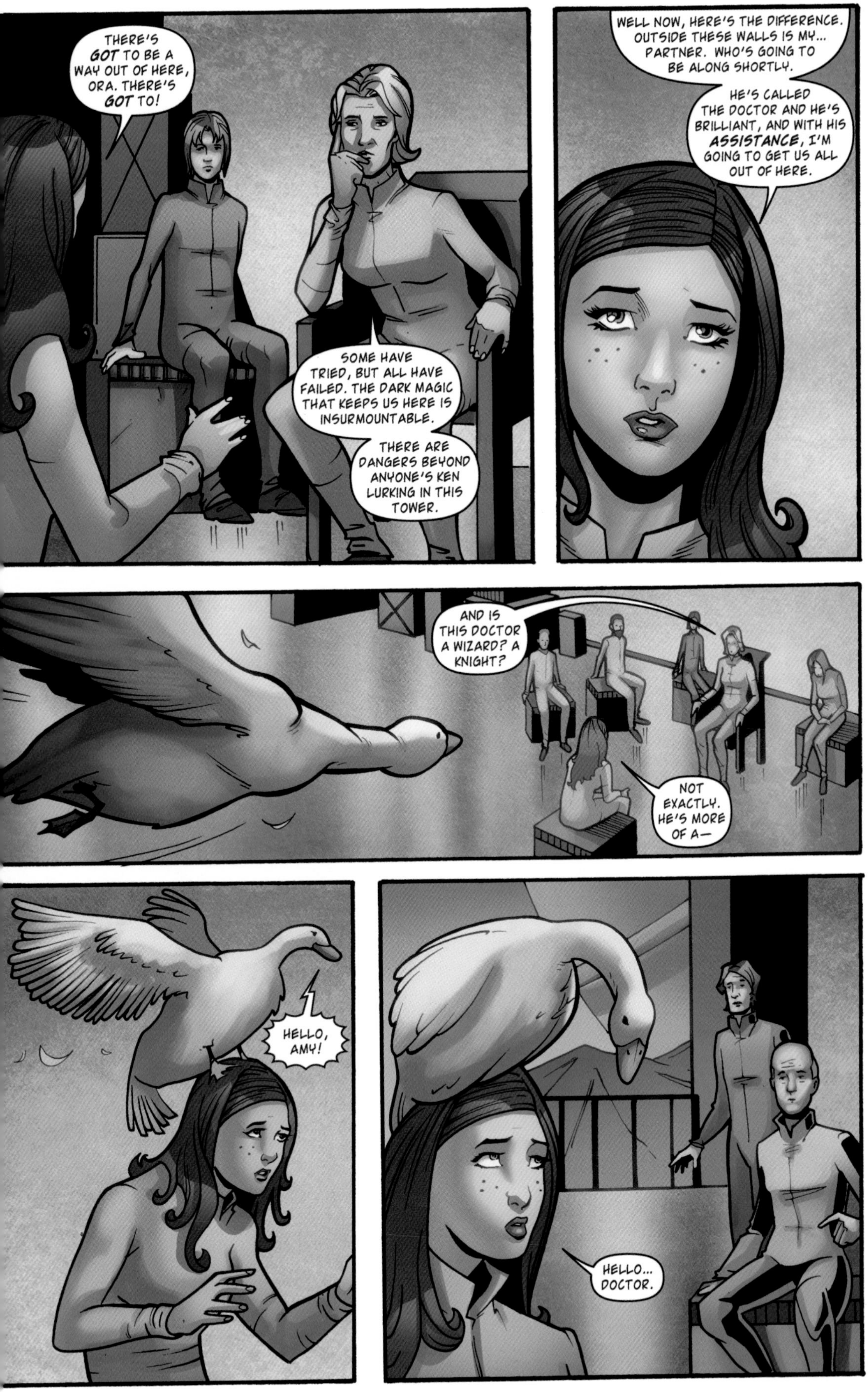
THERE'S GOT TO BE A WAY OUT OF HERE, ORA. THERE'S GOT TO!
SOME HAVE TRIED, BUT ALL HAVE FAILED. THE DARK MAGIC THAT KEEPS US HERE IS INSURMOUNTABLE.
THERE ARE DANGERS BEYOND ANYONE'S KEN LURKING IN THIS TOWER.
WELL NOW, HERE'S THE DIFFERENCE. OUTSIDE THESE WALLS IS MY... PARTNER. WHO'S GOING TO BE ALONG SHORTLY.
HE'S CALLED THE DOCTOR AND HE'S BRILLIANT, AND WITH HIS ASSISTANCE, I'M GOING TO GET US ALL OUT OF HERE.
AND IS THIS DOCTOR A WIZARD? A KNIGHT?
NOT EXACTLY. HE'S MORE OF A—
HELLO, AMY!
HELLO... DOCTOR.

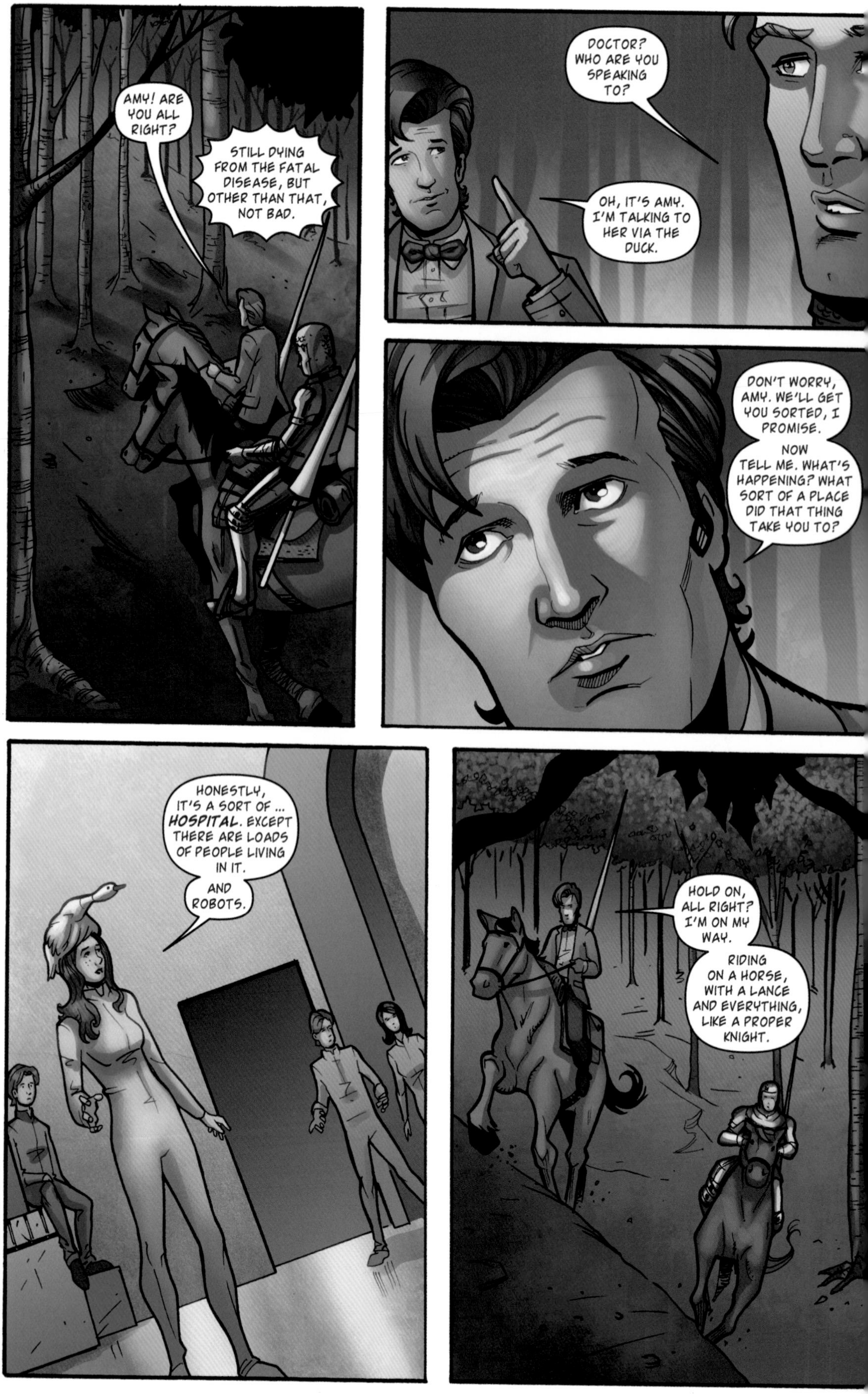

AMY! ARE YOU ALL RIGHT?
STILL DYING FROM THE FATAL DISEASE, BUT OTHER THAN THAT, NOT BAD.
DOCTOR? WHO ARE YOU SPEAKING TO?
OH, IT'S AMY. I'M TALKING TO HER VIA THE DUCK.
DON'T WORRY, AMY. WE'LL GET YOU SORTED, I PROMISE.
NOW TELL ME. WHAT'S HAPPENING? WHAT SORT OF A PLACE DID THAT THING TAKE YOU TO?
HONESTLY, IT'S A SORT OF ... HOSPITAL. EXCEPT THERE ARE LOADS OF PEOPLE LIVING IN IT.
AND ROBOTS.
HOLD ON, ALL RIGHT? I'M ON MY WAY.
RIDING ON A HORSE, WITH A LANCE AND EVERYTHING, LIKE A PROPER KNIGHT.

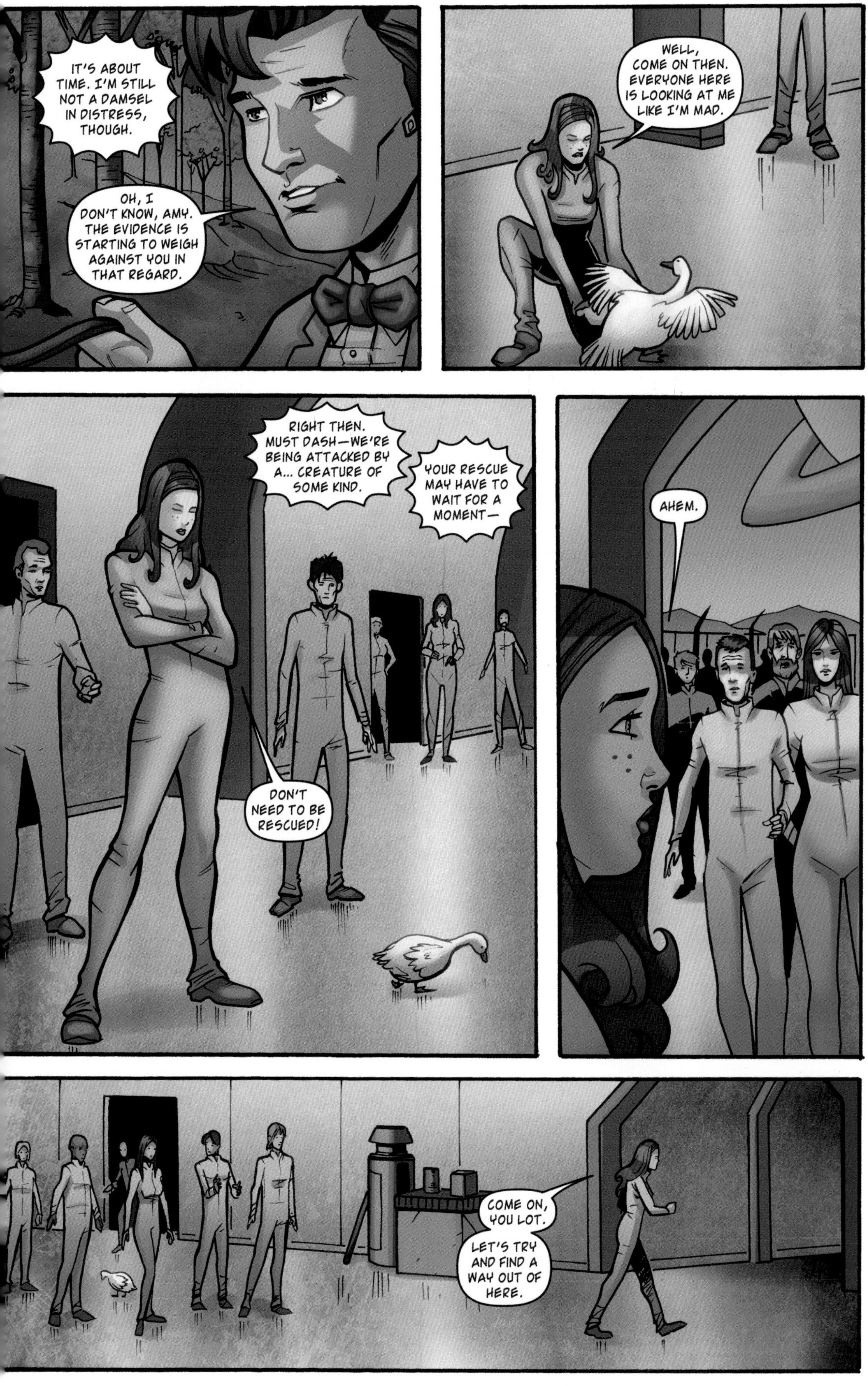
IT'S ABOUT TIME. I'M STILL NOT A DAMSEL IN DISTRESS, THOUGH.
OH, I DON'T KNOW, AMY. THE EVIDENCE IS STARTING TO WEIGH AGAINST YOU IN THAT REGARD.
WELL, COME ON THEN. EVERYONE HERE IS LOOKING AT ME LIKE I'M MAD.
RIGHT THEN. MUST DASH—WE'RE BEING ATTACKED BY A... CREATURE OF SOME KIND.
YOUR RESCUE MAY HAVE TO WAIT FOR A MOMENT—
DON'T NEED TO BE RESCUED!
AHEM.
COME ON, YOU LOT.
LET'S TRY AND FIND A WAY OUT OF HERE.

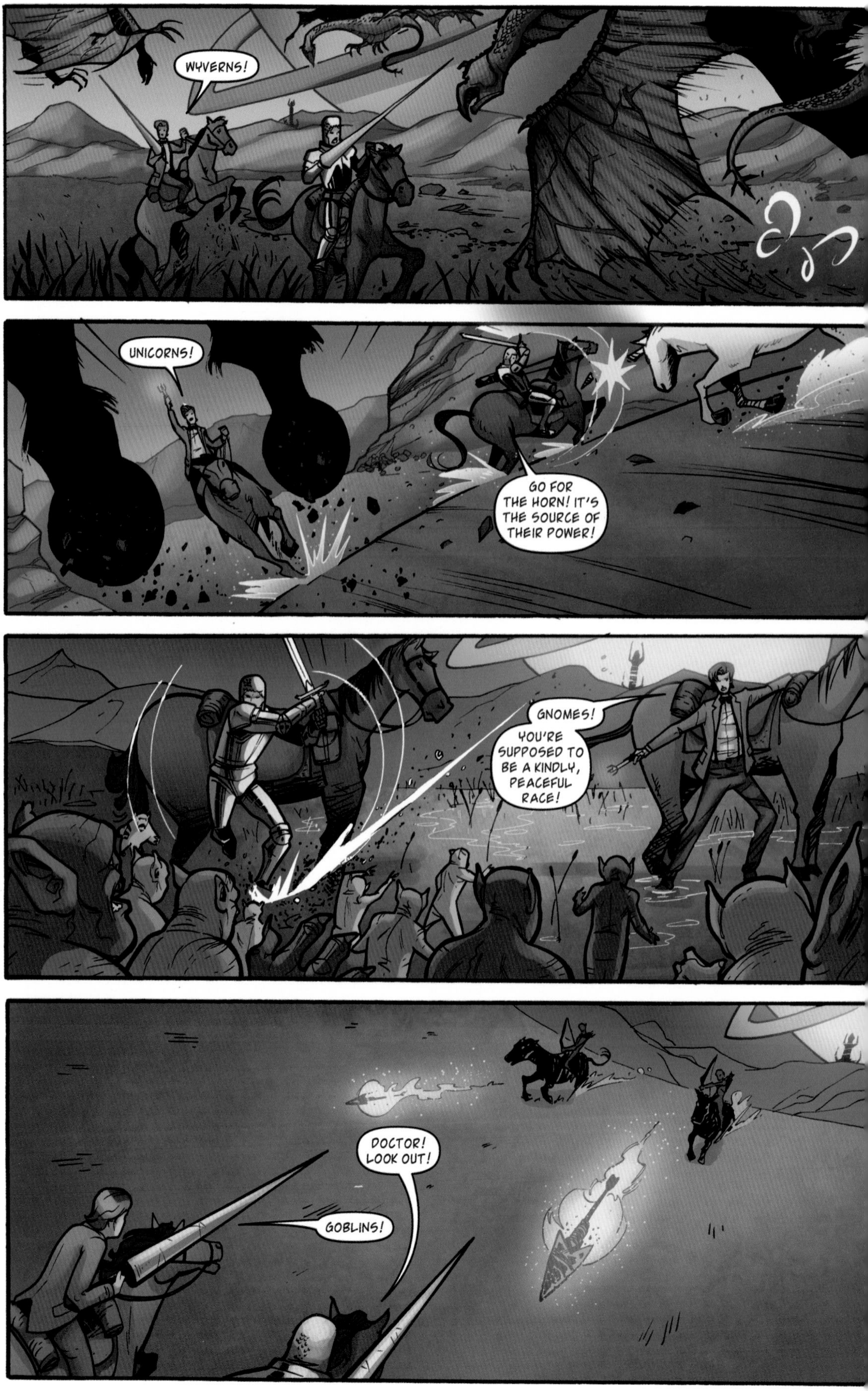
WYVERNS!
UNICORNS!
GO FOR THE HORN! IT'S THE SOURCE OF THEIR POWER!
GNOMES!
YOU'RE SUPPOSED TO BE A KINDLY, PEACEFUL RACE!
DOCTOR! LOOK OUT!
GOBLINS!

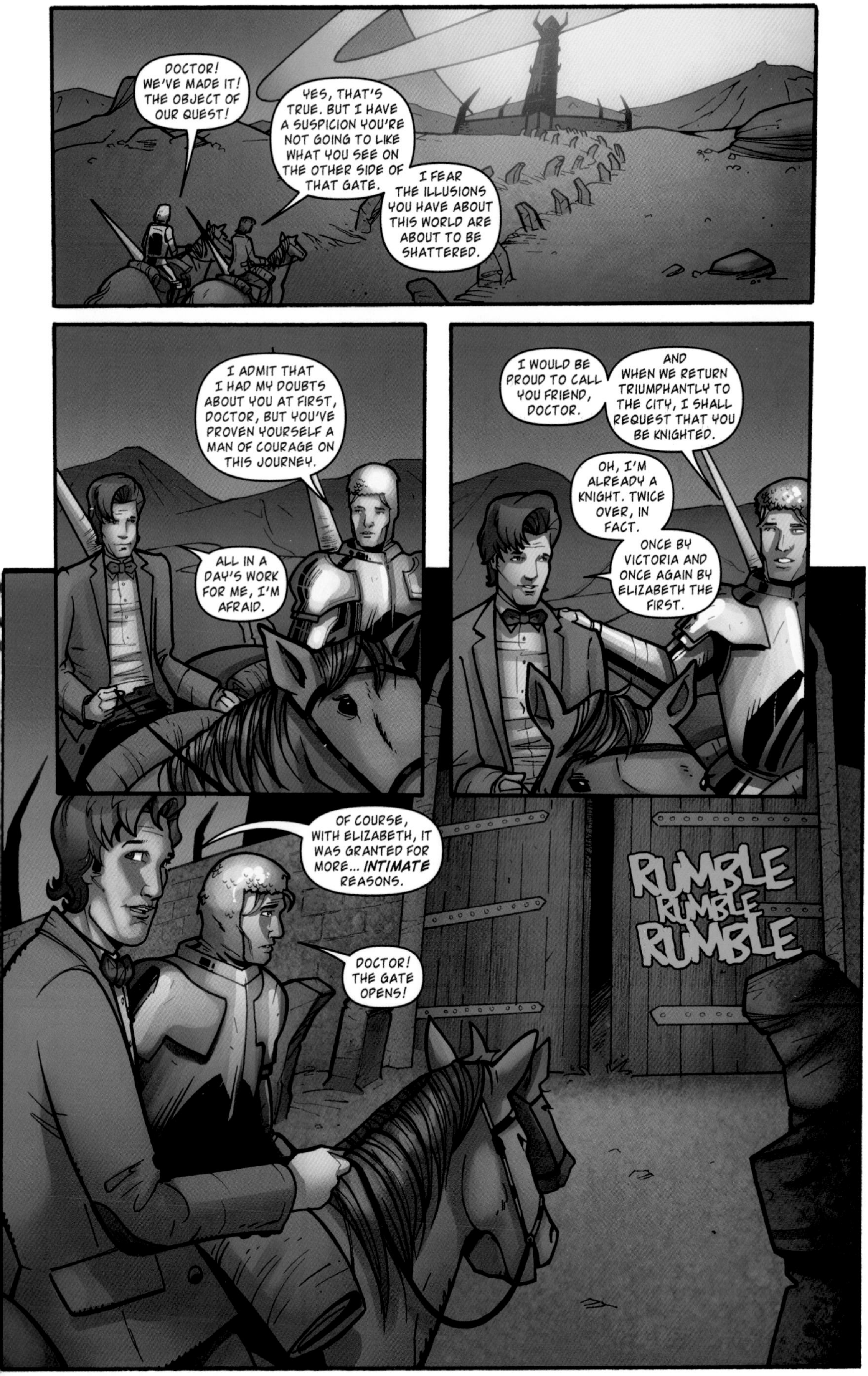
DOCTOR! WE'VE MADE IT! THE OBJECT OF OUR QUEST!
YES, THAT'S TRUE. BUT I HAVE A SUSPICION YOU'RE NOT GOING TO LIKE WHAT YOU SEE ON THE OTHER SIDE OF THAT GATE.
I FEAR THE ILLUSIONS YOU HAVE ABOUT THIS WORLD ARE ABOUT TO BE SHATTERED.
I ADMIT THAT I HAD MY DOUBTS ABOUT YOU AT FIRST, DOCTOR, BUT YOU'VE PROVEN YOURSELF A MAN OF COURAGE ON THIS JOURNEY.
ALL IN A DAY'S WORK FOR ME, I'M AFRAID.
I WOULD BE PROUD TO CALL YOU FRIEND, DOCTOR.
AND WHEN WE RETURN TRIUMPHANTLY TO THE CITY, I SHALL REQUEST THAT YOU BE KNIGHTED.
OH, I'M ALREADY A KNIGHT. TWICE OVER, IN FACT.
ONCE BY VICTORIA AND ONCE AGAIN BY ELIZABETH THE FIRST.
OF COURSE, WITH ELIZABETH, IT WAS GRANTED FOR MORE... *INTIMATE* REASONS.
RUMBLE RUMBLE RUMBLE
DOCTOR! THE GATE OPENS!

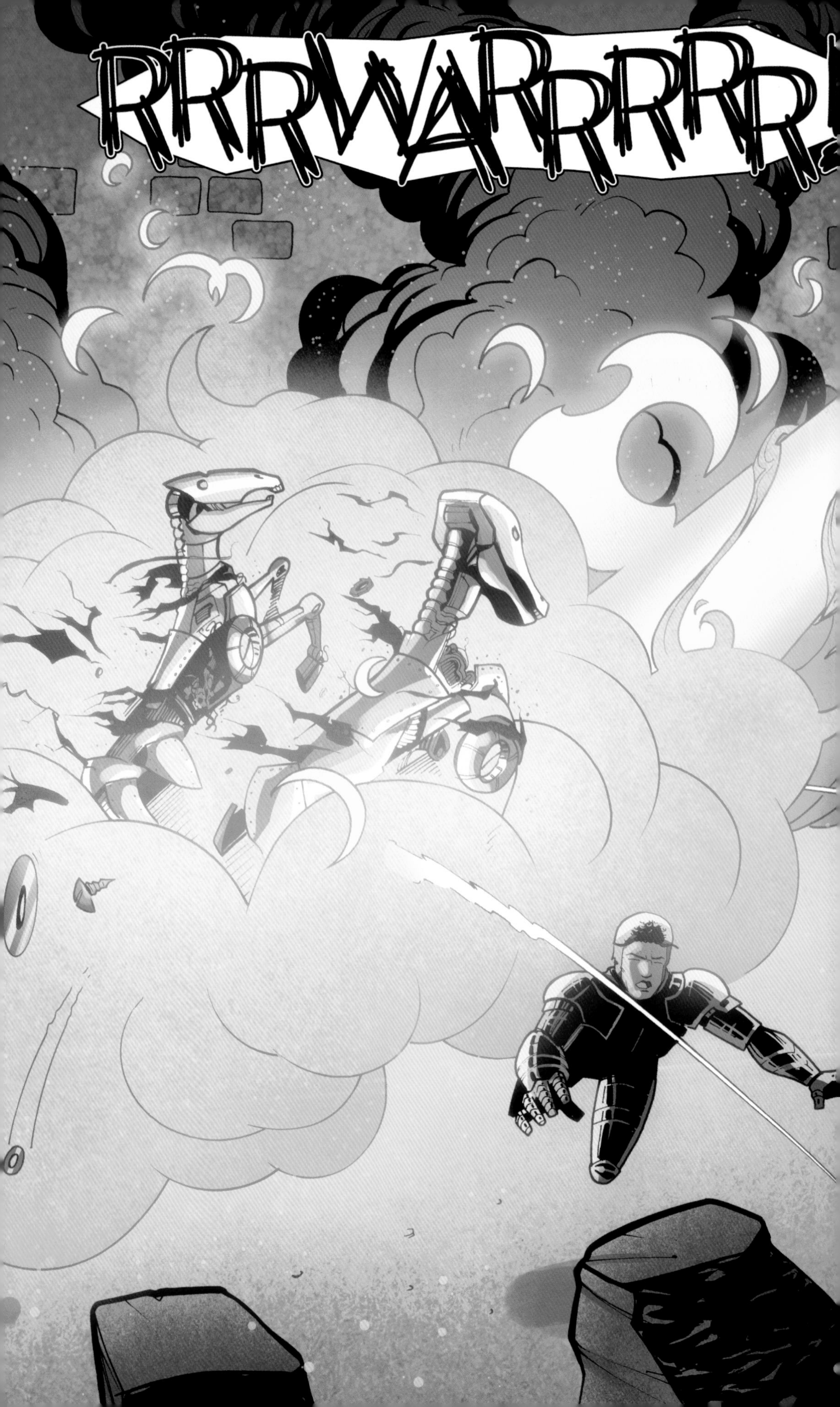
RRRWARRRRR!

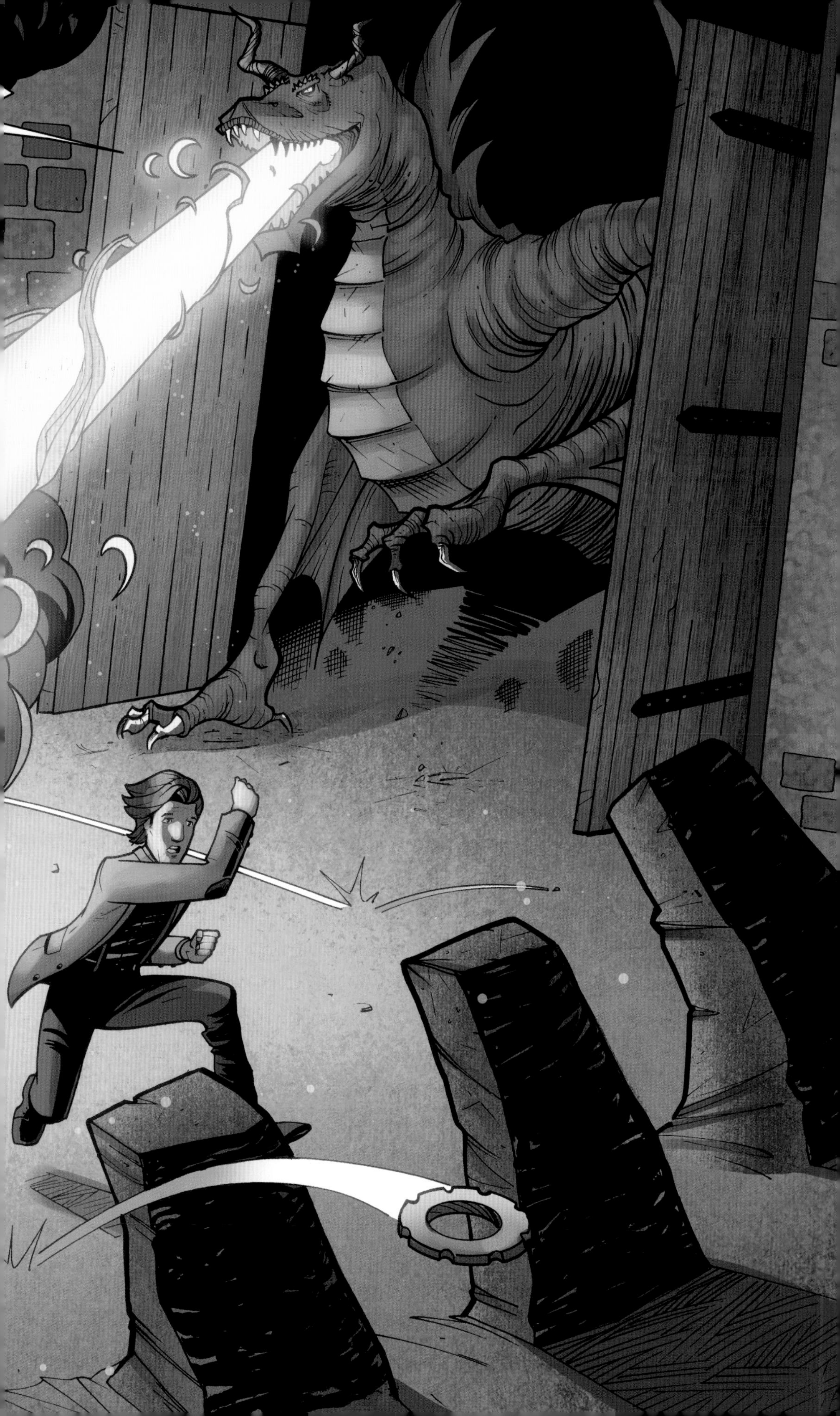

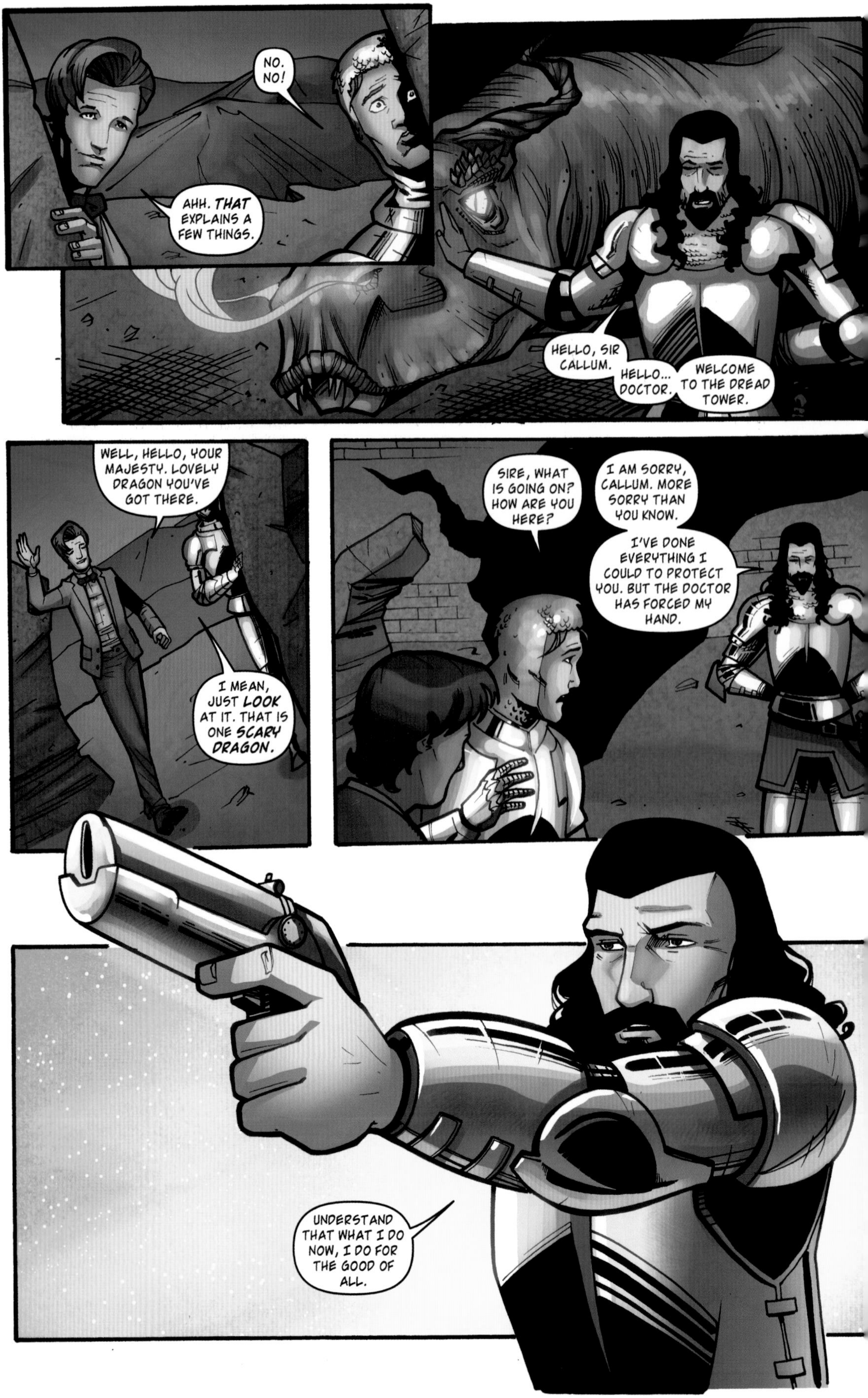
NO. NO!
AHH. THAT EXPLAINS A FEW THINGS.
HELLO, SIR CALLUM.
HELLO... DOCTOR.
WELCOME TO THE DREAD TOWER.
WELL, HELLO, YOUR MAJESTY. LOVELY DRAGON YOU'VE GOT THERE.
I MEAN, JUST LOOK AT IT. THAT IS ONE SCARY DRAGON.
SIRE, WHAT IS GOING ON? HOW ARE YOU HERE?
I AM SORRY, CALLUM. MORE SORRY THAN YOU KNOW.
I'VE DONE EVERYTHING I COULD TO PROTECT YOU. BUT THE DOCTOR HAS FORCED MY HAND.
UNDERSTAND THAT WHAT I DO NOW, I DO FOR THE GOOD OF ALL.

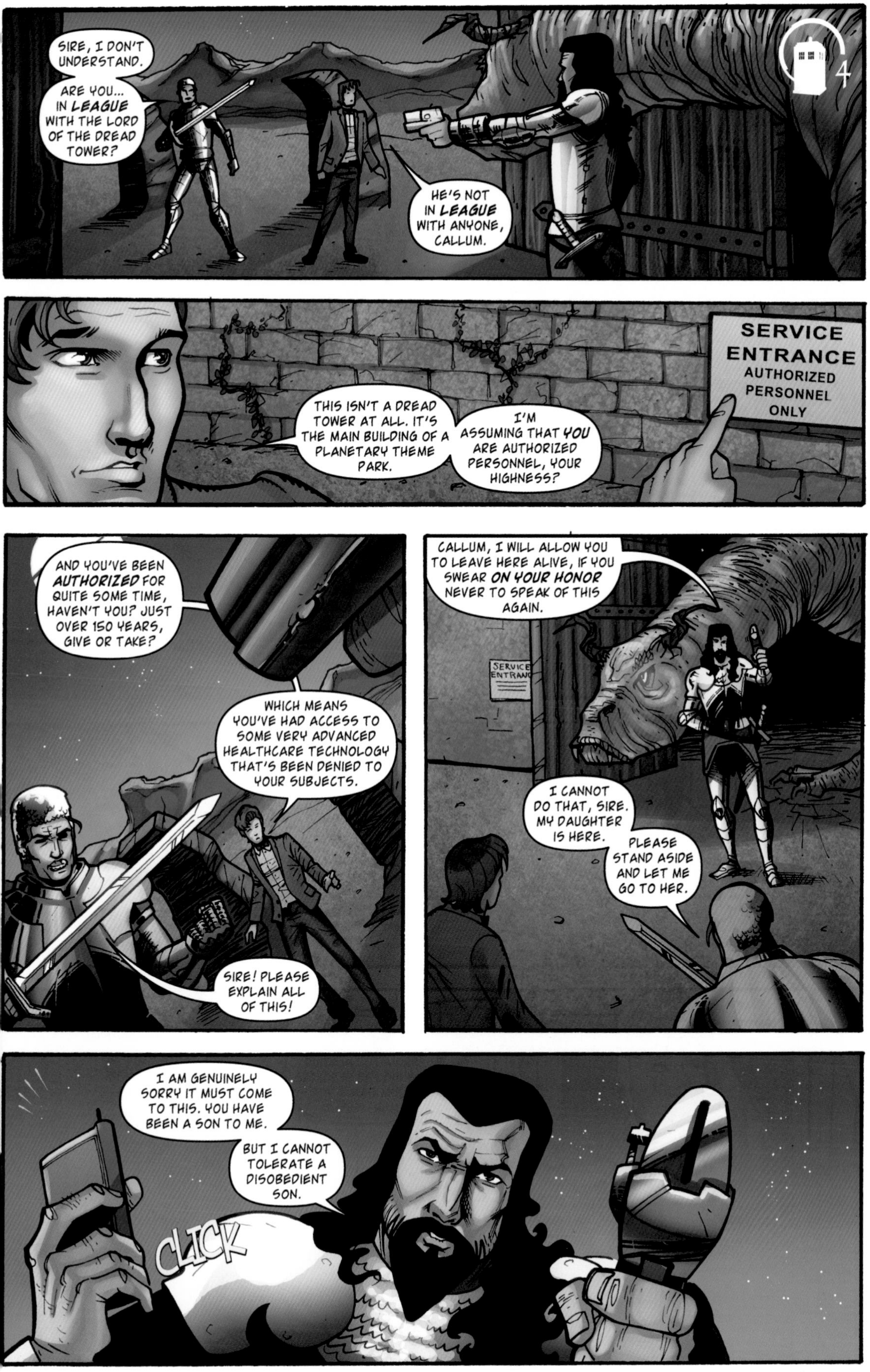
SIRE, I DON'T UNDERSTAND.
ARE YOU... IN **LEAGUE** WITH THE LORD OF THE DREAD TOWER?
HE'S NOT IN **LEAGUE** WITH ANYONE, CALLUM.
SERVICE ENTRANCE AUTHORIZED PERSONNEL ONLY
THIS ISN'T A DREAD TOWER AT ALL. IT'S THE MAIN BUILDING OF A PLANETARY THEME PARK.
I'M ASSUMING THAT ***YOU*** ARE AUTHORIZED PERSONNEL, YOUR HIGHNESS?
AND YOU'VE BEEN ***AUTHORIZED*** FOR QUITE SOME TIME, HAVEN'T YOU? JUST OVER 150 YEARS, GIVE OR TAKE?
WHICH MEANS YOU'VE HAD ACCESS TO SOME VERY ADVANCED HEALTHCARE TECHNOLOGY THAT'S BEEN DENIED TO YOUR SUBJECTS.
SIRE! PLEASE EXPLAIN ALL OF THIS!
CALLUM, I WILL ALLOW YOU TO LEAVE HERE ALIVE, IF YOU SWEAR ***ON YOUR HONOR*** NEVER TO SPEAK OF THIS AGAIN.
SERVICE ENTRANCE
I CANNOT DO THAT, SIRE. MY DAUGHTER IS HERE.
PLEASE STAND ASIDE AND LET ME GO TO HER.
I AM GENUINELY SORRY IT MUST COME TO THIS. YOU HAVE BEEN A SON TO ME.
BUT I CANNOT TOLERATE A DISOBEDIENT SON.
CLICK

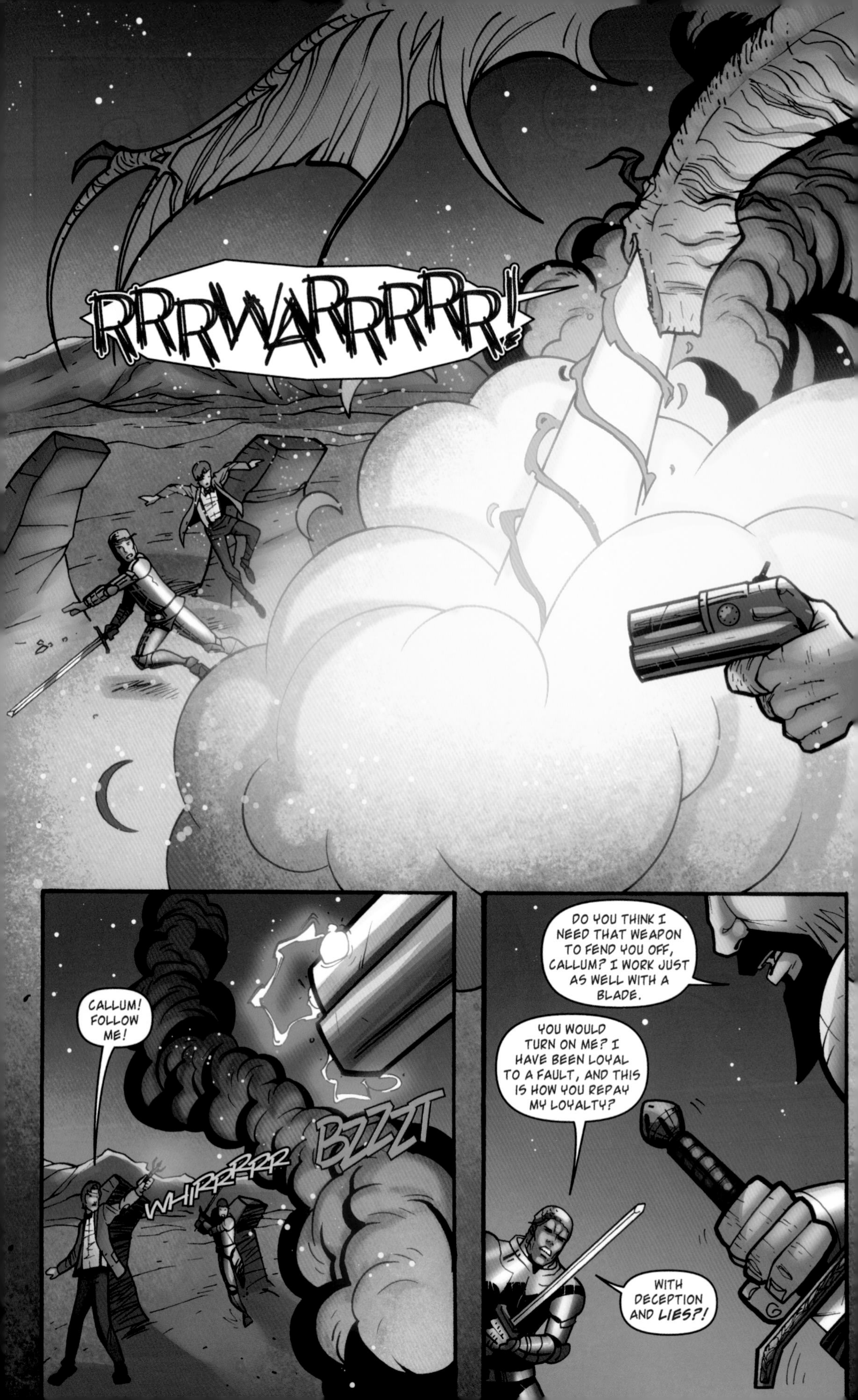
RRRWARRRRRR!
CALLUM! FOLLOW ME!
WHIRRRRR
BZZZT
DO YOU THINK I NEED THAT WEAPON TO FEND YOU OFF, CALLUM? I WORK JUST AS WELL WITH A BLADE.
YOU WOULD TURN ON ME? I HAVE BEEN LOYAL TO A FAULT, AND THIS IS HOW YOU REPAY MY LOYALTY?
WITH DECEPTION AND LIES?!

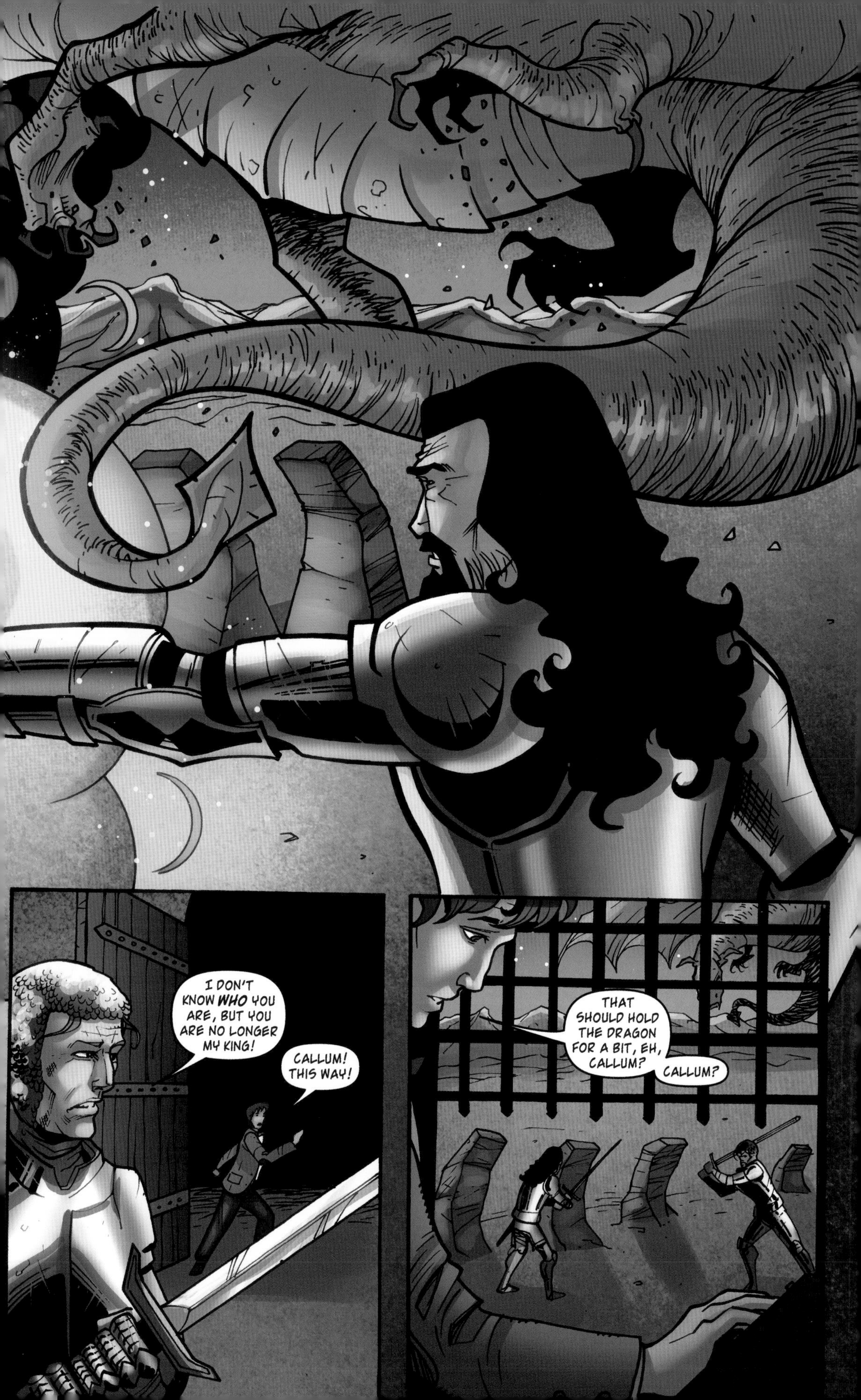
I DON'T KNOW WHO YOU ARE, BUT YOU ARE NO LONGER MY KING!
CALLUM! THIS WAY!
THAT SHOULD HOLD THE DRAGON FOR A BIT, EH, CALLUM?
CALLUM?

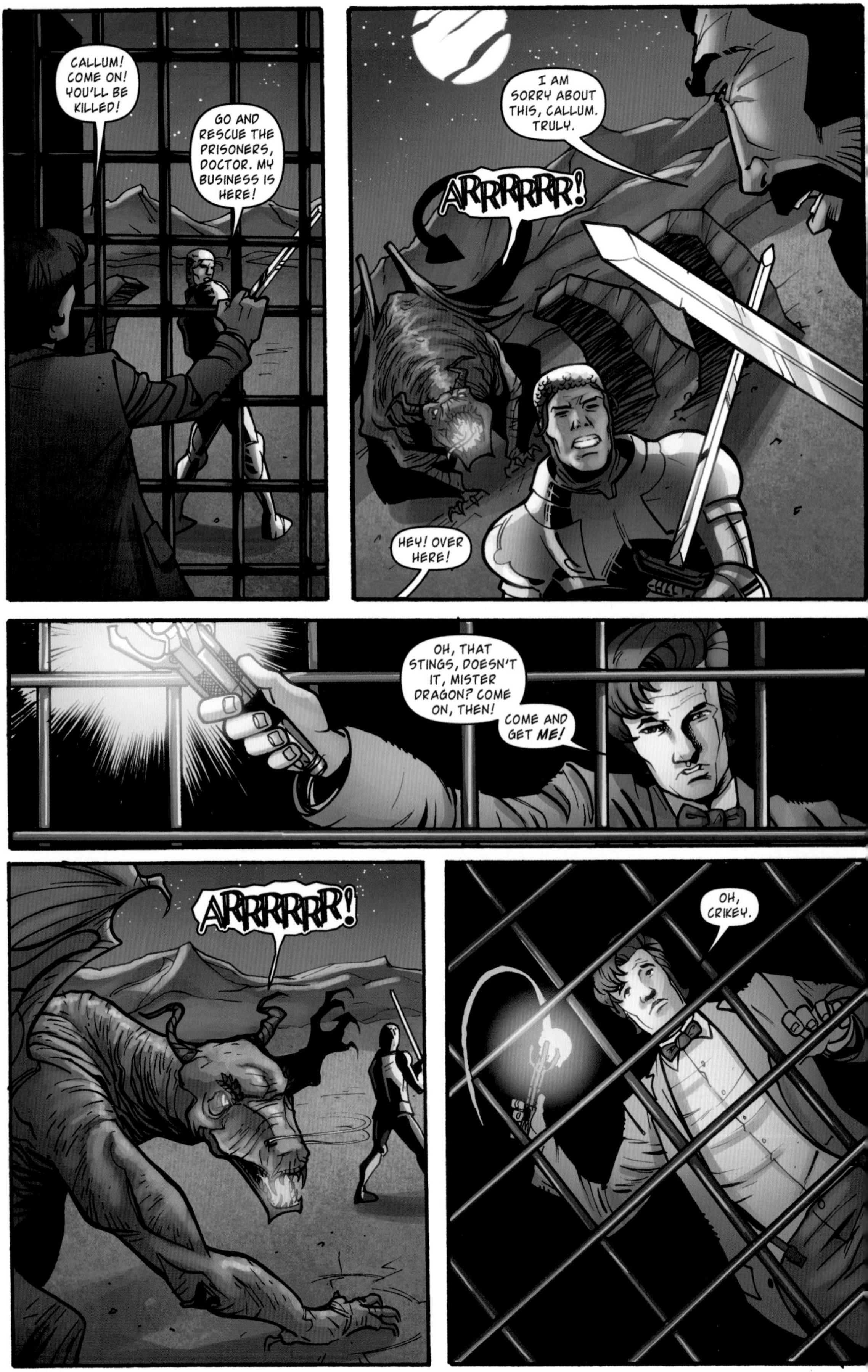
CALLUM! COME ON! YOU'LL BE KILLED!
GO AND RESCUE THE PRISONERS, DOCTOR. MY BUSINESS IS HERE!
I AM SORRY ABOUT THIS, CALLUM. TRULY.
ARRRRRR!
HEY! OVER HERE!
OH, THAT STINGS, DOESN'T IT, MISTER DRAGON? COME ON, THEN!
COME AND GET ME!
ARRRRRR!
OH, CRIKEY.

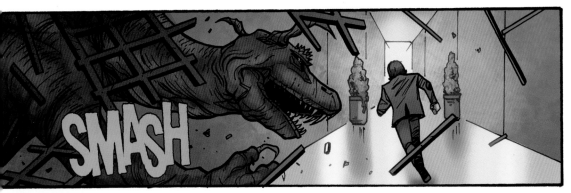

SMASH

FRIEGHT DOCK

ADMINISTRATION

I DON'T SUPPOSE YOU'RE ONE OF THOSE SENTIENT DRAGONS, THE CRAFTY KIND THAT PREFERS A GAME OF RIDDLES, THAT SORT OF THING?

I KNOW SOME BRILLIANT RIDDLES.

NO? WELL, IT WAS WORTH A TRY.

RAAAAR!

SHNK

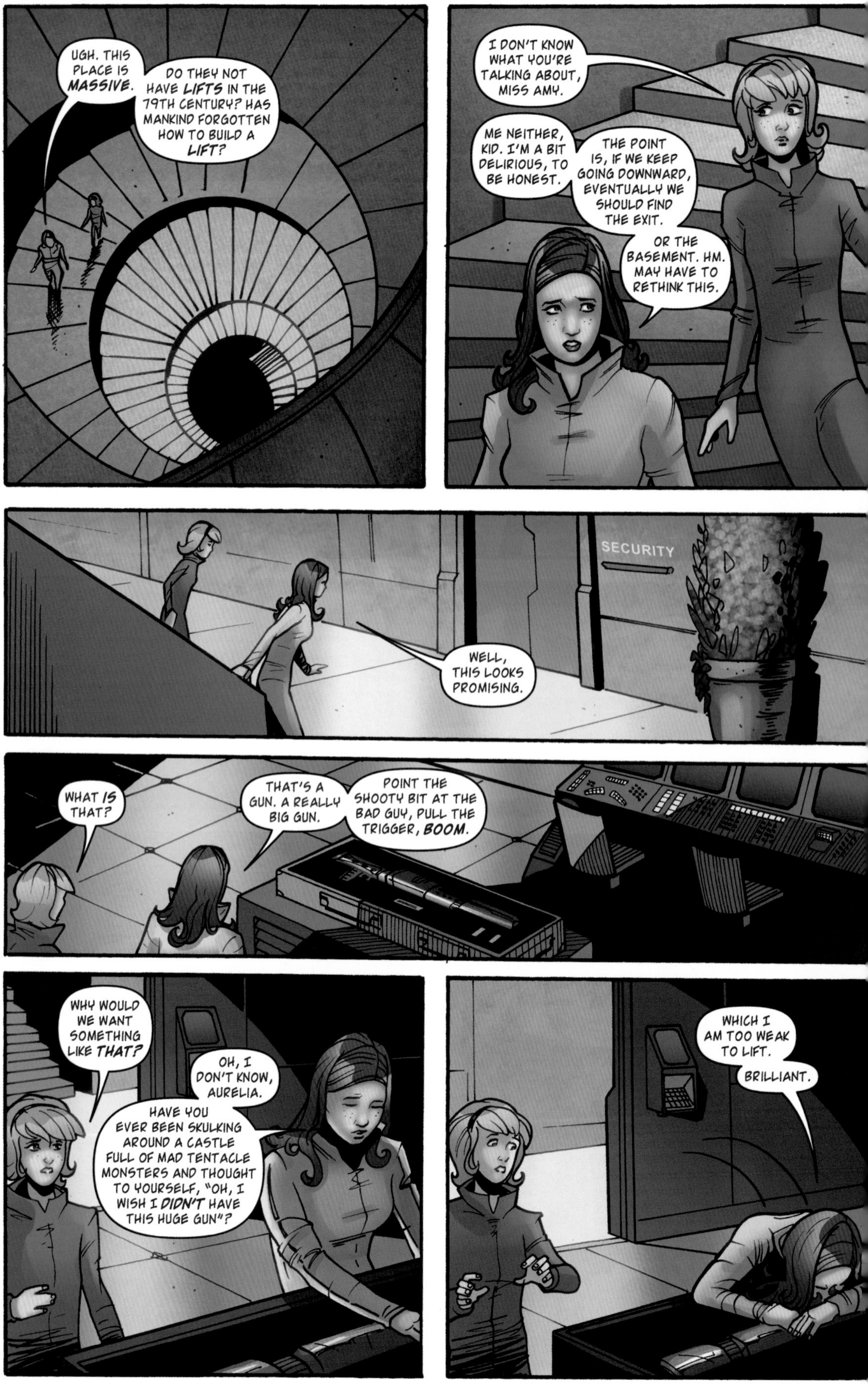
UGH. THIS PLACE IS MASSIVE.
DO THEY NOT HAVE LIFTS IN THE 79TH CENTURY? HAS MANKIND FORGOTTEN HOW TO BUILD A LIFT?
I DON'T KNOW WHAT YOU'RE TALKING ABOUT, MISS AMY.
ME NEITHER, KID. I'M A BIT DELIRIOUS, TO BE HONEST.
THE POINT IS, IF WE KEEP GOING DOWNWARD, EVENTUALLY WE SHOULD FIND THE EXIT.
OR THE BASEMENT. HM. MAY HAVE TO RETHINK THIS.
SECURITY
WELL, THIS LOOKS PROMISING.
WHAT IS THAT?
THAT'S A GUN. A REALLY BIG GUN.
POINT THE SHOOTY BIT AT THE BAD GUY, PULL THE TRIGGER, BOOM.
WHY WOULD WE WANT SOMETHING LIKE THAT?
OH, I DON'T KNOW, AURELIA.
HAVE YOU EVER BEEN SKULKING AROUND A CASTLE FULL OF MAD TENTACLE MONSTERS AND THOUGHT TO YOURSELF, "OH, I WISH I DIDN'T HAVE THIS HUGE GUN"?
WHICH I AM TOO WEAK TO LIFT.
BRILLIANT.

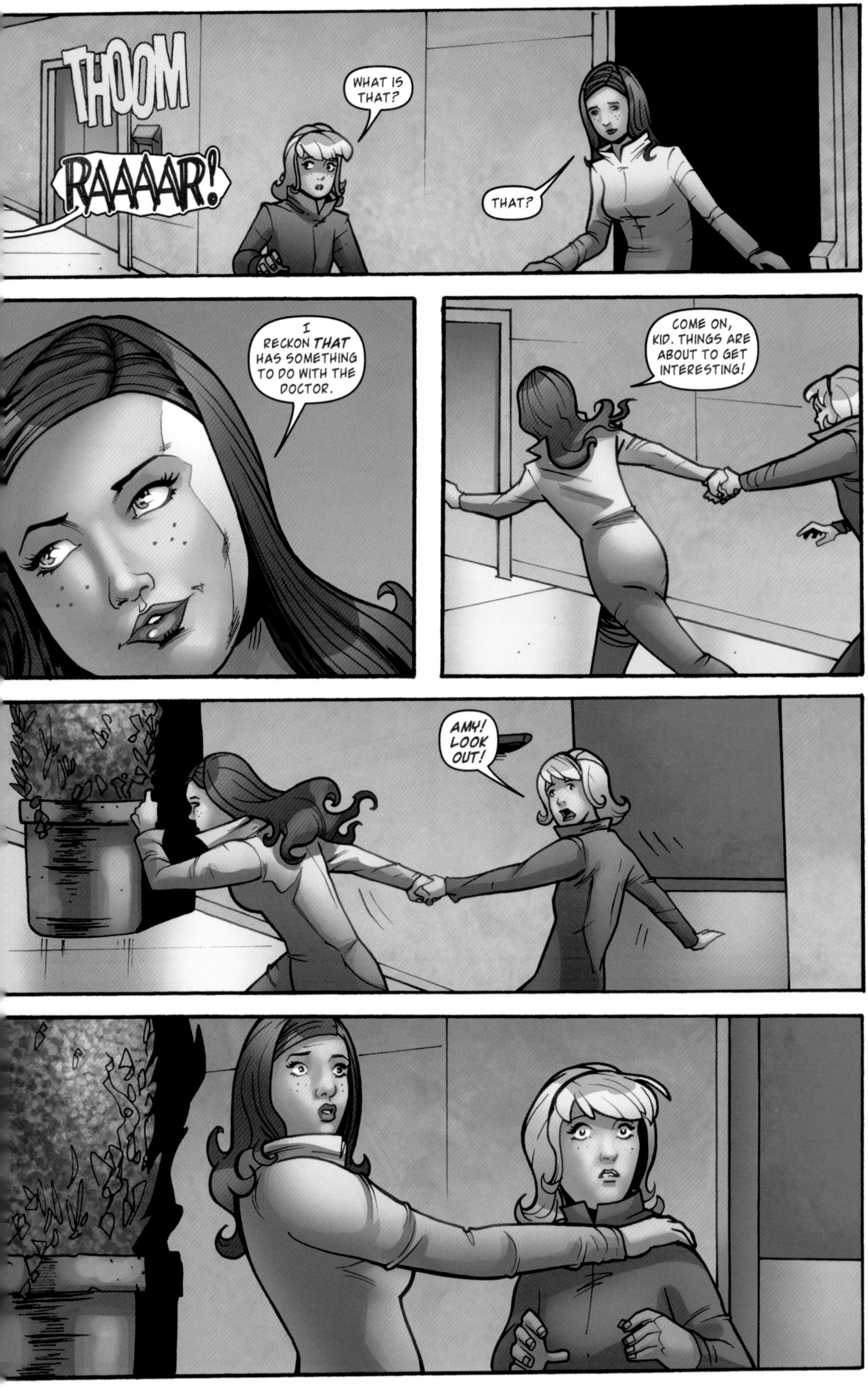
THOOM
RAAAAR!
WHAT IS THAT?
THAT?
I RECKON THAT HAS SOMETHING TO DO WITH THE DOCTOR.
COME ON, KID. THINGS ARE ABOUT TO GET INTERESTING!
AMY! LOOK OUT!

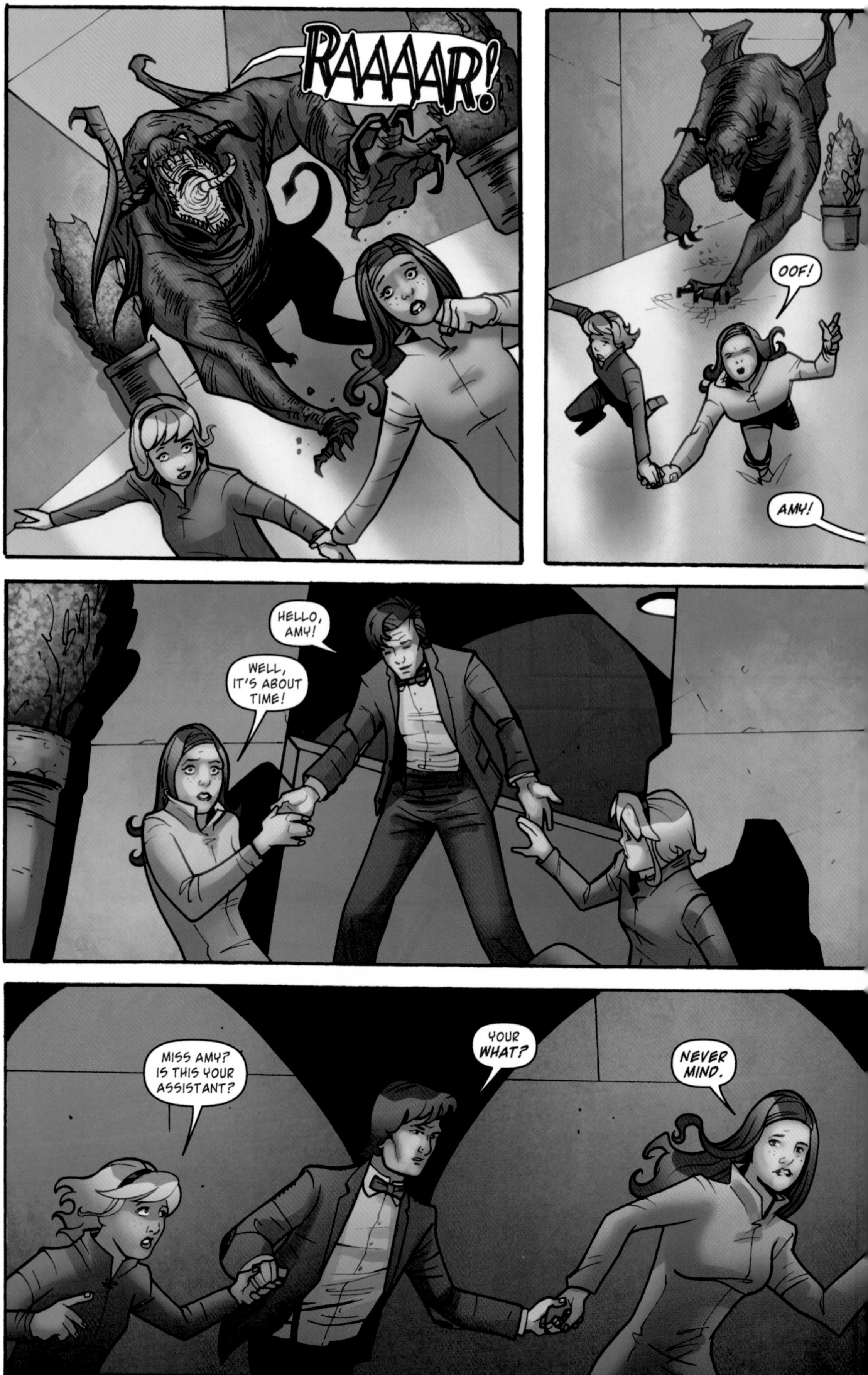
RAAAAR!
OOF!
AMY!
HELLO, AMY!
WELL, IT'S ABOUT TIME!
MISS AMY? IS THIS YOUR ASSISTANT?
YOUR WHAT?
NEVER MIND.

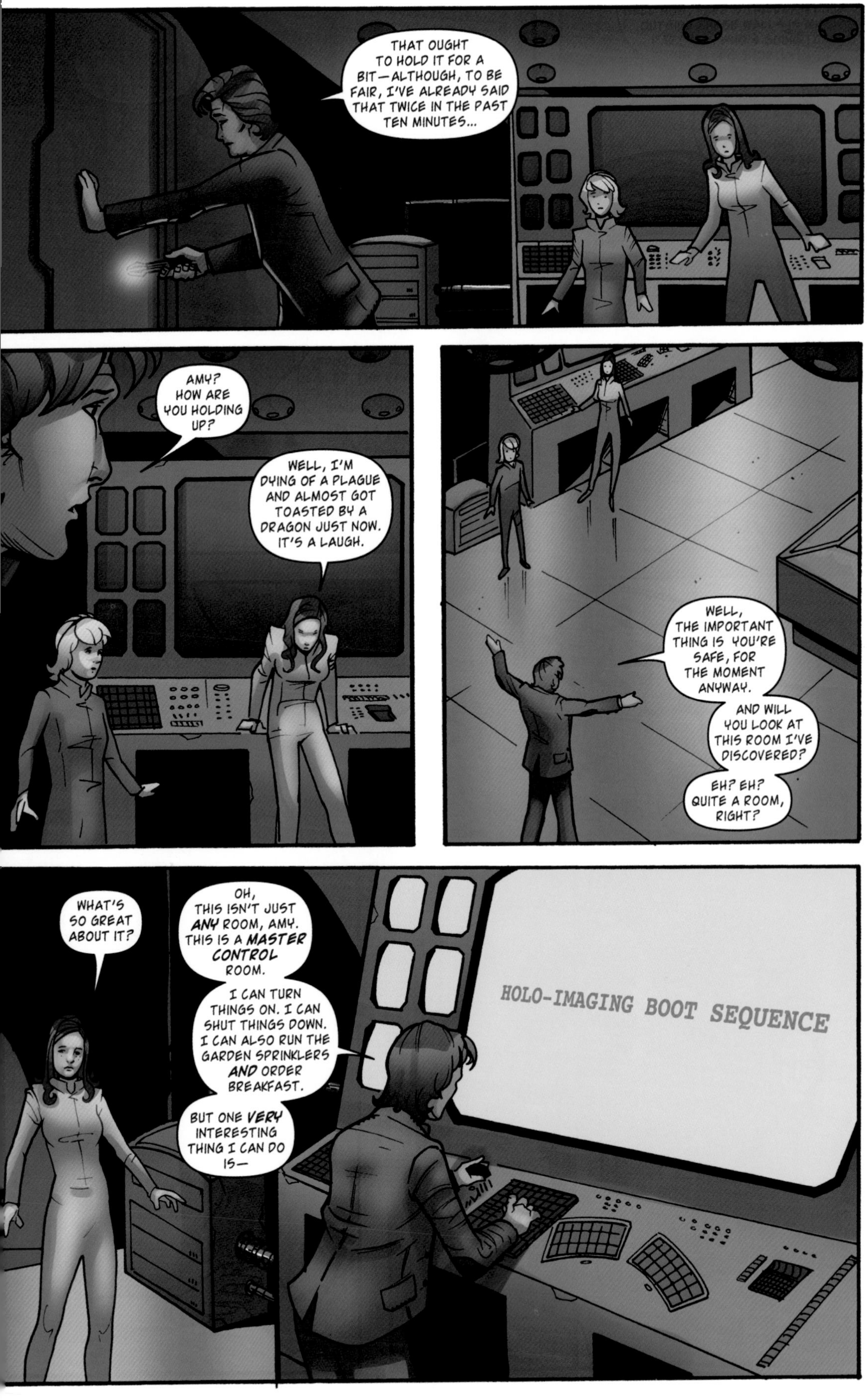
THAT OUGHT TO HOLD IT FOR A BIT—ALTHOUGH, TO BE FAIR, I'VE ALREADY SAID THAT TWICE IN THE PAST TEN MINUTES...
AMY? HOW ARE YOU HOLDING UP?
WELL, I'M DYING OF A PLAGUE AND ALMOST GOT TOASTED BY A DRAGON JUST NOW. IT'S A LAUGH.
WELL, THE IMPORTANT THING IS YOU'RE SAFE, FOR THE MOMENT ANYWAY.
AND WILL YOU LOOK AT THIS ROOM I'VE DISCOVERED?
EH? EH? QUITE A ROOM, RIGHT?
WHAT'S SO GREAT ABOUT IT?
OH, THIS ISN'T JUST ANY ROOM, AMY. THIS IS A MASTER CONTROL ROOM.
I CAN TURN THINGS ON. I CAN SHUT THINGS DOWN. I CAN ALSO RUN THE GARDEN SPRINKLERS AND ORDER BREAKFAST.
BUT ONE VERY INTERESTING THING I CAN DO IS—
HOLO-IMAGING BOOT SEQUENCE

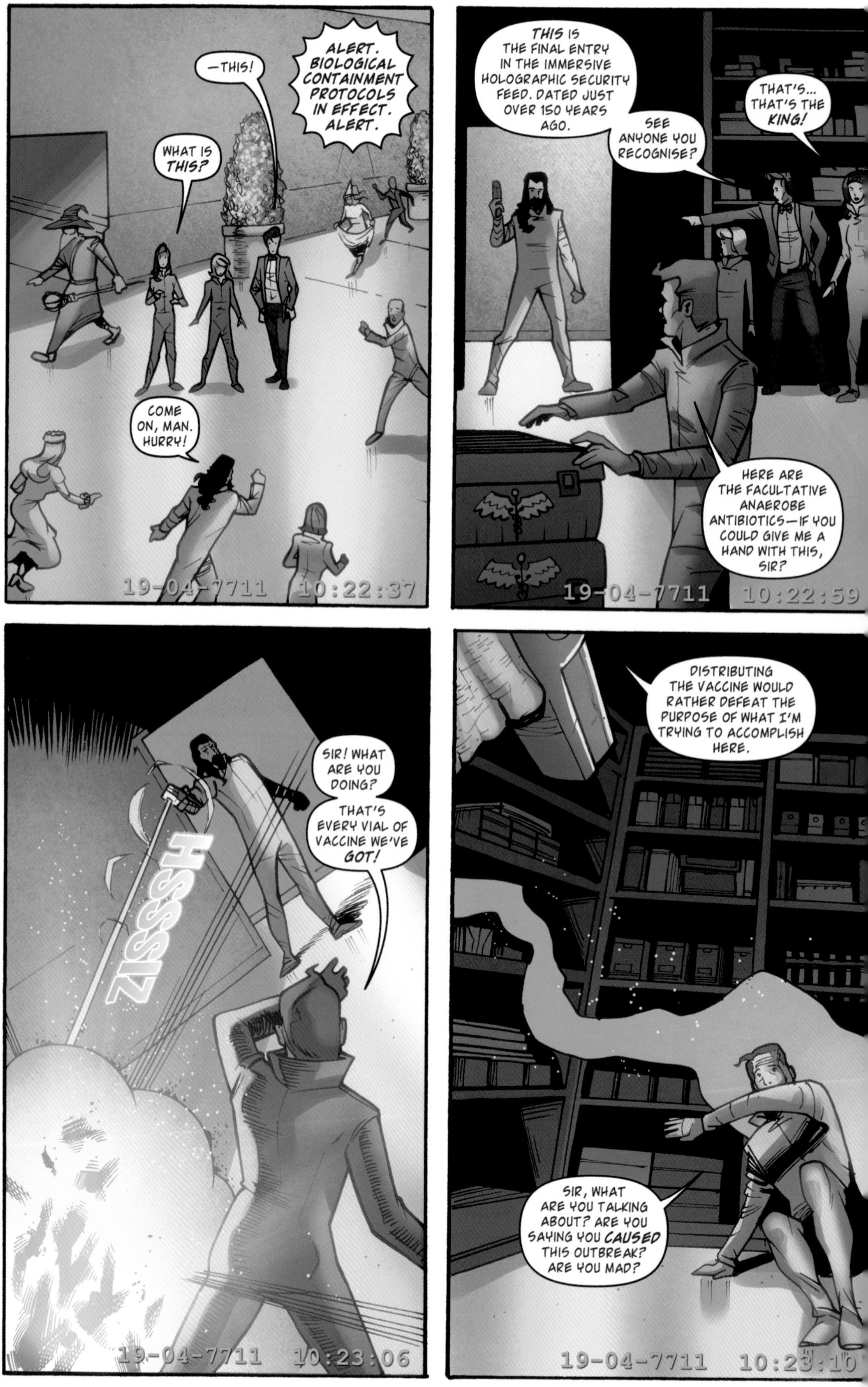

WHAT IS THIS?
—THIS!
ALERT. BIOLOGICAL CONTAINMENT PROTOCOLS IN EFFECT. ALERT.
COME ON, MAN. HURRY!
19-04-7711 10:22:37
THIS IS THE FINAL ENTRY IN THE IMMERSIVE HOLOGRAPHIC SECURITY FEED. DATED JUST OVER 150 YEARS AGO.
SEE ANYONE YOU RECOGNISE?
THAT'S... THAT'S THE KING!
HERE ARE THE FACULTATIVE ANAEROBE ANTIBIOTICS—IF YOU COULD GIVE ME A HAND WITH THIS, SIR?
19-04-7711 10:22:59
SIR! WHAT ARE YOU DOING?
THAT'S EVERY VIAL OF VACCINE WE'VE GOT!
ZISSSHH
19-04-7711 10:23:06
DISTRIBUTING THE VACCINE WOULD RATHER DEFEAT THE PURPOSE OF WHAT I'M TRYING TO ACCOMPLISH HERE.
SIR, WHAT ARE YOU TALKING ABOUT? ARE YOU SAYING YOU CAUSED THIS OUTBREAK? ARE YOU MAD?
19-04-7711 10:23:10

NO. I SIMPLY REPROGRAMMED THE BIOFILTER AT THE SPACEPORT TO STOP SCREENING FOR RECOMBINANT *YERSINIA PESTIS*.

THE SAD PART IS THAT IT ONLY TOOK THREE DAYS FOR AN INFECTED VISITOR TO SHOW UP. A SIGN OF THE TIMES, WOULDN'T YOU AGREE?

19-04-7711   10:23:14

ATTENTION ALL STAFF AND VISITORS. THIS IS... THIS IS CHIEF ADMINISTRATOR AETHELRED.

I AM DEEPLY SADDENED TO INFORM YOU THAT IMPERIAL ORDER 54567 REQUIRES ME TO PLACE THIS PLANET UNDER A STATE OF TOTAL QUARANTINE.

I AM EVEN SADDER TO REPORT THAT OUR BACKUP SUPPLIES OF THE TREATMENT HAVE BEEN SABOTAGED.

ZISSSH

19-04-7711   10:23:18

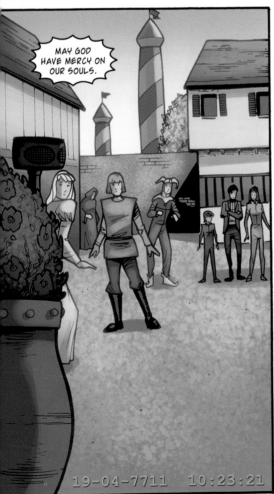

MAY GOD HAVE MERCY ON OUR SOULS.

19-04-7711   10:23:21

IT WAS THE KING. HE DID IT ON PURPOSE. HE LET ALL THOSE PEOPLE DIE.

OF *COURSE*. THAT'S HOW HE PULLED IT OFF!

THE PLAGUE KILLS ALL THE ADULTS, BUT IT LEAVES SMALL CHILDREN ALIVE. SO BY THE TIME THEY'RE FULLY GROWN, HE'S MANAGED TO CONVINCE THEM THAT THIS PLACE IS *REAL*.

THE QUESTION IS—*WHY?*

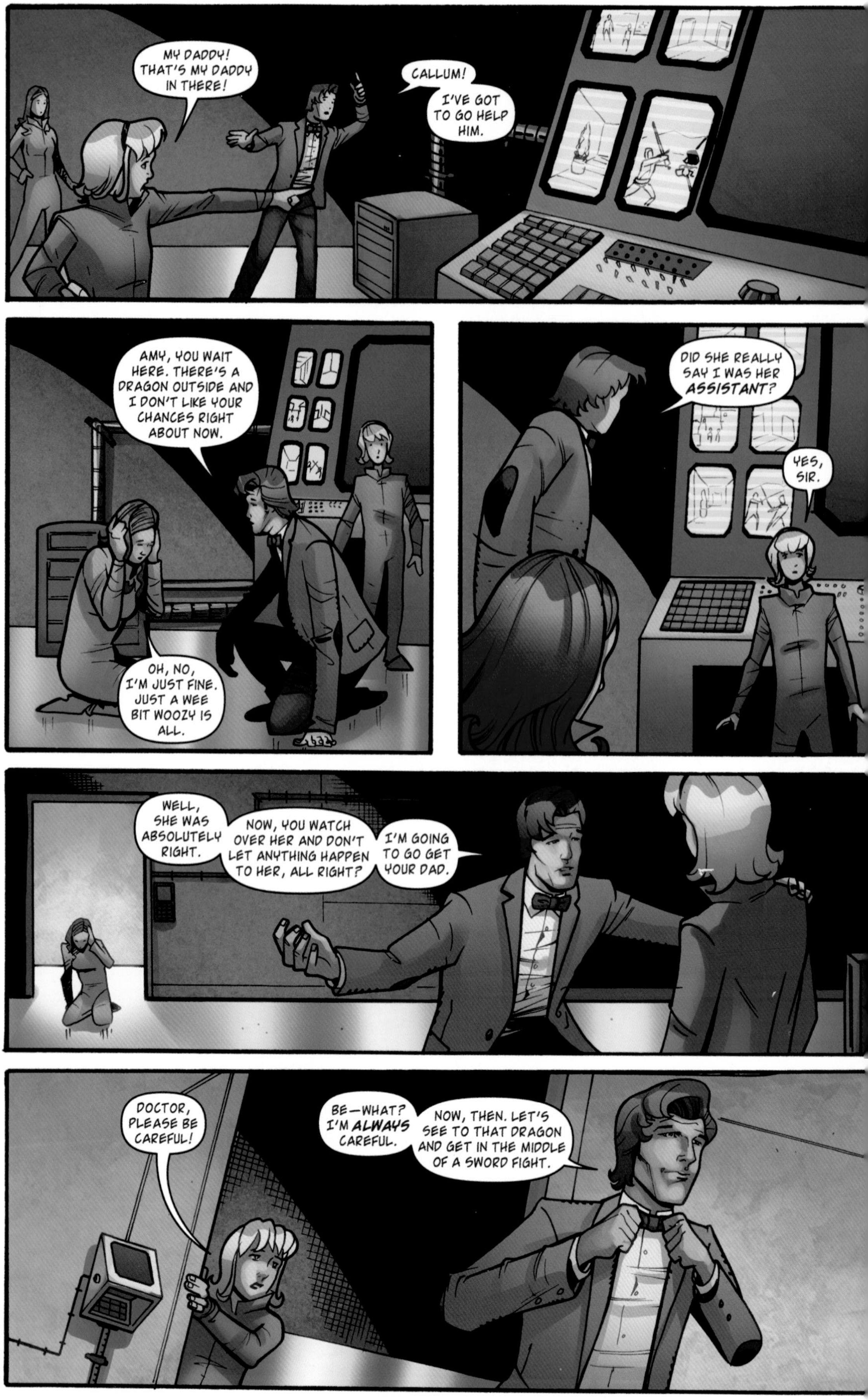

MY DADDY! THAT'S MY DADDY IN THERE!
CALLUM!
I'VE GOT TO GO HELP HIM.
AMY, YOU WAIT HERE. THERE'S A DRAGON OUTSIDE AND I DON'T LIKE YOUR CHANCES RIGHT ABOUT NOW.
OH, NO, I'M JUST FINE. JUST A WEE BIT WOOZY IS ALL.
DID SHE REALLY SAY I WAS HER ASSISTANT?
YES, SIR.
WELL, SHE WAS ABSOLUTELY RIGHT.
NOW, YOU WATCH OVER HER AND DON'T LET ANYTHING HAPPEN TO HER, ALL RIGHT?
I'M GOING TO GO GET YOUR DAD.
DOCTOR, PLEASE BE CAREFUL!
BE—WHAT? I'M ALWAYS CAREFUL.
NOW, THEN. LET'S SEE TO THAT DRAGON AND GET IN THE MIDDLE OF A SWORD FIGHT.

PERHAPS, SIRE, BUT I AM FIGHTING TO PROTECT MY CHILD, WHEREAS YOU ARE ONLY FIGHTING TO PROTECT A LIE.

STAND *DOWN*, SIR CALLUM. WHY WON'T YOU *STAND DOWN*?

YOU KNOW THAT YOU CANNOT BEST ME. I WAS SWINGING A BLADE FOR A HUNDRED YEARS BEFORE YOU WERE EVEN *BORN*.

OH, HELLO!

DOCTOR. YOU YET LIVE.

OH, NOW. YOU CAN DROP THE MEDIEVAL AFFECTATION NOW, *ADMINISTRATOR* AETHELRED.

I'VE JUST BEEN REVIEWING YOUR VERY INFORMATIVE HOLOGRAPHIC SECURITY FOOTAGE.

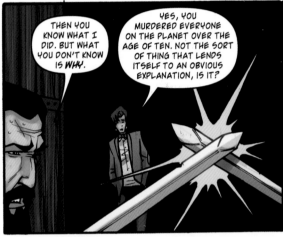

THEN YOU KNOW WHAT I DID. BUT WHAT YOU DON'T KNOW IS *WHY*.

YES, YOU MURDERED EVERYONE ON THE PLANET OVER THE AGE OF TEN. NOT THE SORT OF THING THAT LENDS ITSELF TO AN OBVIOUS EXPLANATION, IS IT?

YOU'RE RIGHT. 7,564 SOULS, TO BE PRECISE.

AND I WILL CARRY THE BURDEN OF ALL THOSE DEATHS TO MY GRAVE. BUT IT WAS *WORTH* IT.

WHAT POSSIBLE REASON COULD YOU HAVE FOR PERFORMING SUCH A *MONSTROUS* DEED?

THE EMPIRE HAD GONE UTTERLY MAD. THERE WAS WAR EVERYWHERE. FAMINE. PLAGUES A HUNDRED TIMES WORSE THAN THE PEST.

ALL OF THOSE PEOPLE WERE AS GOOD AS DEAD ANYWAY, MORE OR LESS.

EXCELLENT POINT, CALLUM. THAT'S WHAT I'M WONDERING EXACTLY.

TO LOOK AT ALL OF THOSE CHILDREN DAY AFTER DAY, HAPPY AND CAREFREE, KNOWING THAT IN A FEW YEARS MANY OF THEM WOULD BE DEAD ON SOME DISTANT PLANET...

...SLAUGHTERED BY THE SYCORAX, OR THE DRAHVINS, OR THE SONTARANS. AND FOR *WHAT*?

I COULDN'T STAND IT ANYMORE!

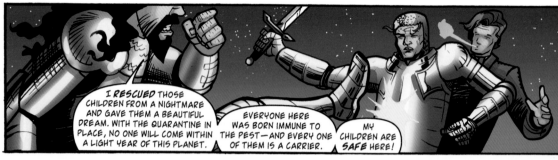

I **RESCUED** THOSE CHILDREN FROM A NIGHTMARE AND GAVE THEM A BEAUTIFUL DREAM. WITH THE QUARANTINE IN PLACE, NO ONE WILL COME WITHIN A LIGHT YEAR OF THIS PLANET.

EVERYONE HERE WAS BORN IMMUNE TO THE PEST—AND EVERY ONE OF THEM IS A CARRIER.

MY CHILDREN ARE **SAFE** HERE!

BUT THEY'RE **NOT** YOUR CHILDREN. IT WASN'T YOUR CHOICE TO **MAKE!**

YOU'RE RIGHT, DOCTOR. BUT I MADE IT ANYWAY. AND I SHALL MOST CERTAINLY BE DAMNED FOR IT.

BUT GIVEN THE CHOICE, I WOULD **DO IT ALL AGAIN!**

CLUNK

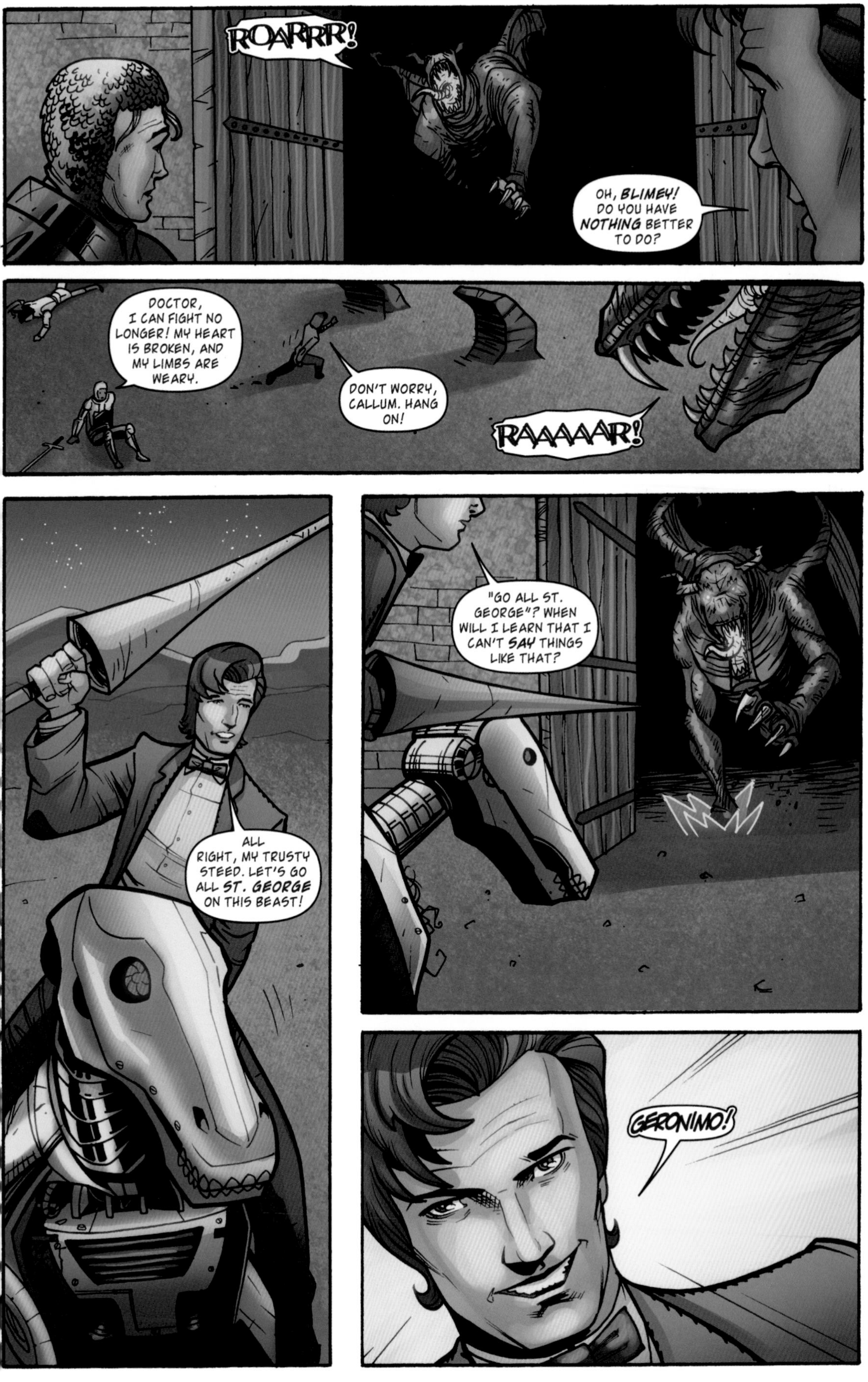
ROARRR!
OH, BLIMEY! DO YOU HAVE NOTHING BETTER TO DO?
DOCTOR, I CAN FIGHT NO LONGER! MY HEART IS BROKEN, AND MY LIMBS ARE WEARY.
DON'T WORRY, CALLUM. HANG ON!
RAAAAAR!
ALL RIGHT, MY TRUSTY STEED. LET'S GO ALL ST. GEORGE ON THIS BEAST!
"GO ALL ST. GEORGE"? WHEN WILL I LEARN THAT I CAN'T SAY THINGS LIKE THAT?
GERONIMO!

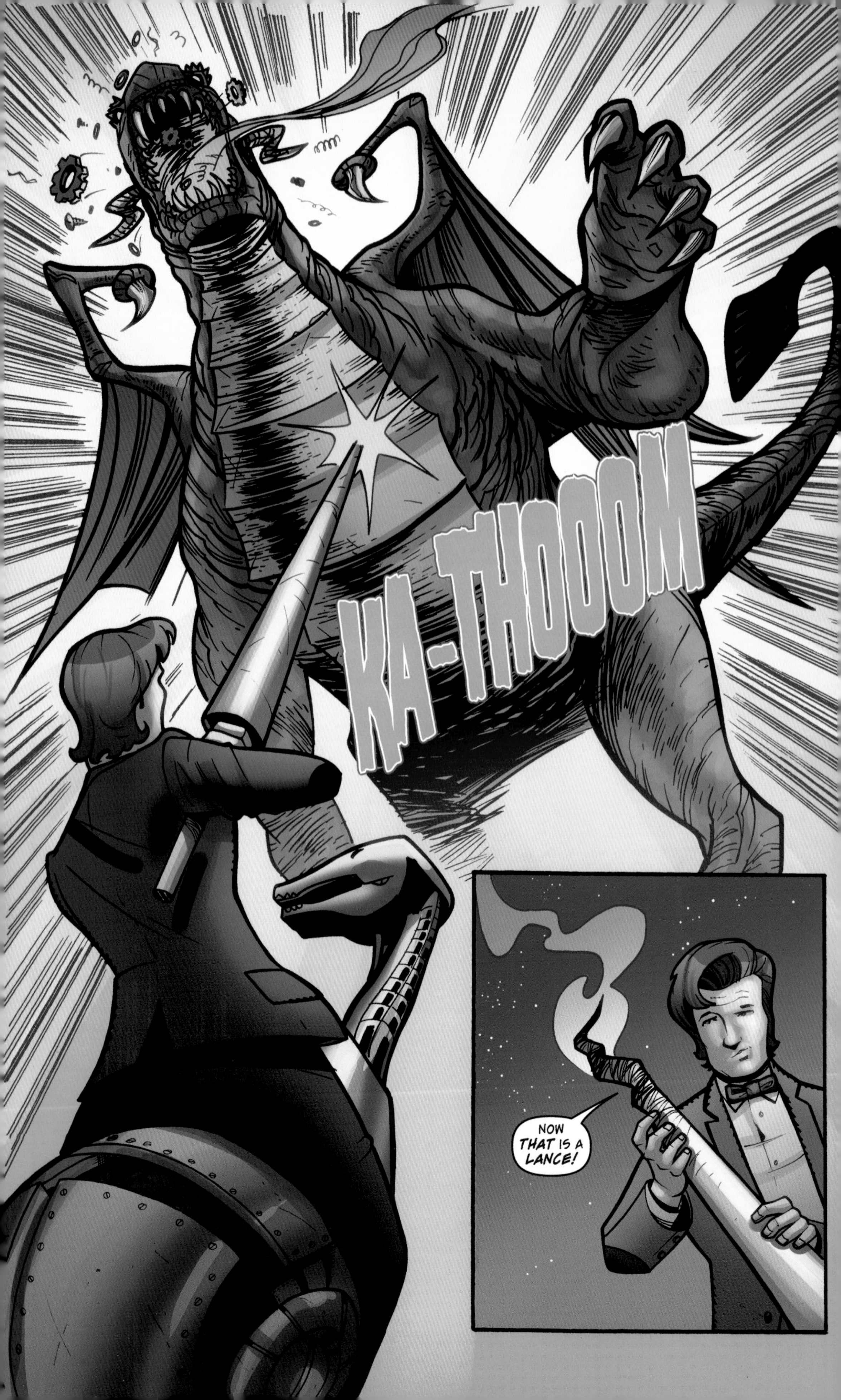
KA-THOOOM
NOW THAT IS A LANCE!

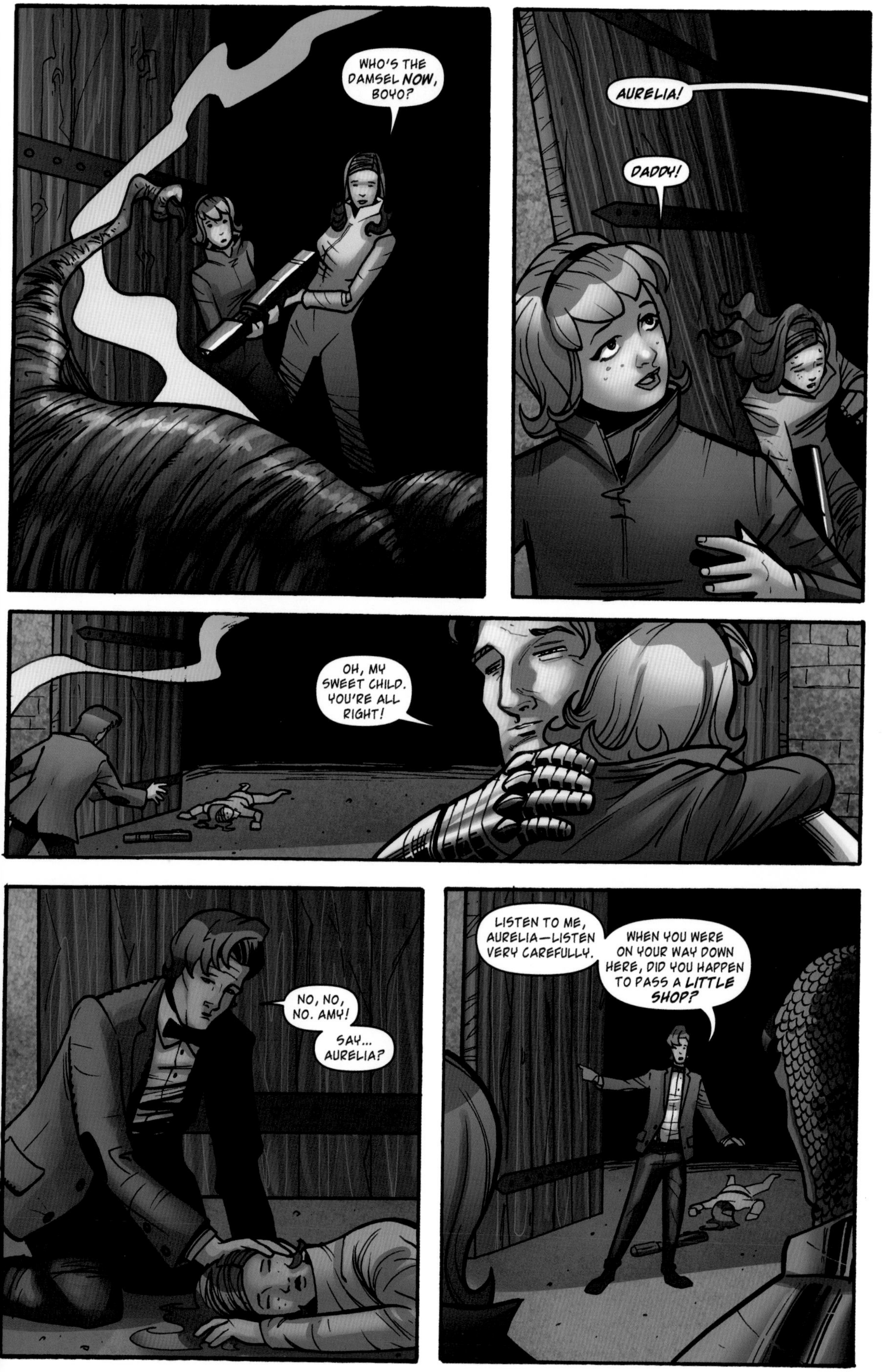
WHO'S THE DAMSEL NOW, BOYO?
AURELIA!
DADDY!
OH, MY SWEET CHILD. YOU'RE ALL RIGHT!
NO, NO, NO. AMY!
SAY... AURELIA?
LISTEN TO ME, AURELIA—LISTEN VERY CAREFULLY.
WHEN YOU WERE ON YOUR WAY DOWN HERE, DID YOU HAPPEN TO PASS A LITTLE SHOP?

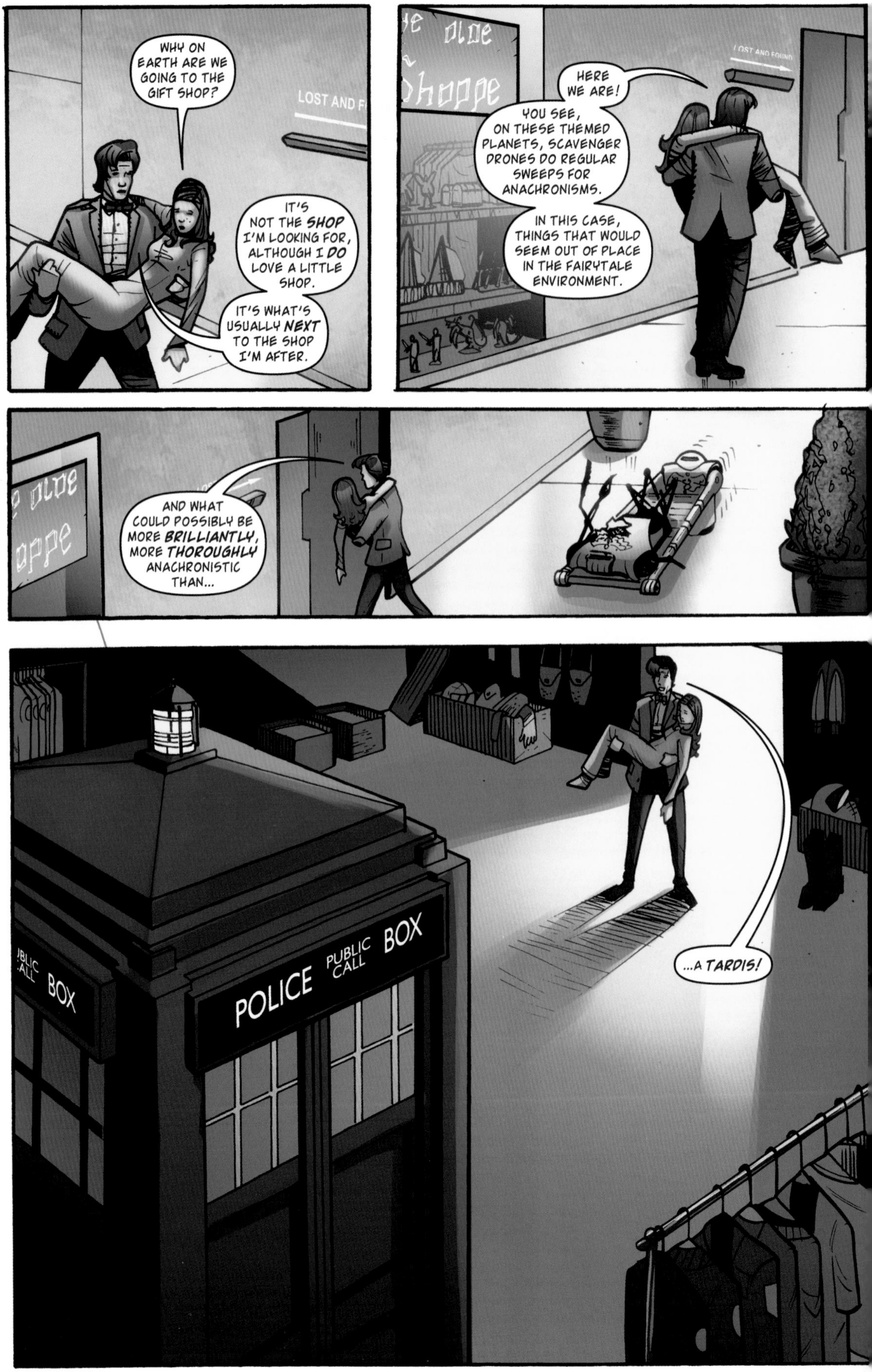
WHY ON EARTH ARE WE GOING TO THE GIFT SHOP?
LOST AND F
IT'S NOT THE *SHOP* I'M LOOKING FOR, ALTHOUGH I *DO* LOVE A LITTLE SHOP.
IT'S WHAT'S USUALLY *NEXT* TO THE SHOP I'M AFTER.
LOST AND FOUND
HERE WE ARE!
YOU SEE, ON THESE THEMED PLANETS, SCAVENGER DRONES DO REGULAR SWEEPS FOR ANACHRONISMS.
IN THIS CASE, THINGS THAT WOULD SEEM OUT OF PLACE IN THE FAIRYTALE ENVIRONMENT.
AND WHAT COULD POSSIBLY BE MORE *BRILLIANTLY*, MORE *THOROUGHLY* ANACHRONISTIC THAN...
POLICE PUBLIC CALL BOX
...A *TARDIS!*

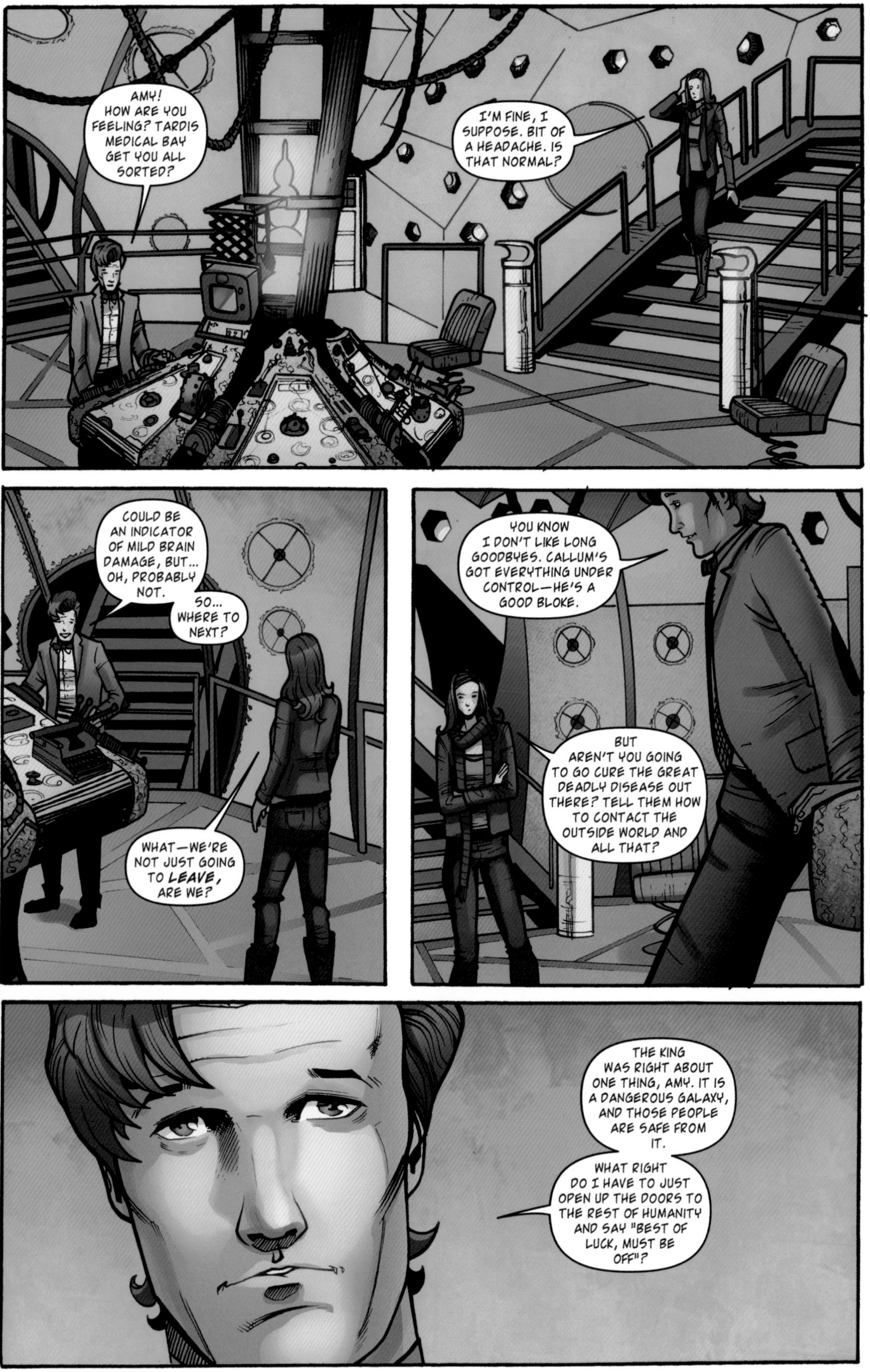
AMY! HOW ARE YOU FEELING? TARDIS MEDICAL BAY GET YOU ALL SORTED?
I'M FINE, I SUPPOSE. BIT OF A HEADACHE. IS THAT NORMAL?
COULD BE AN INDICATOR OF MILD BRAIN DAMAGE, BUT... OH, PROBABLY NOT.
SO... WHERE TO NEXT?
WHAT—WE'RE NOT JUST GOING TO **LEAVE**, ARE WE?
YOU KNOW I DON'T LIKE LONG GOODBYES. CALLUM'S GOT EVERYTHING UNDER CONTROL—HE'S A GOOD BLOKE.
BUT AREN'T YOU GOING TO GO CURE THE GREAT DEADLY DISEASE OUT THERE? TELL THEM HOW TO CONTACT THE OUTSIDE WORLD AND ALL THAT?
THE KING WAS RIGHT ABOUT ONE THING, AMY. IT IS A DANGEROUS GALAXY, AND THOSE PEOPLE ARE SAFE FROM IT.
WHAT RIGHT DO I HAVE TO JUST OPEN UP THE DOORS TO THE REST OF HUMANITY AND SAY "BEST OF LUCK, MUST BE OFF"?

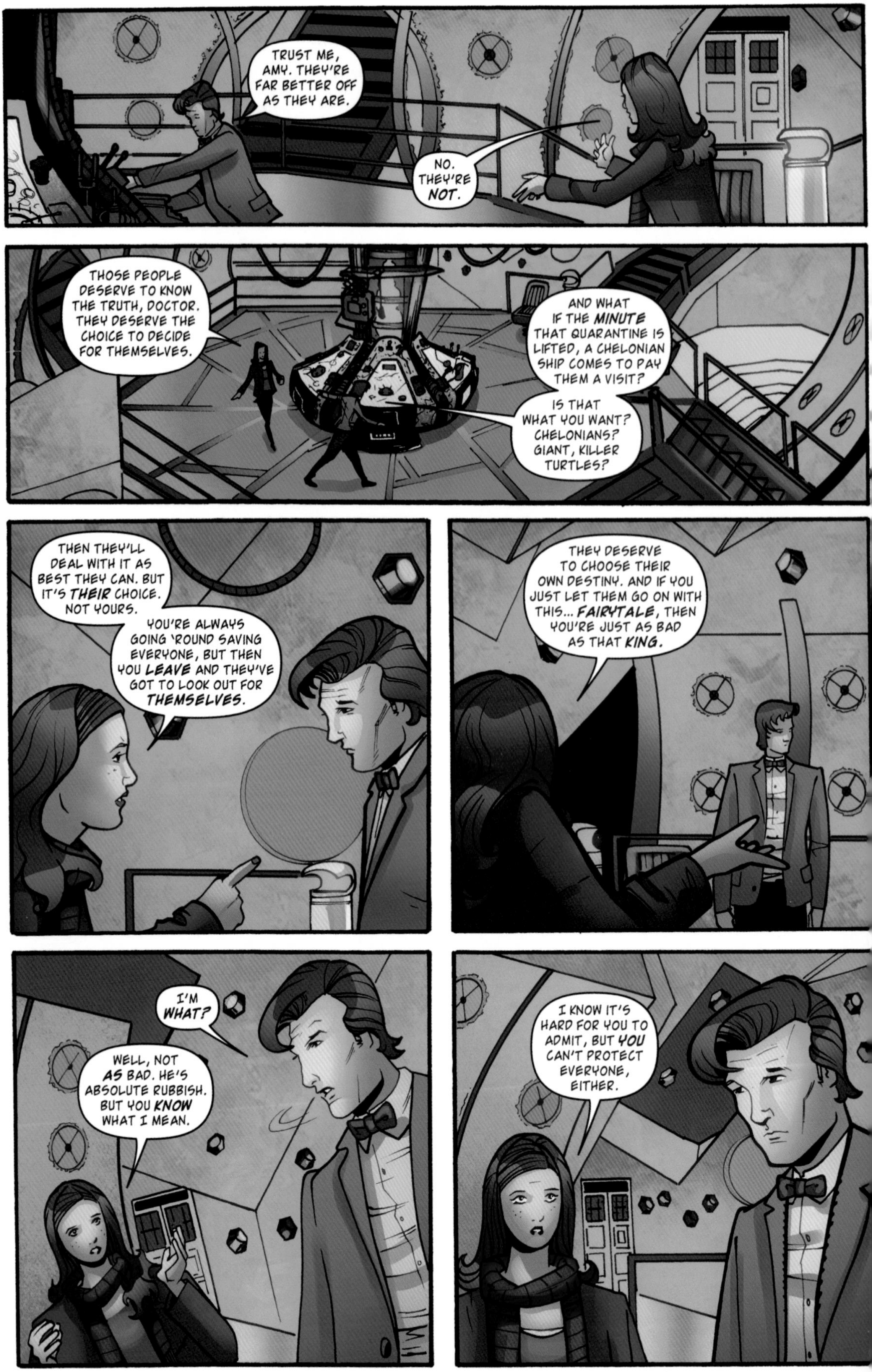
TRUST ME, AMY. THEY'RE FAR BETTER OFF AS THEY ARE.
NO. THEY'RE NOT.
THOSE PEOPLE DESERVE TO KNOW THE TRUTH, DOCTOR. THEY DESERVE THE CHOICE TO DECIDE FOR THEMSELVES.
AND WHAT IF THE MINUTE THAT QUARANTINE IS LIFTED, A CHELONIAN SHIP COMES TO PAY THEM A VISIT?
IS THAT WHAT YOU WANT? CHELONIANS? GIANT, KILLER TURTLES?
THEN THEY'LL DEAL WITH IT AS BEST THEY CAN. BUT IT'S THEIR CHOICE. NOT YOURS.
YOU'RE ALWAYS GOING 'ROUND SAVING EVERYONE, BUT THEN YOU LEAVE AND THEY'VE GOT TO LOOK OUT FOR THEMSELVES.
THEY DESERVE TO CHOOSE THEIR OWN DESTINY. AND IF YOU JUST LET THEM GO ON WITH THIS... FAIRYTALE, THEN YOU'RE JUST AS BAD AS THAT KING.
I'M WHAT?
WELL, NOT AS BAD. HE'S ABSOLUTE RUBBISH. BUT YOU KNOW WHAT I MEAN.
I KNOW IT'S HARD FOR YOU TO ADMIT, BUT YOU CAN'T PROTECT EVERYONE, EITHER.

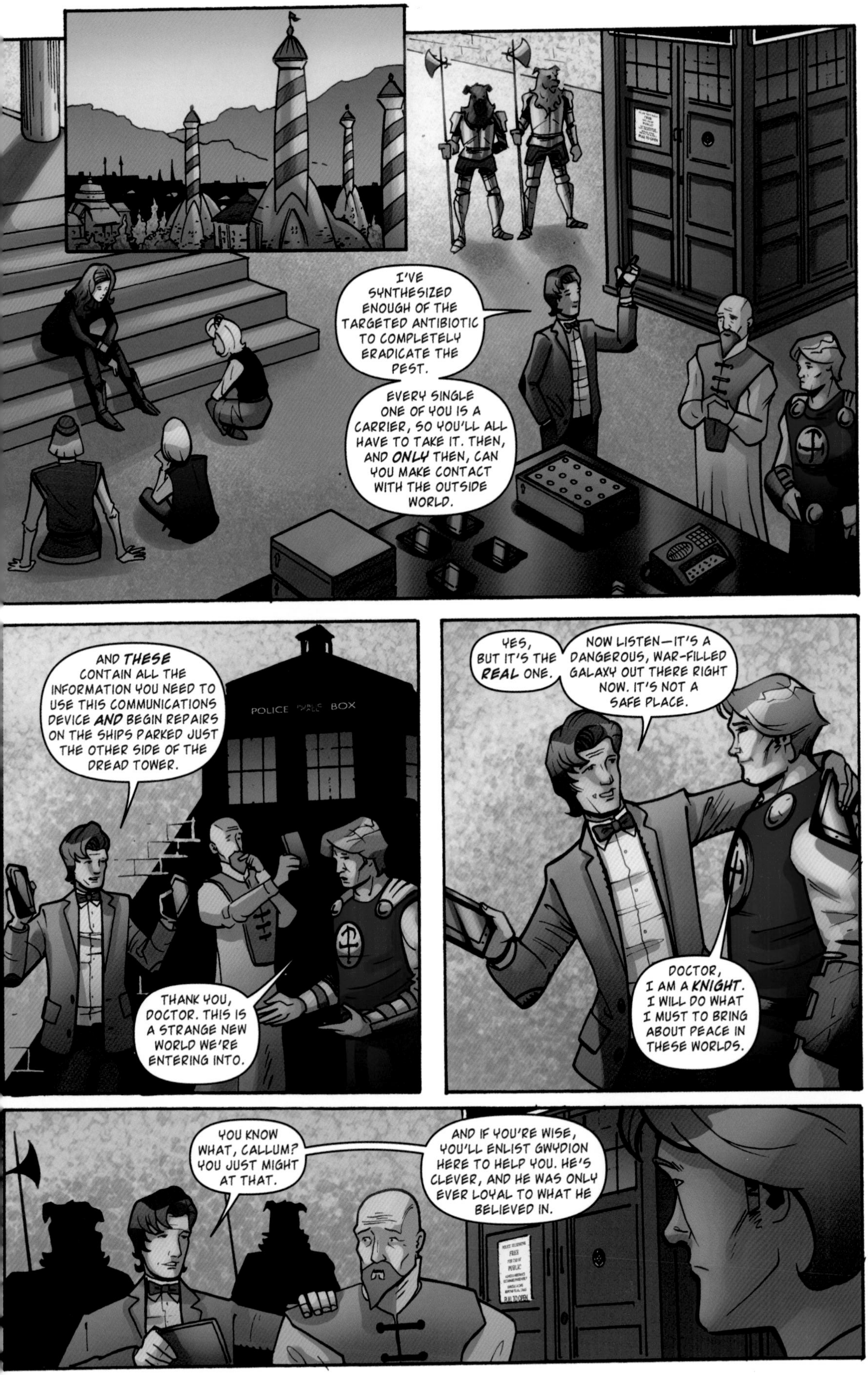

I'VE SYNTHESIZED ENOUGH OF THE TARGETED ANTIBIOTIC TO COMPLETELY ERADICATE THE PEST.
EVERY SINGLE ONE OF YOU IS A CARRIER, SO YOU'LL ALL HAVE TO TAKE IT. THEN, AND ONLY THEN, CAN YOU MAKE CONTACT WITH THE OUTSIDE WORLD.
AND THESE CONTAIN ALL THE INFORMATION YOU NEED TO USE THIS COMMUNICATIONS DEVICE AND BEGIN REPAIRS ON THE SHIPS PARKED JUST THE OTHER SIDE OF THE DREAD TOWER.
THANK YOU, DOCTOR. THIS IS A STRANGE NEW WORLD WE'RE ENTERING INTO.
YES, BUT IT'S THE REAL ONE.
NOW LISTEN—IT'S A DANGEROUS, WAR-FILLED GALAXY OUT THERE RIGHT NOW. IT'S NOT A SAFE PLACE.
DOCTOR, I AM A KNIGHT. I WILL DO WHAT I MUST TO BRING ABOUT PEACE IN THESE WORLDS.
YOU KNOW WHAT, CALLUM? YOU JUST MIGHT AT THAT.
AND IF YOU'RE WISE, YOU'LL ENLIST GWYDION HERE TO HELP YOU. HE'S CLEVER, AND HE WAS ONLY EVER LOYAL TO WHAT HE BELIEVED IN.

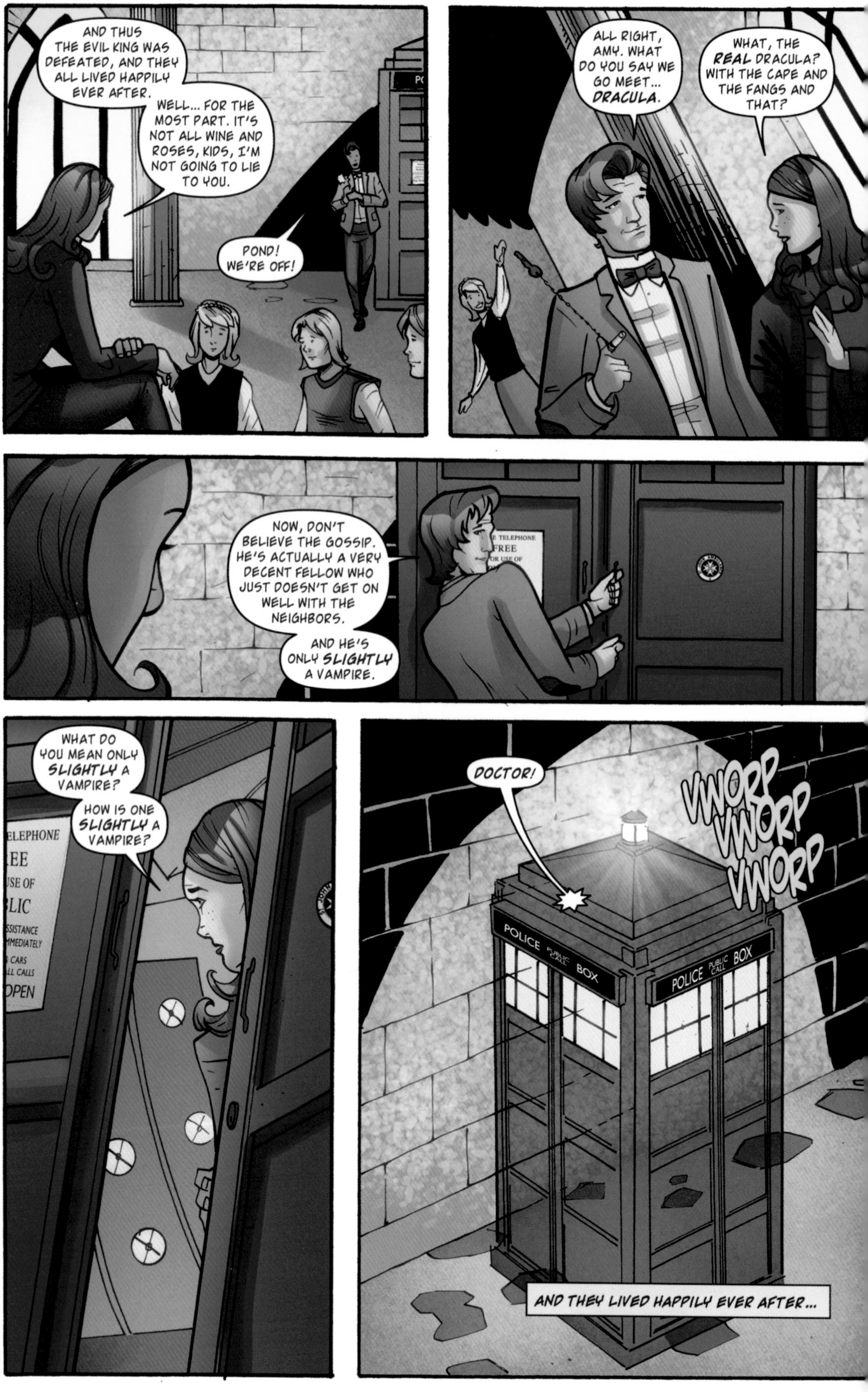

AND THUS THE EVIL KING WAS DEFEATED, AND THEY ALL LIVED HAPPILY EVER AFTER.
WELL... FOR THE MOST PART. IT'S NOT ALL WINE AND ROSES, KIDS, I'M NOT GOING TO LIE TO YOU.
POND! WE'RE OFF!
ALL RIGHT, AMY. WHAT DO YOU SAY WE GO MEET... DRACULA.
WHAT, THE REAL DRACULA? WITH THE CAPE AND THE FANGS AND THAT?
NOW, DON'T BELIEVE THE GOSSIP. HE'S ACTUALLY A VERY DECENT FELLOW WHO JUST DOESN'T GET ON WELL WITH THE NEIGHBORS.
AND HE'S ONLY SLIGHTLY A VAMPIRE.
WHAT DO YOU MEAN ONLY SLIGHTLY A VAMPIRE?
HOW IS ONE SLIGHTLY A VAMPIRE?
DOCTOR!
VWORP VWORP VWORP
POLICE PUBLIC CALL BOX
AND THEY LIVED HAPPILY EVER AFTER...

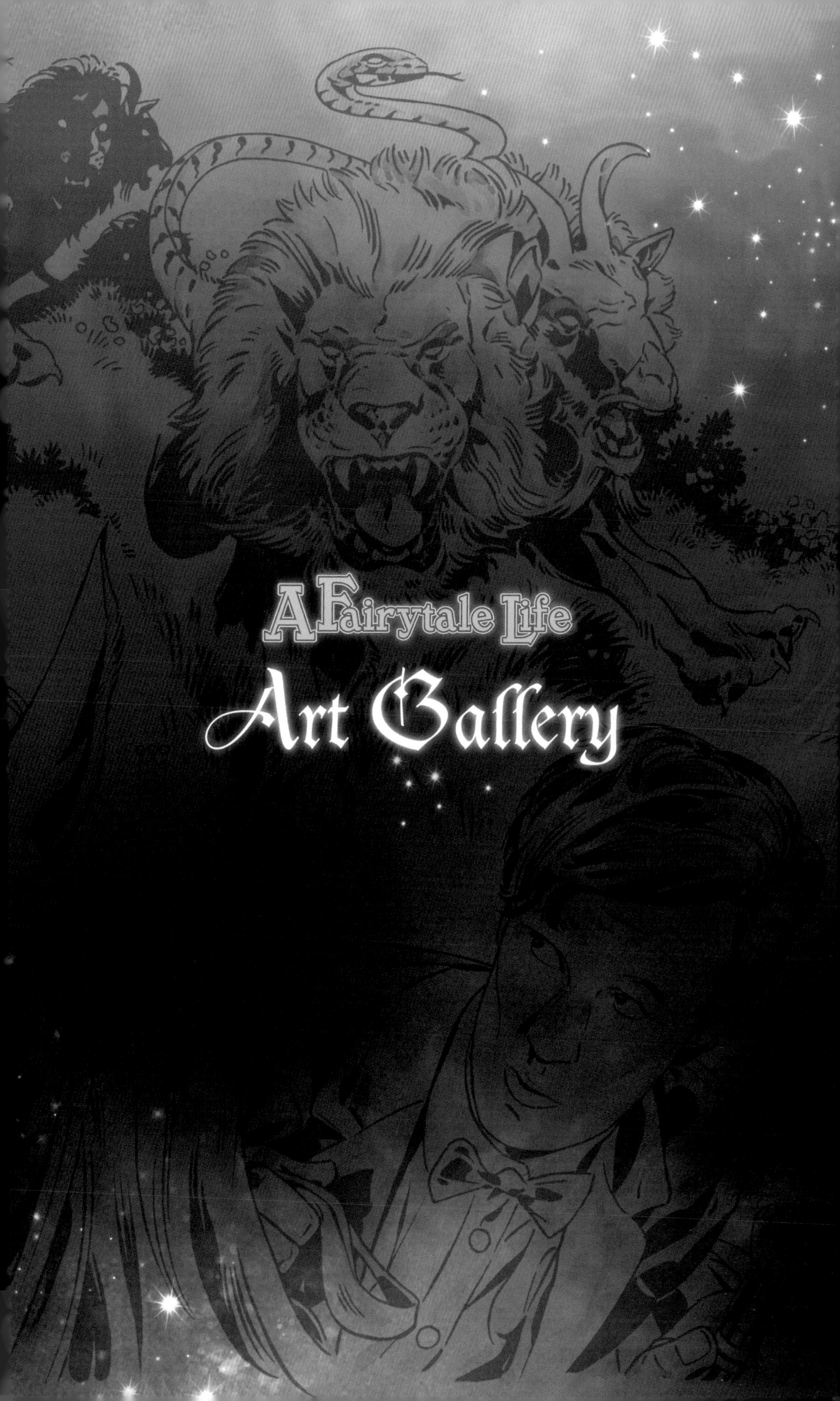

A Fairytale Life
Art Gallery

Art by Mark Buckingham

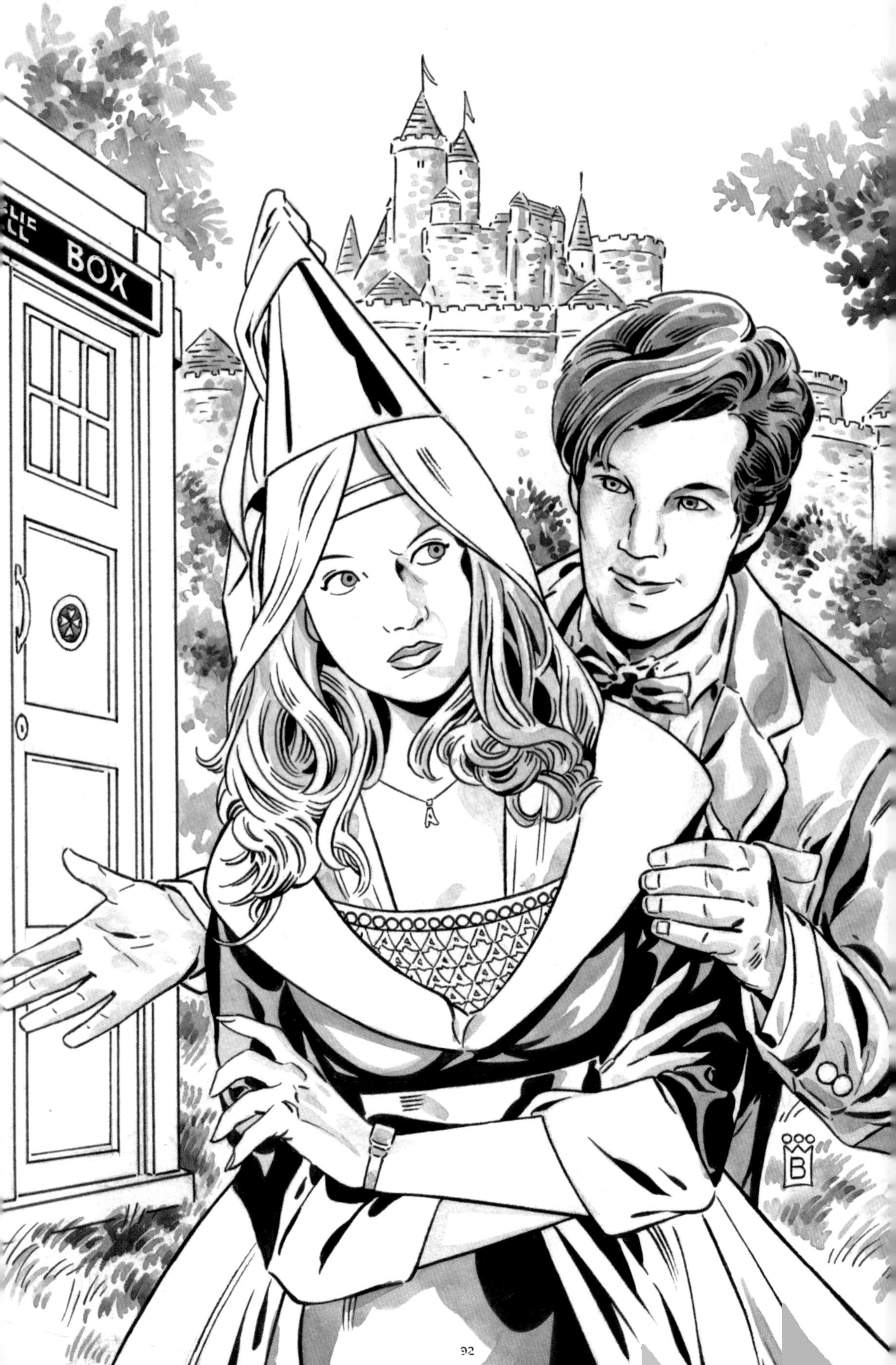
BOX

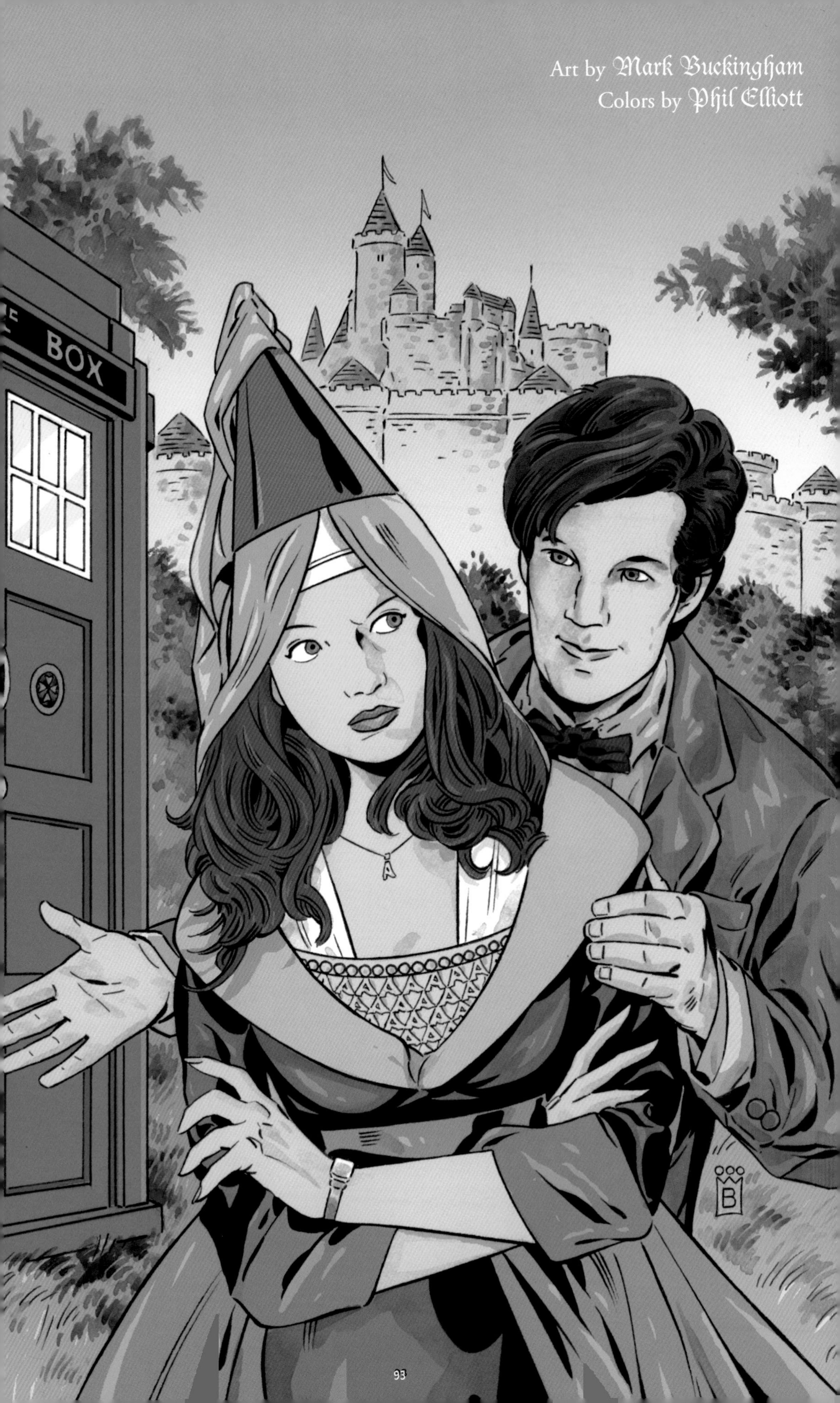
Art by Mark Buckingham
Colors by Phil Elliott
BOX

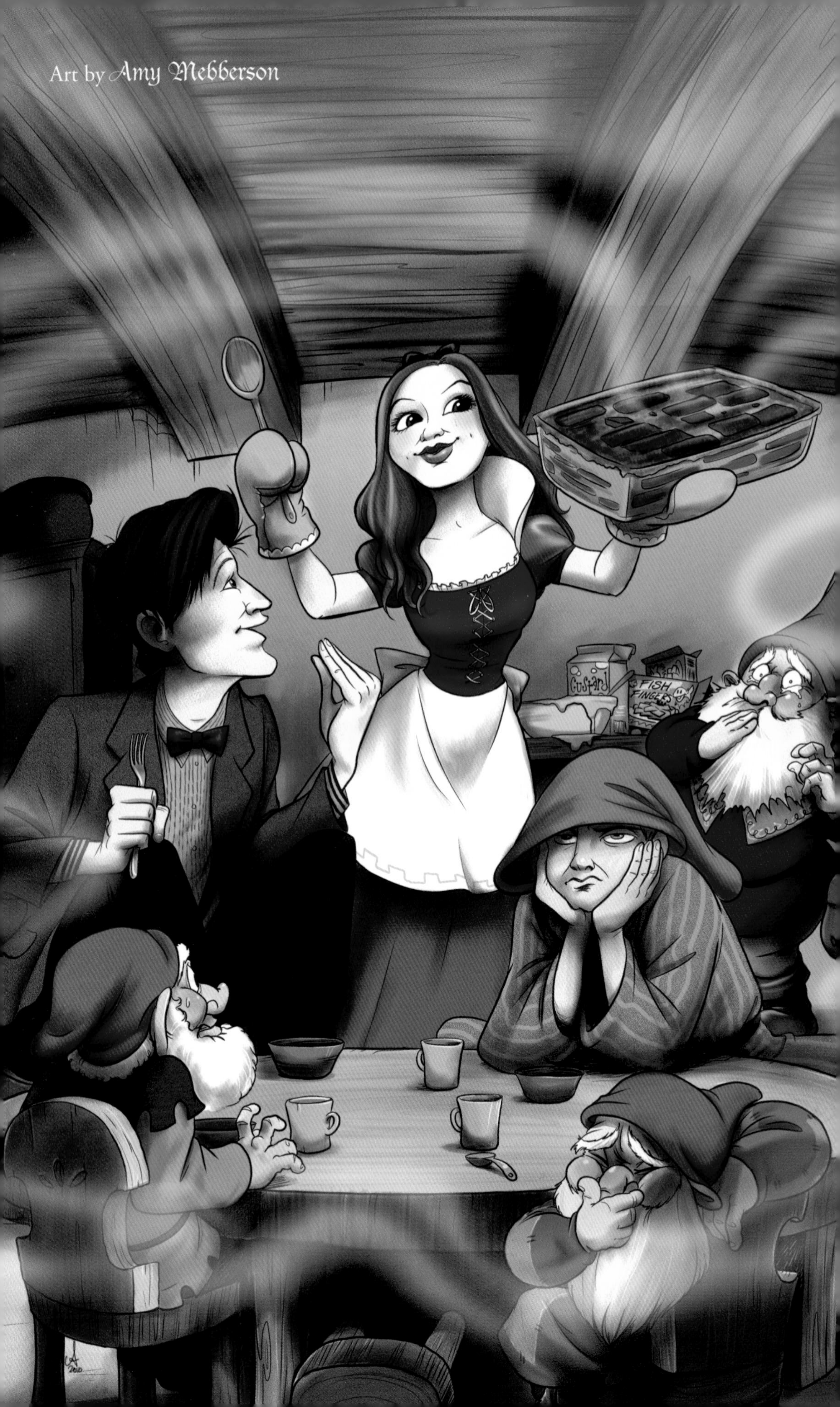
Custard
FISH FINGERS
Art by Amy Mebberson

Art by Mark Buckingham

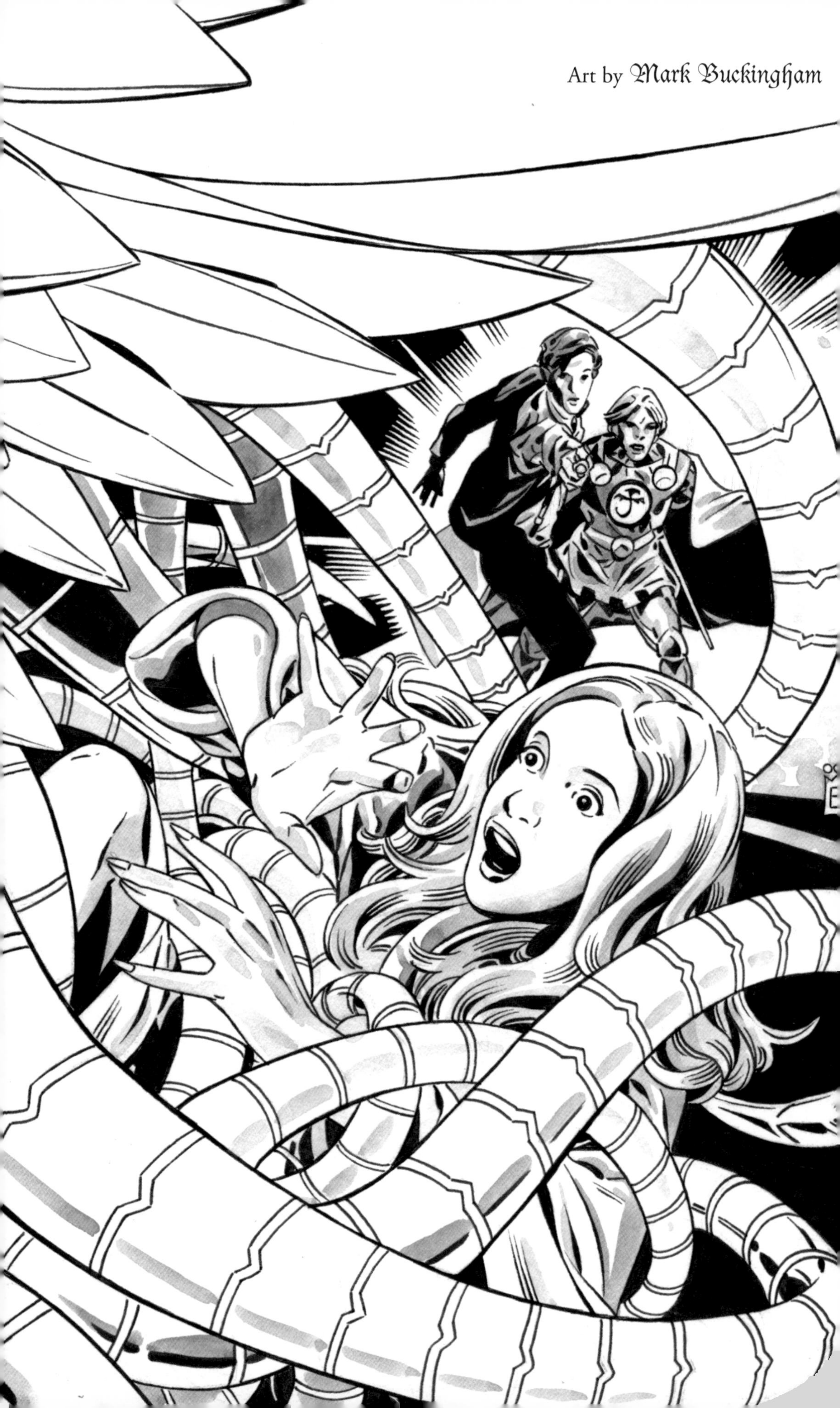

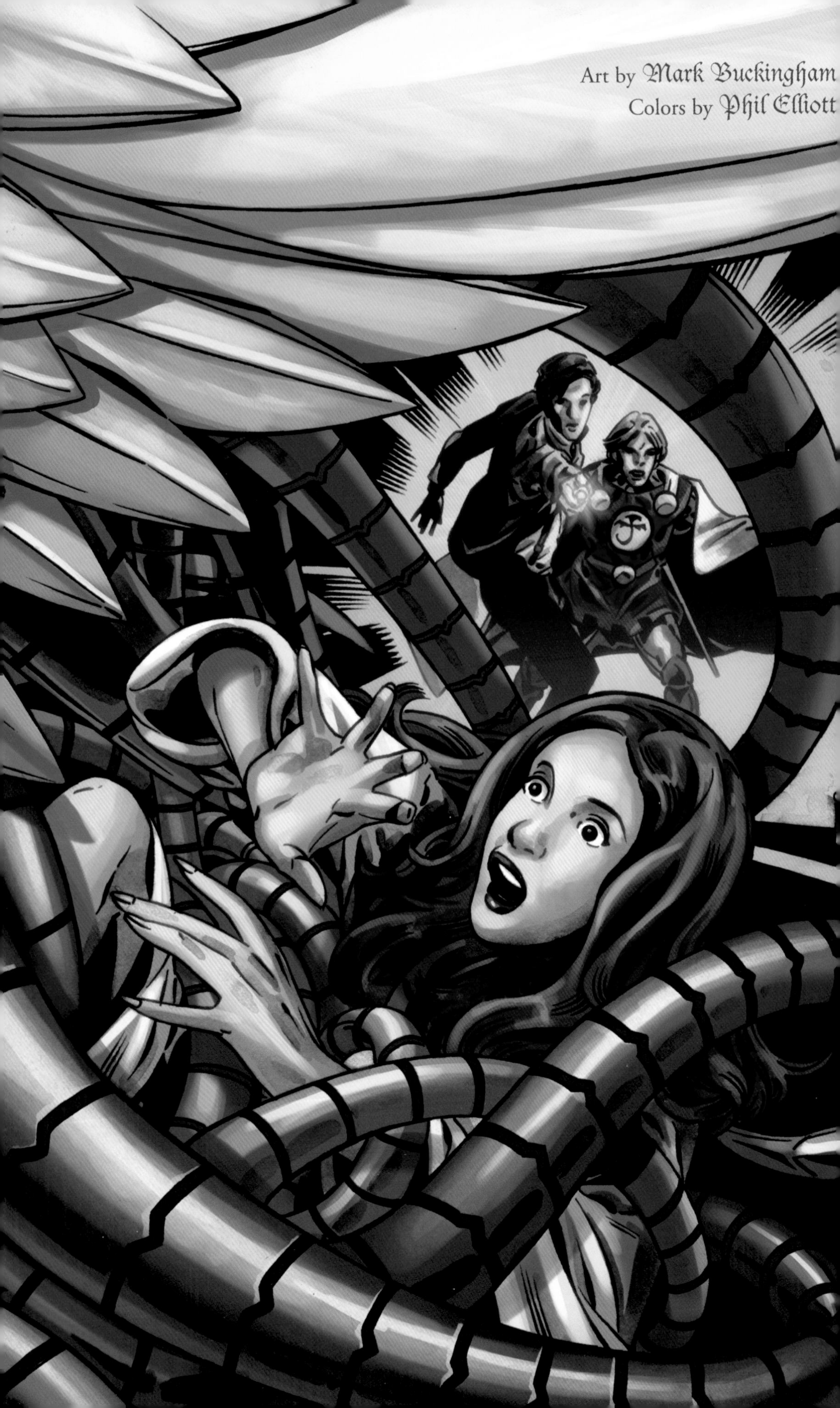
Art by Mark Buckingham
Colors by Phil Elliott

Art by Amy Mebberson

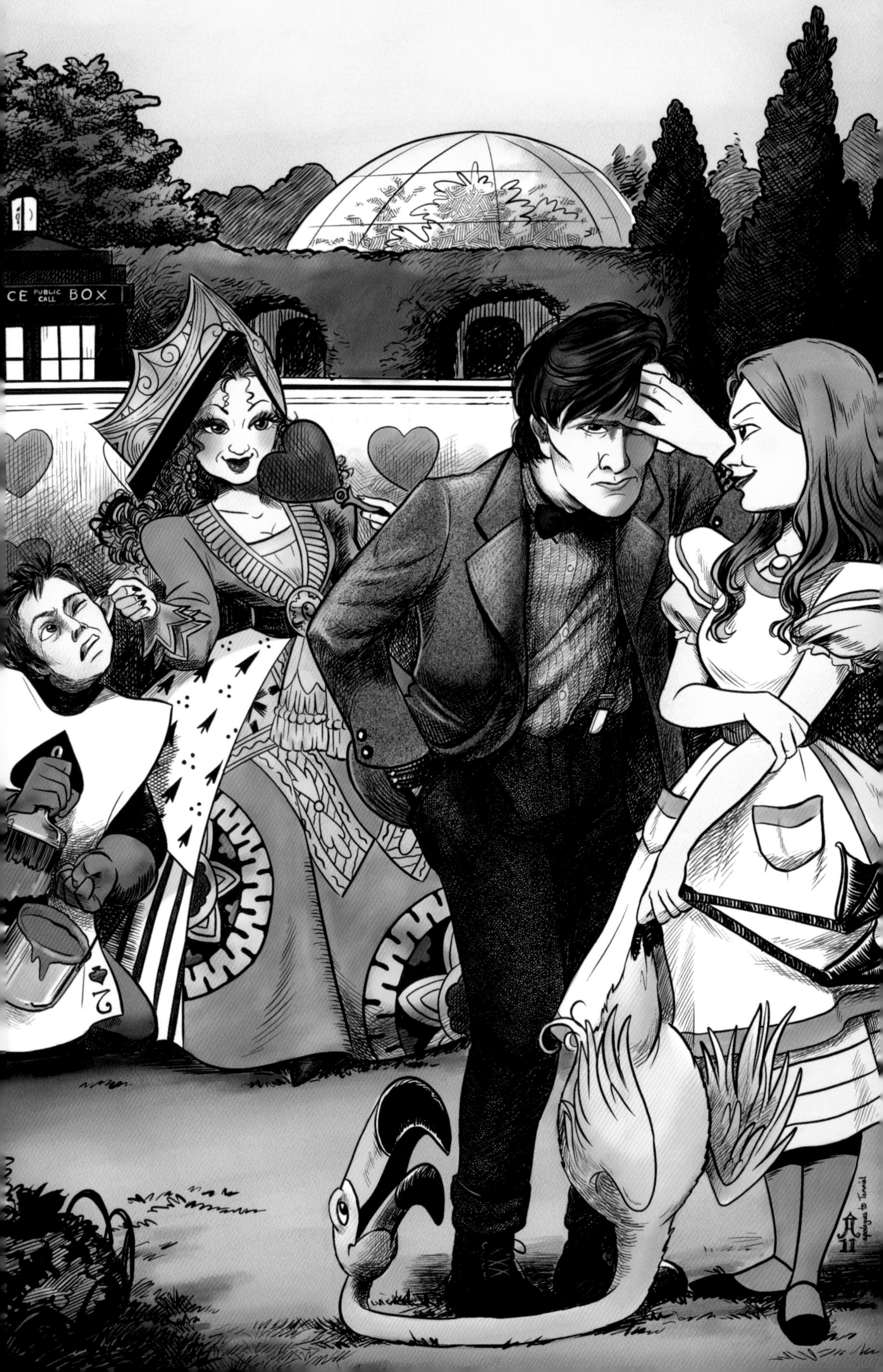
CE PUBLIC CALL BOX
apologies to Tenniel
11

Art by Mark Buckingham

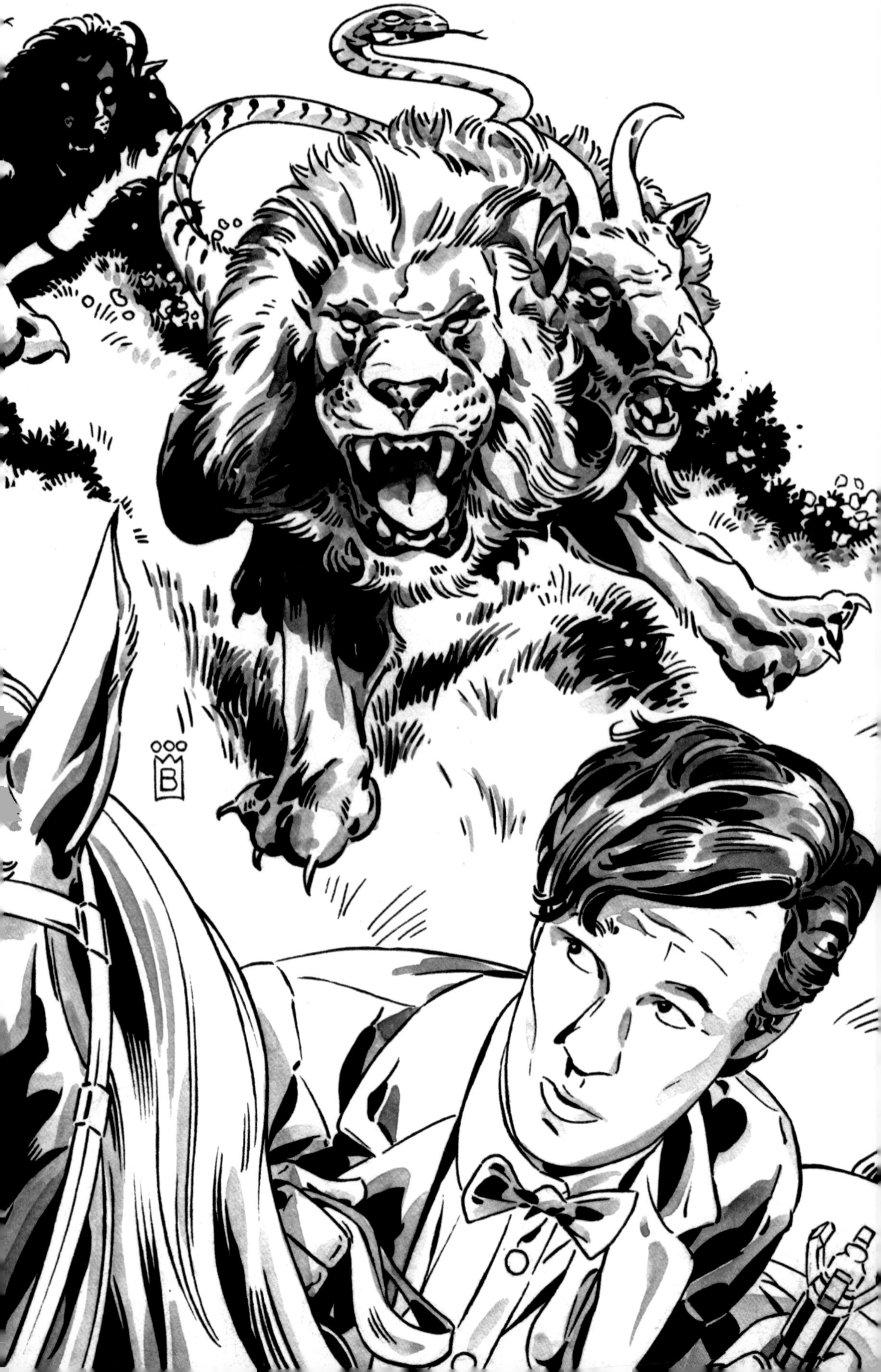

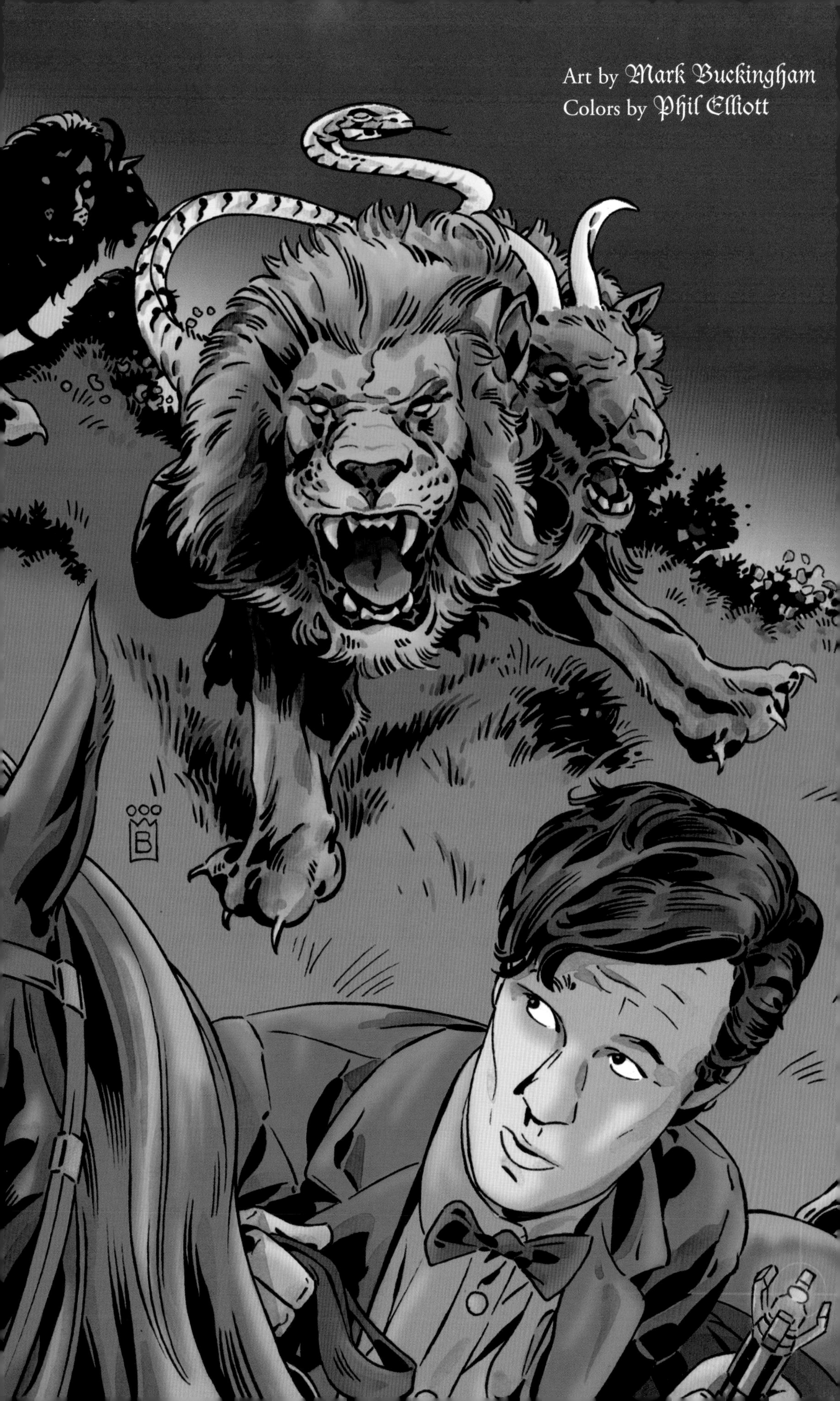

Art by Mark Buckingham
Colors by Phil Elliott

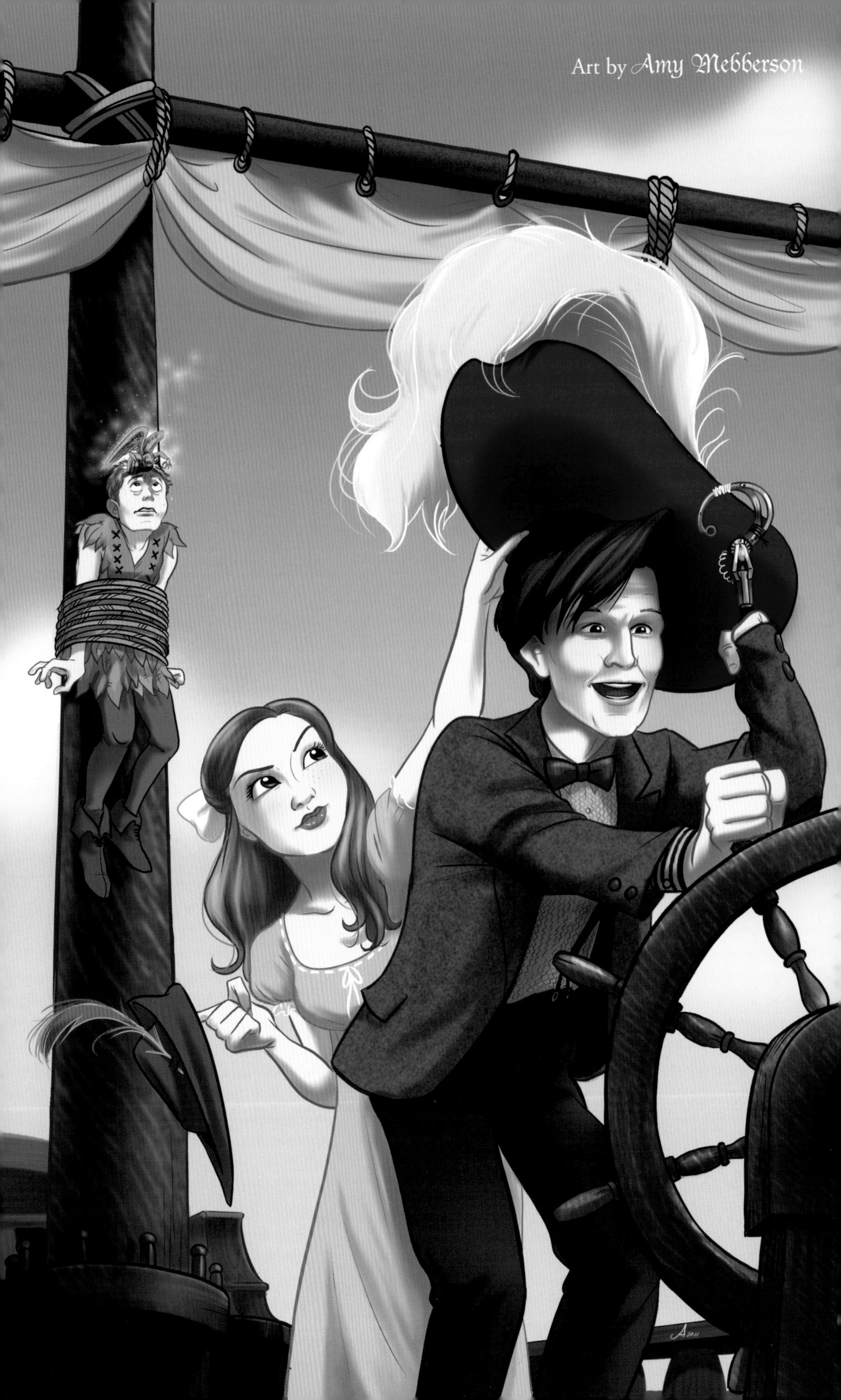

Art by Amy Mebberson

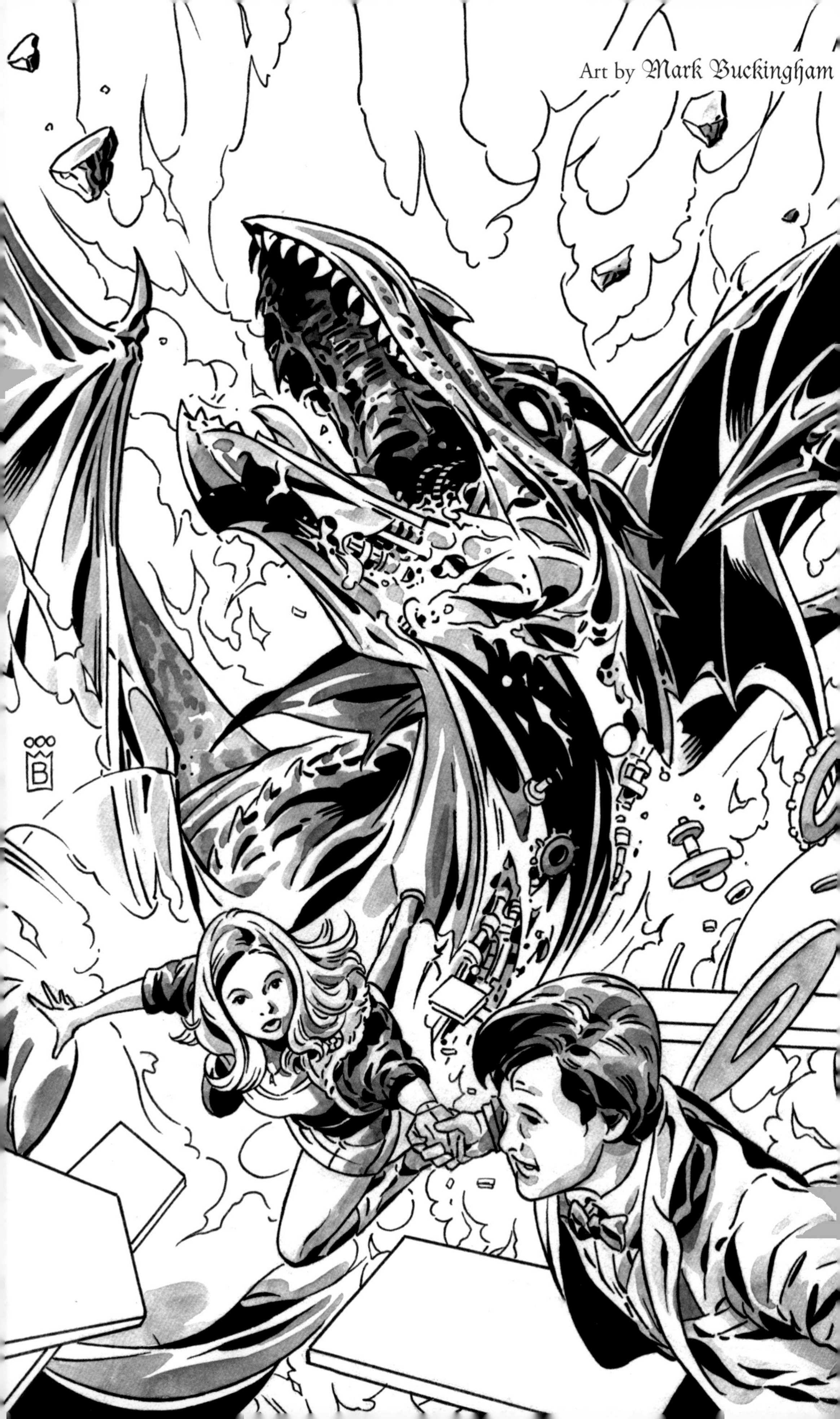

Art by Mark Buckingham

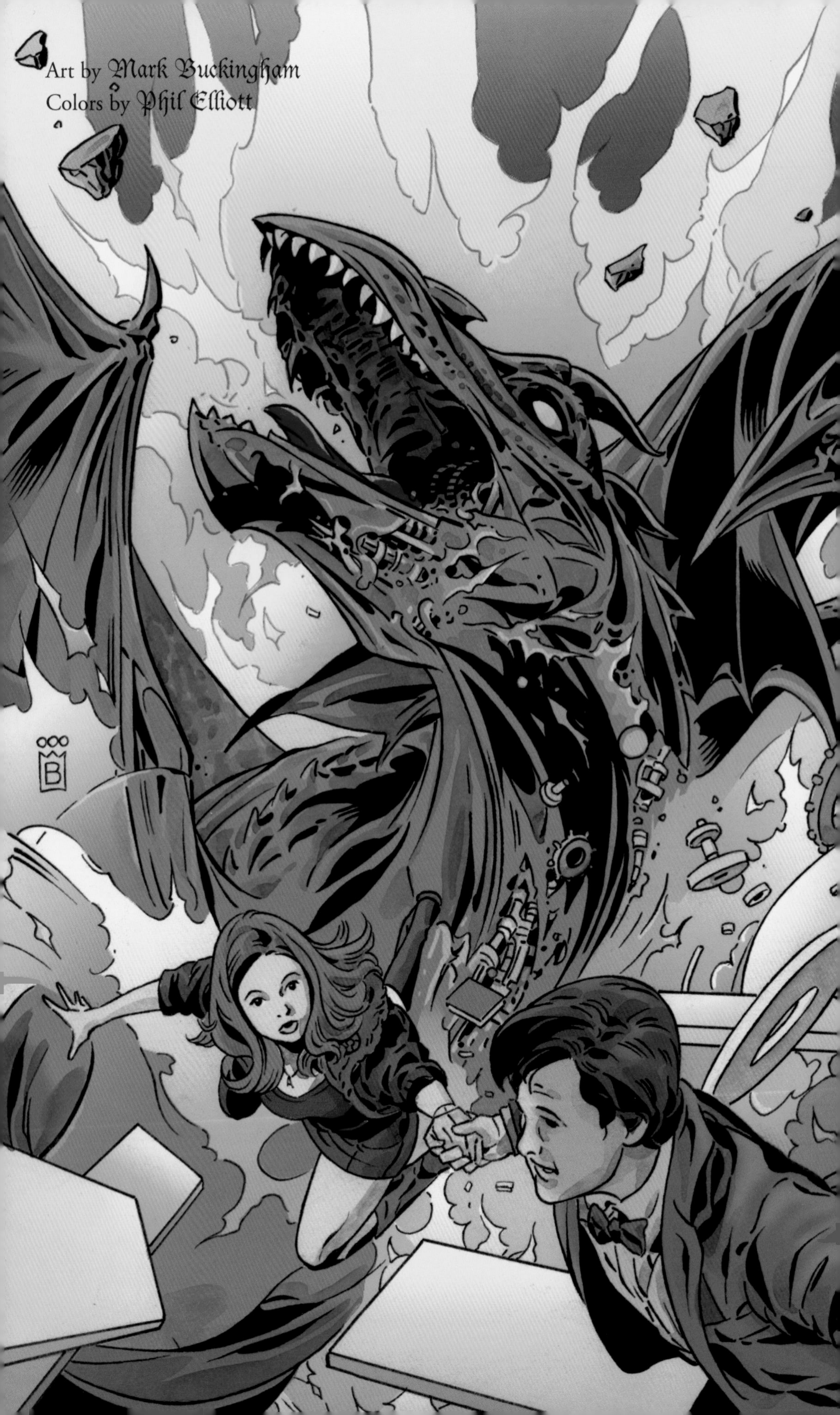
Art by Mark Buckingham
Colors by Phil Elliott

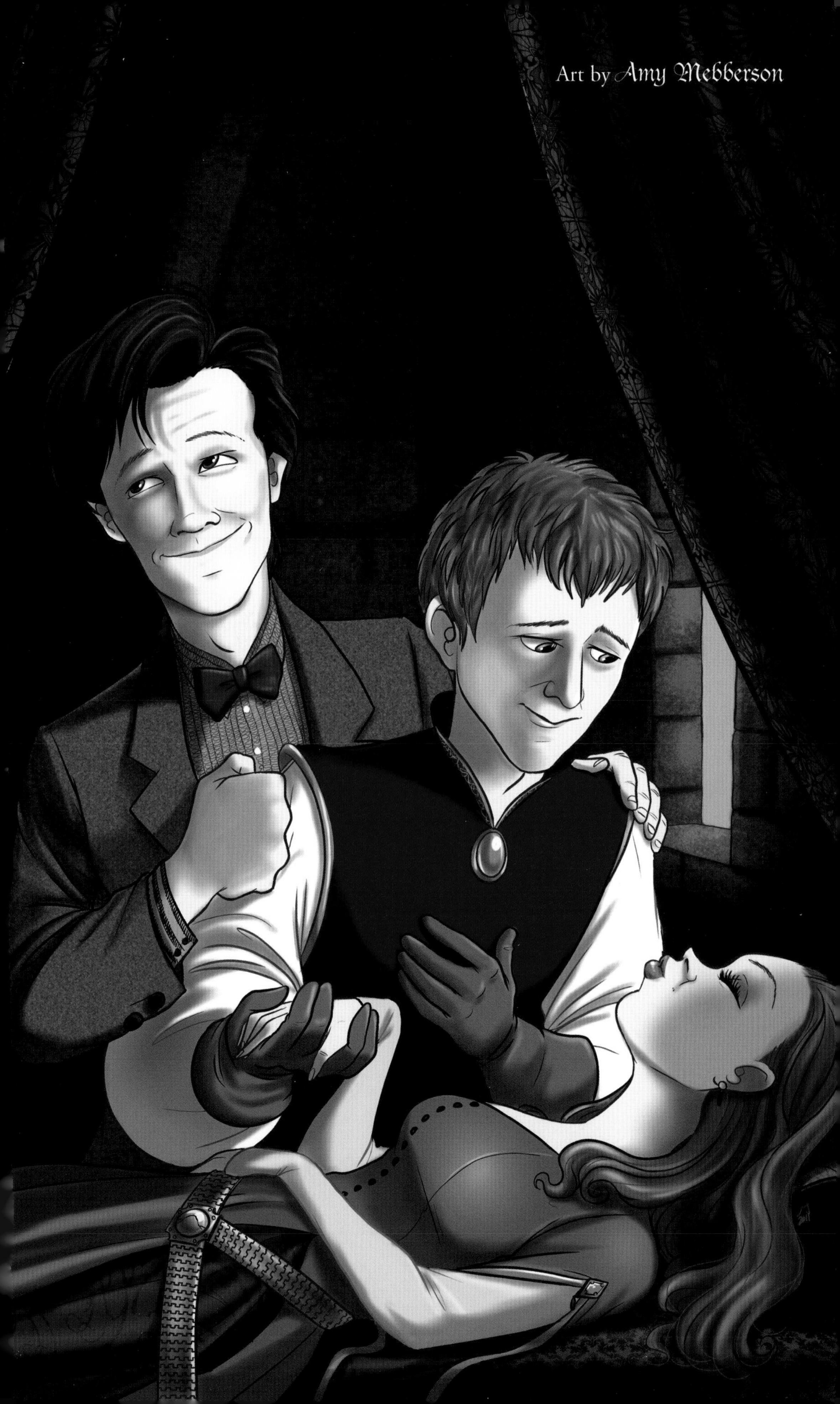

Art by Amy Mebberson

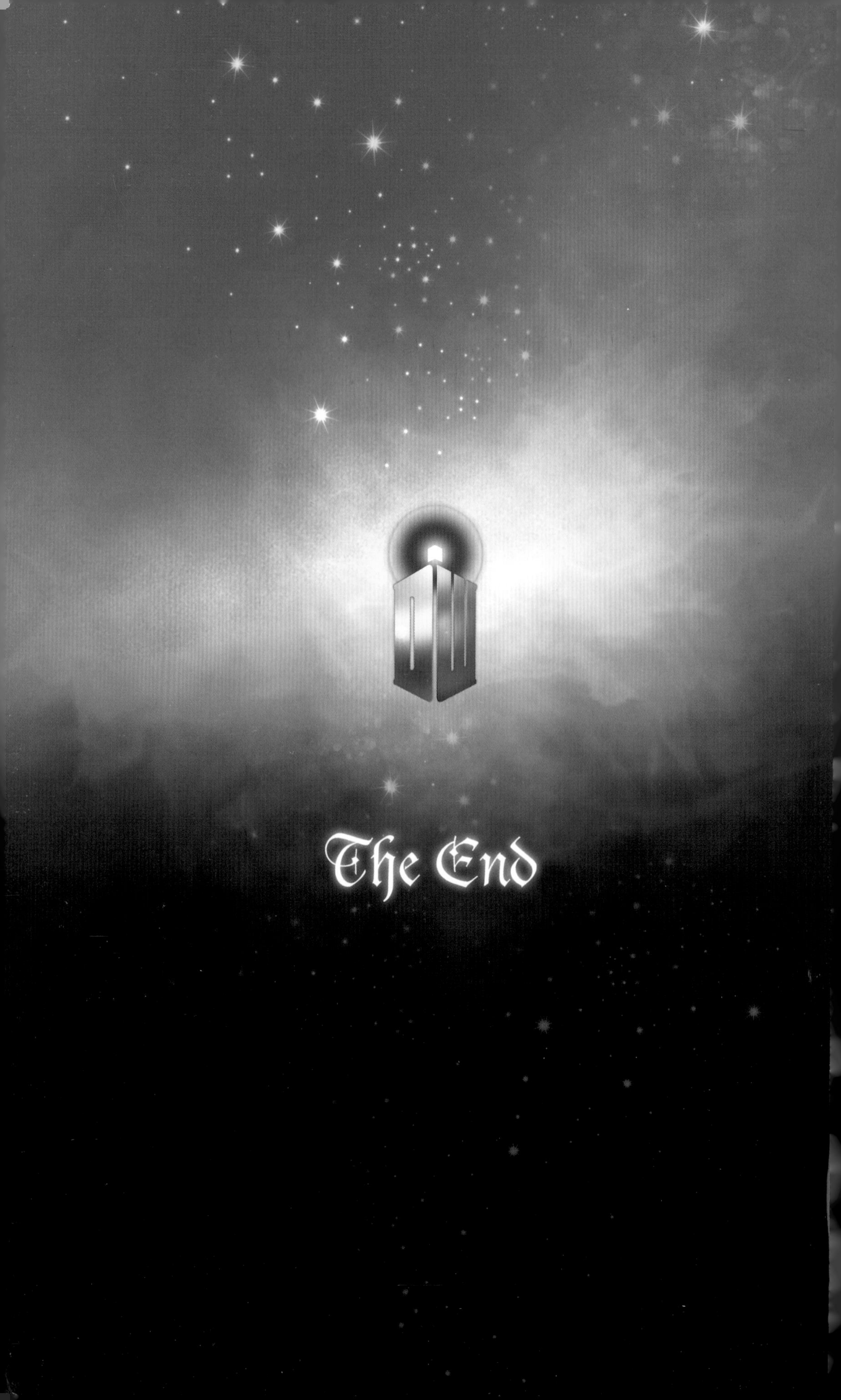
The End